Ana Bence
1.4.05

DENIS WINTER

THE FIRST OF THE FEW

FIGHTER PILOTS OF THE FIRST WORLD WAR

ALLEN LANE

ALLEN LANE
Penguin Books Ltd
536 King's Road
London SW10 0UH

First published 1982

ISBN 0 7139 1278 2

Set in 11 on 12pt Ehrhardt
Printed and bound in Great Britain

CONTENTS

LIST OF ILLUSTRATIONS

BBC Hulton Picture Library 18, 21, 27, 29

Illustrated London News Picture Library 15

Imperial War Museum 1-14, 16, 17, 19, 20, 22-26, 28, 30-41

*

The drawings on pages 32, 34, 35 and 48 are taken from *Military Aeroplanes* by Grover Loening, published in 1918.

ACKNOWLEDGEMENTS

The original spark for this book came from Eleo Gordon at Penguins, when she pointed out that the manuscript of my first book, *Death's Men: Soldiers of the Great War*, contained very little reference to the air. Checking the vast basement collection of Great War material at West Hill library, Putney, I was surprised to find that there was indeed a substantial body of personal writing by Great War pilots. Going on to the Cambridge University library, I discovered that there was in addition a large amount of printed material on aircraft construction, aero engines, aviation medicine and so on from that period. This led on to archive collections at the Public Record Office, the RAF museum at Hendon and the Imperial War Museum, with a final benediction from a visiting fellowship at the Australian National University which allowed me to check on the War Memorial, Canberra. The courtesy and helpfulness of all these institutions was so great that one was often in danger of taking it for granted. My thanks finally to the present Lord Trenchard, who gave generous permission to go through that part of his father's papers which are lodged at Hendon. If, in using material from there and from other sources, I have been critical at times of the conduct of the air struggle in the Great War, it is in full knowledge that it is one thing to fight a war in France between 1914 and 1918, quite another to dissect it from an easy chair sixty years and another world war later.

I am also grateful to the following for permission to reproduce material: Bailey Brothers and Swinfen Ltd for W. Bishop, *Winged Warfare*; Doubleday and Co. Inc., for E. V. Rickenbacker, *Fighting the Flying Circus*; Newnes-Butterworths for W. McLanachan, *Fighter Pilot*, and E. Udet, *Ace of the Black Cross*; Peter Davies Ltd for C. Lewis, *Sagittarius Rising*; Nicholson and Watson for I. Jones, *King of the Air Fighters*; and Jonathan Cape Ltd for V. Yeates, *Winged Victory*.

I
INTRODUCTION: THE FIGHTER AEROPLANE

Speaking as Commander in Chief, Aldershot, just one month before the outbreak of the Great War, Sir Douglas Haig told a military gathering: 'I hope none of you gentlemen is so foolish as to think that aeroplanes will be able to be usefully employed for reconnaissance in the air. There is only one way for a commander to get information by reconnaissance and that is by the use of cavalry.'

As Commander in Chief of the British Expeditionary Force when the war ended, Haig saw no reason to change his general opinion on the military value of aircraft. In his personal draft for a final dispatch, just two sentences were given to the air: 'Though aircraft and tanks proved of enormous value, their true value is as ancillaries of infantry, artillery and cavalry.' The reason he gave for this poor rating was that 'the killing power of the aeroplane is still very limited as compared to the three principal arms'.

More imaginative than Haig, more radical in his evaluation of the role of machinery in war, and writing about the same time, Winston Churchill gave only two of the 1,400 pages of his text in *The World Crisis* to the work of the air service. There was therefore nothing peculiarly obtuse about Haig's dismissal of aerial work. Indeed, even that passionately forward-looking military writer Basil Liddell Hart, writing with the advantage of the greater availability of material a decade later, gave only six of his 450 pages on the Great War to the air and this in the form of a postscript inserted apparently at random in the middle of his text.

Most statistics would seem to support this slighting treatment. Numerically the Royal Flying Corps, or Royal Air Force as it became on 1 April 1918, had always been insignificant. Taking September each year as the point of comparison, manpower between the arms of the expeditionary force was distributed as follows:

	infantry	artillery	cavalry	engineers	air
1914:	64%	19%	9%	6%	0.6%
1915:	70%	17%	4%	8%	0.4%
1916:	65%	19%	3%	10%	1%
1917:	62%	19%	2%	12%	2%
1918:	58%	24%	1%	10%	3%

The aeroplanes involved seemed, too, pitifully weak by the side of the killing machinery of the ground war. Comparison with the piston-engined fighter machines of less than a generation later makes the same point more clearly to our generation. A Sopwith Camel, among the best of Great War fighters, was powered by a 130 hp engine and could reach 20,000 feet in thirty-six minutes or achieve a maximum speed of 125 mph in level flight. The American P47 Thunderbolt of the second war housed a 2,800 hp engine, reached 32,000 feet in just thirteen and a half minutes and on the level could touch 473 mph. In relative punch, the Camel mounted two 0.303-inch machine guns and 50 pounds of bombs; the Thunderbolt eight 0.5-inch machine guns and 1,500 pounds of bombs or rockets.

A strong case can nevertheless be made, notwithstanding such statistics, that a tiny number of flimsy aircraft equipped with such limited 'killing power' still gave the war on the west front its two basic features for most of the duration.

First, the roles of day and night were reversed, night becoming the time of action, day that of rest. So new was this pattern in war and so unexpected that even if it was noted in memoirs it was certainly not then traced to its root. Fighter pilot Cecil Lewis thus wrote of summer 1916:

By day the roads of France were deserted. As soon as dusk fell they were thick with transport, guns, ammunition trains and troops all moving up through the town of Albert to take their positions in the line. We used to lean over the window sill of our aerodrome mess and watch them, dim and fantastic silhouettes passing in the flicker of oil lamps, solid-tyred lorries bumping and rattling over the potholes, the grinding of gears, the rattle of equipment, the shouted orders, the snatches of song. The noisy nightmare gave us the illusion of victory. We took some pride in the evidence of strength. The sinister ghosts hailed us as they passed and we shouted back to them the catch phrases

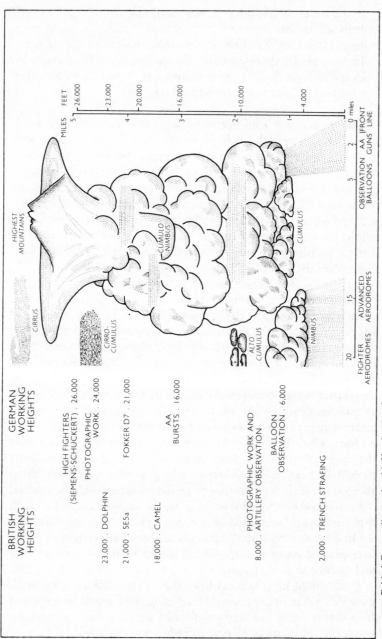

FIGURE 1. Behind German lines – the chief battleground

of the time, the ribald greetings, sardonic cheers – all equally drowned in the clatter of their passing. Endlessly, night after night it went on. Yet when dawn came, all signs of it were gone. There was the deserted road, the tumbledown farmhouse, all serene and silent in the summer morning. Never do I remember a time when night so contradicted day.

The reason for this nocturnal activity was straightforward. Flying about five miles behind the enemy front lines and spaced two miles apart were German observation balloons from whose baskets, 6,000 feet above the ground, trained observers using high-powered telescopes wirelessed information direct to gunpits. At the same time, low-flying two-seater aircraft equipped likewise with radio and protected by fighter top cover circled the battle area in low, leisurely figures of eight at quarter-mile intervals, accurately directing artillery fire and filling in those gaps left by the balloons. Only when the night blinded such eyes was movement safe within twenty miles of the front line.

The other basic feature was the sustained stalemate which seemed to follow upon the impossibility of achieving surprise in attack. Here again, the air played the critical role. Right at the start of the war RFC information had prevented the encirclement of the BEF at Mons. Later it spotted the gap developing between the advancing German armies beyond Paris and initiated the battle of the Marne, which finally broke the Schlieffen impetus. When anti-aircraft fire drove aeroplanes above the range of visual observation, cameras at once proved a superior substitute. Measuring three feet by four, wind-driven and fixed vertically downward to eliminate the effect of vibration, semi-automatic plate cameras produced twice daily a sequence of photos the length of the west front. From 16,000 feet, an area measuring two miles by three would be covered with remarkable sharpness in a single exposure. When such exposures were assembled on wooden boards in mosaic form and studied, all the latest developments in trench geography could be over-printed on to mass-produced trench maps of 1:10,000 scale and circulated to divisions.

Little could be concealed from the camera and anything indicating a change in the enemy's level of activity would be answered by a gathering of one's own defensive artillery. Such indications would be the V nicks of new machine-gun positions or the grey lines and trampled grass associated with newly erected barbed wire. Additional artillery could be detected from the shadows of gun barrels, breaks in surrounding country at the edges of gunpits or tracks leading to the new positions. Muzzle-blasted bleached grass would anyway reflect more light and show up white, like newly dug earth. The light railway tracks always put down to move accumulations of shells for a barrage could never be hidden however well camouflaged trenches or artillery positions were, and would always confirm suspicions weeks before the start of any offensive.

However, there was nothing infallible about the eye in the sky. Low cloud or high wind, together with print grain, confusing shadows or incorrect orientation of photos, meant that the evidence of listening posts, spies or captured prisoners was necessary for the confirmation of photographic information and, even then, poor staff work was always able to abuse the best intelligence information. A good example was in May 1918, when five divisions were resting on a 'quiet' part of the French front. When dust was reported above roads in the German rear, the RE8s of 52 Squadron stayed on the ground, since no enemy activity was expected. The Germans attacked three days after the warning with a barrage from 1,000 guns and complete surprise was achieved.

The importance of aerial observation overall is nevertheless suggested by the activity of the US camouflage corps. During an average month in 1918 this corps used 4 million square yards of burlap material, 200,000 gallons of paint, 7,700 fish nets and 2 million square yards of poultry wire to conceal gunpits and trenches. In practice such a quantity of assorted material did nothing more than register anxiety, because concealment of trench systems was always beyond the capacity of engineers. A single square mile of such systems, after all, contained about 900 miles of barbed wire, 6 million sandbags, 1 million cubic feet of timber and 36,000 square feet of corrugated iron. Quantities like these could defeat any human ingenuity.

The tactical conclusion had already been drawn two years before the war, when aerial observation cut short the annual British manœuvres and allowed Grierson's invading 'Germans' to embarrass Haig's defending 'British'. 'Warfare will be impossible unless we have mastery of the air,' Grierson concluded. When the Great War began, therefore, means had to be found to achieve such mastery, with RFC chief Hugh Trenchard the mouthpiece. The RFC policy statement of August 1916 said:

It is sometimes argued that our aeroplanes should be able to prevent hostile aeroplanes from crossing the line and this idea leads to the demand for defensive measures and a defensive policy ... supposing we had an unlimited number of machines for defensive purposes, it would still be impossible to prevent hostile machines from crossing the lines if they were determined to do so because the sky is too large to defend ... the sound policy which should guide all warfare in the air would seem to be this – to exploit the moral effect of the aeroplane on the enemy. This can be done by attacking and continuing to attack.

In March 1917 the nature of this policy of attack was rather more clearly defined. 'The further our patrols penetrate, the greater the moral effect ... and the more they will interrupt the work of the enemy's machines.' In short, there was to be constant offensive flying across the line to so harass and pin down the enemy that his own observation work would be hindered and British observation work simplified.

The means for carrying out such a policy were already to hand, though originally the development had had other ends in view. Speaking to the Aeronautical Society in 1912, the director of the army aircraft factory, Colonel Capper, had said that the gaining of information and the rapid transmission of that information were the chief functions of aircraft working with the army. Two types of reconnaissance machine were therefore developed. The first was the fast single-seater which would serve as a rapid probe of a wide area. The second was the slower, more stable two-seater which would be sent to take a closer look at the most promising sightings of the single-seaters.

There was little thought of arming such aeroplanes. RFC staff officer Sykes said at the start of the war that 'There should be no attempt at aerial conflict', and the Germans agreed with him. In 1913 their general staff had pronounced that seeing, not fighting, was the role of the air. The mounting of light machine guns on fast single-seaters and the gathering of such machines into compact fighting units followed logically nevertheless, with the object of securing one's own information and attacking the enemy's reconnaissance capability.

Such developments meant that the single-seater fighter became the crucial aeroplane of the Great War, because it was thought to hold the key to what one authority called 'the war of the lenses'. The importance of this role can be expressed in statistical form. In June 1918, for example, fighters constituted 58 per cent of the RAF's aeroplanes against the 27 per cent of two-seater reconnaissance machines and 15 per cent of bombers. The growth of fighter squadrons as registered in April of each year suggests in addition the progressive realization of such importance:

> 1915 – 0 squadrons
> 1916 – 3 squadrons
> 1917 – 13 squadrons
> 1918 – 30 squadrons

Looking beyond the fighters to the overall importance of the air war, the fact that one quarter of Britain's military budget in 1918 was spent on the air force and that half of the £160 million in contracts outstanding at the end of the war were air contracts puts the matter in a fresh perspective. The low rating of Haig, Churchill and Liddell Hart seems comprehensible only in terms of a tendency to explain the Great War in comparison with previous wars. Since the first flight of the Wright brothers had been made a year after the Boer war was concluded, air, as a new aspect of war, was always likely to be left out of the final reckoning. Post-mortem argument was conducted in the language of infantrymen and artillerymen. Had the writers looked at financial accounts, they might have paid greater attention to a war which centred around the eyes of those infantry and artillery.

2
ENLISTING PILOTS

The critical decision concerning pilot supply in the Great War was taken as early as 1909. In that year the Committee of Imperial Defence reported that 'it had yet to be shown whether aeroplanes are sufficiently reliable to be used under unfavourable weather conditions. The committee has been unable to obtain any trustworthy evidence to show whether any great improvement was to be expected in the immediate future.' They noted too the high cost of an aeroplane – £1,000 – and recommended instead that £45,000 should be invested in airship research. As a result of this recommendation it was soon announced by the War Office that experiments with aeroplanes had ceased, 'as the cost has proved too great, namely £2,500'. Meanwhile by 1909 the French had spent £47,000 on aeroplanes for its army, the Germans £400,000 on aeroplane research alone.

The result was that the Royal Flying Corps formed only the smallest fragment of the BEF and went to war with just 197 pilots. A fortnight after war had been declared, Sefton Brancker, as Director General of Military Aeronautics, drew up a list of all men left in the UK able to fly and discovered that only 862 men held the Royal Aero Club's certificate, and that of these just fifty-five were sufficiently advanced to leave immediately for active service, including middle-aged men such as Hugh Dowding, who was recorded as 'having had no practice lately'.

For some time such slender resources were not considered a great handicap, since all combatants discounted aerial combat, mounted no guns and therefore anticipated few losses. As late as the summer of 1915 there were only 200 pilots in training on the eleven flying stations in Britain, and it was assumed that gentlemen weekend fliers would keep the supply topped up. The War Office therefore laid it down that 'Members of the RFC who own their own aeroplanes should be encouraged to bring them to the Central Flying School when they undergo their training there.' Candidates had moreover to obtain the necessary Aero Club certificate of competence before RFC acceptance, the £75 fee coming from their own pocket. For the sort of men the RFC wanted, this was a small sum indeed, because the cheapest engine available to power an aeroplane cost £700, with running costs thereafter 4d. a mile, or 6½d. if an engine overhaul every 5,000 miles was included. At any time, forced landings (new spars £1 each from the frame maker), blown piston rings (£2 9s. for a set of seven) or other costly mechanical breakdowns had to be taken into account, as had the cost of renting an aerodrome shed (£100 per annum) and the wages of a good mechanic (£175 per annum), at a time when many were living, in the title of a well-known book of the period, on 'Round about a pound a week'.

The likeness of aeroplanes to cavalry horses in function and of the pilot class to the cavalry class seemed to make the selection from within this small group of men a simple matter. As late as 1917 Brancker said: 'There are very few Englishmen who won't make good pilots so long as they have sufficient experience. Flying is perhaps a little easier than riding a horse because you sit in a comfortable armchair in a quiet machine instead of a slippery saddle on a very lively horse.' From such assumptions it followed that almost any gentleman was acceptable for training. When Norman Macmillan wished to transfer from infantry to flying corps after getting the necessary clearance from his commanding officer, he was merely asked whether he could ride a horse, sail a boat or ride a motor cycle. Men who had done any of these gentlemanly things were reckoned able to go solo within two hours. Then, after picking out strands of differently coloured wools, Macmillan was pronounced medically fit to fly.

By the end of the war there had been great change from this casual state of affairs. Scale alone, quite apart from increased complexity in machinery and tactics, determined such change, for by the armistice the original 197 pilots had become 26,000.

The change most immediately apparent to contemporaries was the promotion of plebeians from two-seater squadrons to the fighter ranks. Even during 1916 disgruntled gentleman-pilot Reid noted disapprovingly 'what a mixed crowd' the RFC had become, and by 1918 news of the broadening had reached Westminster. On

20 June 1918 the Secretary of State was questioned and had to admit that 'for some time the proportion of public school entrants to the RAF has been decreasing but steps are now being taken to improve this by arrangement with the army and by popularizing the service within the schools'.

Demand for pilots was however always far beyond the scope of such popularization. This was reflected in the rate of pay: on top of the basic 7s. 6d. daily, officers got an additional daily 4s. as flying pay, the bonus rising to 12s. 6d. when they won their wings. Such figures represented a formidable inducement to leave the mud and artillery barrages of the ground war or to apply for transfer from the rear seat of a reconnaissance squadron – quite apart from the prestige of wearing the RFC maternity jacket (5½ guineas from Dunhill).

The problems which accompanied this unexpected degree of social mobility were never solved. Fry noted how hard it was for NCO pilots to win acceptance in 65 Squadron and sardonically described Albert Ball's spontaneous and patronizing remark when he saw McCudden's medal ribbons: 'By jove, that fellow's wonderful.' McCudden after all had been an army bugler at fourteen while Ball had been working his way through Trent College public school, yet both men had won the same decorations. In two-seater Bristol Fighter squadrons, the cleavage was even more graphically expressed. On leave in London, NCO pilot Butcher wrote of going to see *Chu Chin Chow* in the Haymarket and of being literally kicked out by officer cadets who insisted that all NCOs should use the side door regardless of what they might be doing at the front. Butcher then went on to observe that officer killings on active service were scored against that officer's name while NCO successes went to the squadron collectively, and that combat reports, which could only be made by an officer, recorded the pilot as 'Mr' but his observer as a simple surname, in the same way as cricket scorecards used to distinguish between the amateur 'gentleman' and the professional 'players'.

Less disturbing to the social conventions of the time and less often remarked on was an even greater change than social broadening – the Dominion intrusion. Of 145 pilots listed in 24 Squadron's history, twenty were Canadians, five Australians, four South Africans, two New Zealanders (and eight Americans). Reflecting after the war with less statistical precision, Gibbs reckoned that by

1918 about 70 per cent of 29 Squadron pilots were Dominion men, and he doubted whether the RAF could have kept its cutting edge without such a transfusion.

Canadians formed much the biggest contingent. The reason for this was that in late 1916, when RFC wastage was running at about 25 per cent monthly, the War Office approved an offer made by Canadian industrialists to build at their own expense an aviation factory and school (their commercial sharpness reflected in the fact that the $6\frac{1}{2}$-acre factory at Toronto was then built from scratch in under three months). By 1918 this school was sending 200 pilots over monthly, and by the end of the war a Dominion with 10 per cent of the Empire's population was producing a third of the British air force. Raymond Collishaw, the ace Canadian pilot, later thought that many Canadians joined under false pretences, brought in by the pressure of a press campaign calculated to generate enthusiasm for the defence of the weak and oppressed rather than for a place in the European racial war which, in his opinion, was at the root of the Great War.

Canadians came in quantity, nevertheless, and brought with them a new vigour. Typical was Lieutenant Hambley. In England, the CO of his training squadron wrote of him: 'In my opinion this officer is completely untrustworthy and casual. During the period he was with the squadron he was a continual source of trouble and personally I should hesitate to believe anything he said.' On active service, men saw another side to Hambley. A British pilot wrote:

> Old Hambley is a very bad Canadian and if I wasn't out here I should have difficulty in seeing any good in him at all. But he is one of my best comics. He used to pull the major's leg and say things to him that no subaltern should say to a CO. He was uncouth and used to bring terrible Canadians into the Mess and the major wanted me to get rid of him at one time but I said I would rather not. He drinks too much, wears sidewhiskers and sometimes a dirty stock. But he is a splendid fellow and I have the utmost confidence in him over the line. Best of all, although he used to pull my leg a bit, he would do just anything I asked him and he never worried me in the slightest. I could never refrain from bursting into laughter whenever I spoke to him.

RNAS ace Rochford recalled similar vigour in Canadians: 'In addition to seven Canadians from 3 Wing, our CO was also a Canadian (Collishaw). They were a wonderful bunch of fellows to be with and the more I got to know them, the better I liked them although coming as I did from a rather sheltered home, they did at times shock me.' Men from across the Canadian border seemed to have had the same flavour. McFarlane Reid, who handled the first sixty of the 210 Americans at Stamford training squadron, described them as 'a strange, rough crowd' but approved their 'wild, keen spirit'. Bigger, richer, more self-assured, North Americans remained distinct to the end.

More talented, too. By the end of the war Canadian pilots had the lion's share of killings: Bishop 72, Collishaw 60, Barker 59, Maclaren 54, McEvoy 46, Claxton 39, McCall 37, Quigley 34, Carter 31, McKeever 30 – without such scores the RAF list would have been thin gruel, and such precocity was noted even during the war. In June 1918 the Secretary of State remarked on the 'very high standards of the semi-trained Canadians' as 'a most striking feature'. Like the performance of the Australian Corps on the ground, superior Dominion achievement is not easily accounted for. Chief aeromedicine researcher Dr Flack put it down to the open-air life, the wearing of minimal clothing and lack of coddling, together with cold baths in the morning and cross-country tramping in all weathers. Since so many came from the big towns, Flack's suggestion hardly fits the facts. Probably more important was the lack of social preconceptions, the absence of a belief in the unique fighting qualities of an 'officer' class. Writing confidentially to the Australian official historian, British analogue Sir James Edmonds remarked in 1936: 'To my mind the great advantage the Australian Corps possessed was the provision of officers by promotion of experienced and tried men from the ranks. The British to a great extent kept up class distinction and sent out many inexperienced lads from home as officers.' In terms of the air, the Dominion outlook meant selection initially from a much wider social pool, Other Ranks being likely to gain approval for transfer from the infantry as officers, and, back home, fewer men considering pilot status as above their station in life. Characteristically, after the war the RAF made no attempt to research into the discrepancy between British and Dominion capacity or to find out why during the war the Canadians spent $9,835 per man just on the preliminary flying course as against British expenditure of £1,030 for the whole process of training a pilot.

The third great change was in health. In 1915 air journalist Turner wrote drily of

> a medical school near London where pupils who had failed to do well at the aerodromes were examined and catechized in order to obtain data for future guidance. A series of questions was put to these subjects, reminding one of those autograph albums in vogue twenty years ago. What is your favourite amusement? Who is your favourite poet? Do you mind solitude? The selection of Kipling or Stevenson was supposed to indicate greater promise than of Shelley or Meredith. A football player stood better with the examiners than a pianist.

By the autumn of 1916 this examination had been put on a sounder basis, which followed contemporary French practice. A team of sixteen doctors examined 200 applicants daily, first checking the heart. A pulse rate of 60 was thought good and one over 100 bad. Examination of the lungs with a manometer followed, suitable candidates being those able to hold their breath for 45 seconds; one man in seven had to be marked down as unable to fly above 8,000 feet without artificially supplied oxygen. Then came the spinning test: the candidate was revolved ten times in twenty seconds on a typing chair to see if his eye movements stabilized within half a minute. Finally a fifteen-minute interview sorted out the slow-witted, the timid, the unstable and the unreliable by a rule-of-thumb method. Lecturing during the war on his techniques, chief research adviser Dr Flack said: 'There is a type of facial expression one gets well acquainted with carrying out this sort of interview. It consists of a furtive look as if always expecting something unpleasant to happen, in marked contrast with the straight, decided expression of the crack fighter pilot.' In a vaguely scientific way, Flack picked out impulsives, paranoids and psychopaths as marked character types an examiner might expect. The first were men who would insist on picking their own type of job and their own CO; they were men whose lives bordered on criminality, often very brave but never suited to leadership. The second type were the critical and the hostile, who would complain constantly of inefficiency in the system, of uncaring COs and of poor living conditions. The third were the line-shooters, the aeroplane wreckers. These were moody and reclusive or violent and aggressive by turn. What Flack did not make clear was that these three types held up for official disapproval produced a disproportionate number of aces, for all their presence as grit within the oyster.

By the end of 1917 this embryonic science of aviation medicine was already rejecting 6 per cent of applicants to the RFC on psychological grounds and a further 12 per cent on physical. Just as in the second war, however, when only 35 per cent of those who passed the medical tests made good pilots as against the 11 per cent who became good pilots after failing the medical, so in the Great War Flack was surprised how many of his low-classified men were returned 'good' by instructors. As Sefton Brancker put it in an address to the Aeronautical Society in 1916:

> The most unexpected people make good pilots and very often the most promising ones never attain more than mediocrity in the air and for this reason it has always seemed to me undesirable to lay down a stereotyped process of training. Personally I think any sound man with sound nerves (and women too for that matter) can make a good, useful pilot but it is only the exceptional individual who will make a really brilliant fighter pilot. Even the unsound, for we have deaf people and people with wooden legs who frequently make very useful pilots.

The trend nevertheless was towards a narrower range in physical and mental type. By 1917 there were few forty-year-olds actively flying. Nor were there so many like Lieutenant Voge of 64 Squadron, of whom a commanding officer wrote: 'He suffers from double astigmatism and short sight. In consequence he finds it difficult to keep formation, frequently loses his way and, I am certain, would be unable to spot an enemy aircraft. I do not consider him suitable for a scout pilot in the field.' In the second part of 1917 Lieutenant Voge would not even have reached the training squadron.

By then pilots had become fitter men – and younger. Here was the fourth big difference from the early days. The average age of 65 Squadron's pilots in 1918 was twenty and in 100 Squadron twenty-two and a half, while Lee wrote of feeling old at twenty-two and Burge reckoned twenty-five too old for the making of a good fighter pilot. Put statistically, of 100 officers certified dead by the autumn of 1917 and taken as a random sample, 60 per cent were twenty-two or under. The reason for such youth was that quite early in the war it had become clear that air was a new type of war which involved constant high-speed manœuvre in an unbounded three-dimensional medium for which there were no manuals or established rules. It meant too the manipulation of heavy machinery without power assistance and from within an open cockpit at high altitude. Survival required speed and certainty in response, which simply eliminated older men with their slow reflexes, by killing them off. Nevertheless, some did go on fighting. Lee wrote of 'Daddy' Heath, aged thirty-six, while American ace of aces Edward Rickenbacker only started flying at twenty-seven. But Rickenbacker was a prize-winning racing driver (he had started his war as Pershing's chauffeur) and such men were exceptional. More typical of the pilots of 1917 was Ira Jones of 65 Squadron, arrested in Cardiff by military policemen while on leave, on the grounds that no man so young could have lawfully gained the ribbons he was wearing on his chest.

There was protest of course from many who saw the growing number of young pilot officers, many of whom were in addition of plebeian origin. Thus *Aeroplane* editor Grey was already writing in June 1915:

> There is an idiotic theory that a man is too old at 30 if he wants to fly and that a howling little bounder of 20 is going to make a better officer aviator than a thoroughly sound sportsman of 32. The youngster may certainly fly more recklessly till his nerve breaks just as a mongrel dog will go yapping into a fight till he gets a damned good hiding but he will never make an officer and will never fly after a bad smash in the way the better class of man will do. Blood tells in a man as much as it does in a horse or dog. Many a good chaser has come out of the shafts where it has found its way by bad luck and many a better officer aviator can be found in the ranks than among the brats of the well-to-do shopkeepers and business-like merchants such as are now entitled to swagger round in uniform and draw salutes from their social, mental and moral betters.

But the demands of war were greater than the conventions of generations. Young certainly, rich probably, Dominion perhaps, the fighter pilots of the Great War were able to claim a level of pay, a responsibility for complex machinery and a latitude in the interpretation of orders which in the ground war belonged only to Dominion brigadiers or British corps commanders. Little wonder then that recruiting officers of RFC and RAF were never short of applicants even during the bloodiest days of April 1917.

3
LEARNING TO FLY

A prospective pilot's first experience of the RFC was most unpromising. He would first be ordered to remove any previous rank badges or flashes from his khaki uniform and then be given a white cap band to indicate reversion to cadet status. For up to six weeks he would hang about at the depot waiting for a vacancy on the first rung of the training ladder and under the charge of regular soldiers either too old for active service or, in the peculiarly British way, given command of training establishments because they had already been proved inadequate in field command.

Depot tone was therefore old army tone. 'If your pupils are slack,' said the depot manual, 'give them drill and see that it is carried out vigorously.' Future ace Ira Jones recalled such vigour when a depot corporal kicked away his bowler hat on his first parade, and thereafter there was constant verbal abuse by NCOs during depot drill.

A typical day began with gunfire tea and two biscuits at 6 am, followed by a cross-country run. Then came breakfast and inspection. Serving his depot phase at Hastings in the summer of 1918, Cheesman wrote of several periods confined to barracks for omitting to polish the soles of his spare boots, the omission coming to light during such an inspection. Afterwards came PE, with much marching at 140 paces to the minute, hands brought up to shoulder level at each swing, before marching off to lectures in mapwork, rigging, use of compass and so on.

By way of contrast, during the initial training period the French cadet would have been sent straight to an aerodrome, with the obligation to watch all flights and analyse faults with the instructor. Inability to answer questions would be punished by the loss of forty-eight hours of leave.

From the depot pool, the British cadet would pass on to the School of Military Aeronautics at either Reading or Oxford, his gain in status indicated by permission to replace regimental and rank badges. It meant too an allowance of 7s. 6d. weekly, together with the issue of £50 as kit allowance. On the strength of signing a form, the cadet would be able to anticipate the payment of this kit allowance and order one uniform, khaki usually being the chosen colour because of its capacity to camouflage grime. Only the well-to-do could also purchase the new blue uniform introduced in the spring of 1918. The material of this uniform had ironically become available just at this moment because the Russian Revolution had put that country out of the war, with the result that Russian officers' uniforms, hitherto manufactured in Britain, had lost their market.

The ethos of the school was made clear on the first day, when newcomers were each given a pamphlet. 'Every pupil on arrival will make himself thoroughly familiar with the contents of this pamphlet. Ignorance of its contents cannot be accepted as an excuse for neglect of duty or disobedience of orders.' Reading on, the newcomer might well be surprised to discover that all work on parade, in lectures and on aerodromes came under the category of 'parades', which meant that cadets had to salute an instructor all the time they spoke to him and that no cadet could speak with an air mechanic or NCO while being instructed. Cadets were also specifically forbidden to damage maps, spill ink, break pencil points or otherwise 'waste the resources of war'. Slacks were never to be worn on parades, or shorts and socks at any time.

Lieutenant Burn, who did this training at Oxford, described a typical day. After reveille there would be PE in the quadrangle of Christ Church College. After breakfast the 500 cadets and fifty officers marched the mile or so to university lecture rooms, where from 9 until 12.30 and again from 2 until 5 lectures were absorbed. Notes had to be written up and learnt in the evenings. Burn remembered all these lectures, apart from those on engines, as being mostly dull and valueless, and consisting of masses of unrelated information – 'valves are made of alloy steel' and the like. Lee wrote also of being 'dazed' by the amount of factual information laid down for memorizing at Oxford.

Lee was probably rather unusual in taking it all seriously. Burn used to slip out of the lectures at 11 and 4 to take coffee at the Cadena café, anticipating that the exams at the end of the course would be in the usual military style. And so they were. 'The exam of course was a farce', he wrote. Scripts were passed around to allow gaps to be filled, while the capacity to draw neat diagrams made success anyway a formality. Failing the practical work on a morse buzzer, Burns was nevertheless given the official benediction 'proficient in wireless'. The cost of the Haig–Trenchard policy of constant offensive flying made the Oxford exam necessarily a formality. Enterprising cadets like Burn could still make something of the period at Oxford. Using his Douglas motor cycle (bought for £32) Burn used to ride out to Port Meadow aerodrome and take fifteen-minute flips in Maurice Farman Shorthorns, describing the sensations of low flying as 'the most beautiful things in the world'.

Burn's French counterpart at the same stage would have been dismounting engines, stripping carburettors, dismantling magnetos and acquiring the closest feel and understanding of the most important sections of his war aeroplane.

After Oxford came the training squadron. There, after the Smith-Barry training system was adopted late in 1917, the trainee escaped the worst of the old army tradition. Indeed, in many ways the experience seemed so aptly conceived, the assault upon personal dignity so slight, that training squadron days recalled after the war seemed something of a dream-time. Compared with the illogicalities and accumulations of the unexpected which came before and after, Smith-Barry's logic was such that few pilots wrote of their first taste of practical work. Indeed, in many ways it must have seemed like going back to well-remembered civilian routines. Gathered in small numbers to learn a skilled trade which carried with it the certainty of officer status and membership of an elite fighting unit, training squadron work had the flavour of an old public school or university about it. Certainly the relation of instructor and cadet had the subtlety and gently humorous equality of don and student, and, as at school or university, training was a thing of gentlemanly hours – 10 am to midday and 2 to 4 in the afternoon, with no flying at weekends. After work, time was always a trainee's own. The records of 64 Squadron show that slacks could be worn after 4.30 pm and that Lewis guns could be borrowed for duck shooting. Even aeroplanes could be borrowed. Butcher once chauffeured an officer in a DH4 to a remote country house, where the butler was waving a tea towel to indicate that the coast was clear. While the officer courted the young lady of the house, Butcher, as an NCO, was taken down to the servants' quarters for tea. A trainee could even sleep off the aerodrome if the CO had been asked, then turn up for breakfast with his tunic and flying boots worn over pyjamas. Naturally first-class rail warrants were issued against leave, and weekend leave freely given though at the students' expense. ('I can hardly live here on the pay. The Mess is awfully expensive. I shall be glad when I get out to France,' wrote one prospective pilot in December 1916.)

There was nothing casual about the practical side of training, however gentlemanly the off-duty style. First came the test flight to eliminate poor fliers from among those who had done part of their training before the acceptance of the Smith-Barry system. Such men were weeded out in a ninety-minute period of dual flying. One method for detecting the inadequate was to stall the aeroplane so as to be able to talk with and observe the passenger. Wrote Smith-Barry: 'This gives a useful indication of the state of the pupil's nerves. Those who are likely to prove unsuitable for single-seater flying generally cling to the side with an unintelligent expression instead of conversing fluently and with confidence.' Overall, about 45 per cent of those whose first experience had been with Farmans would be rejected, joined by another 5 per cent from those who had started on other machines.

If he passed this test, the trainee would be handed over to his instructor. These were always chosen from men whose ability had been first proven in war flying and then withdrawn to instruct as a full-time job. Every step of their work had been laid down in Smith-Barry's forty-two-page manual, which, measuring just four inches by three, was the invariable pocket companion of both teacher and taught throughout the course.

The Avro 504K training machines had been selected with similar care. Possessing the tricky rotary engine of the most taxing front-line fighters, they were nevertheless tame enough for novices. Yet, while they could be flown safely with ease, they could be flown accurately only by the best pilots, so that able men stood out clearly while dark areas in the knowledge of other pupils were magnified to the benefit of all. In the Hendon RAF museum today, this classic aeroplane strikes one as a large machine with the feel of a bomber about it, but to the eye of the time, in Bridgman's words, 'it had classical simplicity of conception. It was a machine with nothing unnecessary about it which achieved a sudden, inexplicable

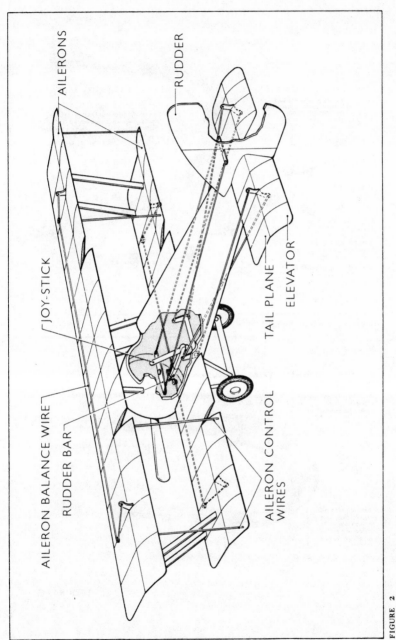

AILERONS

RUDDER

JOY-STICK

TAIL PLANE

ELEVATOR

AILERON BALANCE WIRE

RUDDER BAR

AILERON CONTROL WIRES

FIGURE 2

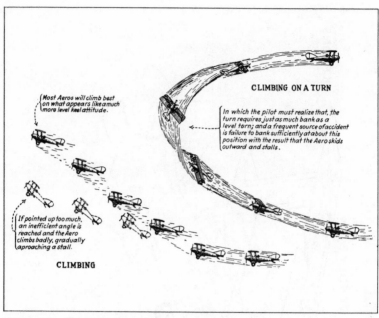

CLIMBING ON A TURN

Most Aeros will climb best on what appears like a much more level keel attitude.

In which the pilot must realize that, the turn requires just as much bank as a level turn; and a frequent source of accident is failure to bank sufficiently at about this position with the result that the Aero skids outward and stalls.

If pointed up too much, an inefficient angle is reached and the Aero climbs badly, gradually aproaching a stall.

CLIMBING

FIGURE 3△   ▽FIGURE 4

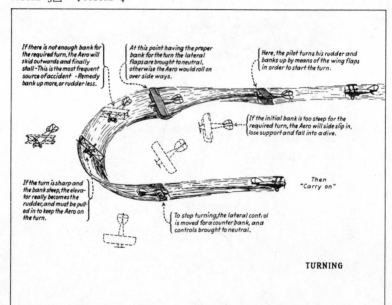

If there is not enough bank for the required turn, the Aero will skid outwards and finally stall - This is the most frequent source of accident - Remedy bank up more, or rudder less.

At this point having the proper bank for the turn the lateral flaps are brought to neutral, otherwise the Aero would roll on over side ways.

Here, the pilot turns his rudder and banks up by means of the wing flaps in order to start the turn.

If the initial bank is too steep for the required turn, the Aero will side slip in, lose support and fall into a dive.

If the turn is sharp and the bank steep, the elevator really becomes the rudder, and must be pulled in to keep the Aero on the turn.

To stop turning, the lateral control is moved for a counter bank, and controls brought to neutral.

Then "Carry on"

TURNING

1. A new fighter pilot poses after being awarded his wings. Sam Browne belt and uniform show him to have been on transfer from the army, while his youthfulness is typical. The average age of fighter pilots was little over twenty. Statistically there is a better than evens chance of him having come from a public school. There is every prospect, too, that he will soon be dead, since 80 per cent of casualties were amongst those with fewer than twenty missions at the front.

2. Trainee pilots learning about the rigging of aircraft. In the middle distance some cadets are examining the tailplane of a well-worn Sopwith Camel. In the foreground the desked ranks of trainees suggest the peculiarly theoretical bias of the prospective pilots' early stages.

3. Though experiments were made with metal or plywood construction, the urgent demands of war kept the factories to spruce, ash and linen, which precluded mass production methods. Even at the end of the war, Britain could produce only 3,000 machines monthly – though keeping pace with the Germans. Here the 200 hp Hispano Suiza engine is being married to the SE5a.

4. Left, squadron commander Major Waldron and right, 'the great Smith-Barry, the man who taught the world to fly', in Trenchard's phrase. As a boy, Smith-Barry's Eton report described him as 'an awful little boy. He has no aptitude whatever.' Learning to fly before the war in the same class as Trenchard, he became 60 Squadron's commander at the front and devised the training programme which remained basic through two world wars. Its result was to halve the death rate immediately in training and produce more aces than any other country in 1917 and 1918, by which time the 'awful little boy' had taught himself seven languages fluently. Plain speaking and a ferocious personality led the RAF to get rid of him and ignore his achievements as soon as it decently could.

5. Avro produced the classic training machine, the 504K. Easily flown but difficult to fly accurately, the Avro's tricky rotary engine gave novices the feel of a real war machine. In training, the cadet always had full control and sat in the front seat, linked with his instructor by a speaking tube. The credit for the idea of using a single type of machine for training and with this configuration belongs to Smith-Barry.

6. Training at the gunnery school. The Vickers is being aimed at a one-twentieth-sized model. Since neither trainee nor target is moving and since the exercise is being performed without flying kit, utility is questionable.

7. Vert Galand, one of the most famous aerodromes in France, just south of Doullens. The defending gunpits have been erased by the censor. The immaculate (and useless, since it had no barbed wire) trench system indicates a 1918 date when there were great fears of massive German infantry attacks for half the year. The separate officer and NCO compounds stand out clearly. By the road is parked a mobile pigeon loft. The crossroads location, typical of RAF aerodromes, was perhaps to make the German bomb aimer's task easier.

harmony of parts.' One can sense the biased affection of all veterans for those stable rotary machines of the war's middle years.

Seating configuration was just as important as engine type. The Avro was a two-seater with the pupil in the front seat from the beginning and in touch with his instructor at first by a waggled control column and later in the war through a speaking tube modelled on the device popularized by continental waiters in Soho.

This use of dual training aeroplanes represented a new conception. Throughout the war the French used the Blériot system, in which the individual taught himself through a carefully planned evolution towards expertise. The French cadet initially spent two months on the ground analysing flight theoretically before going to the 'frogs' meadow where 'Penguins' with sawn-off wings careered about at 40 mph with convulsive little jumps into the air. Six straight runs meant gradation to 30 hp Blériots. Right circuits followed left at 50-feet altitude, crashes assigning pilots to the glasshouse for ten days. The final test was with the 110 hp Nieuport, instructors working from the ground and sending their pupils up to execute specific manœuvres in short five-minute flights.

In the UK, by way of contrast, Smith-Barry's pupils were in full control immediately and airborne with an instructor. The order of procedure was then strictly laid down – demonstration of controls, straight and level flying, turn, misuse of controls in a turn, action of controls with motor cut off, slow flying and glide turns and, finally, take-off and landing. Each flight was preceded by half an hour of theory and followed by half an hour of discussion. During flight, every movement of each control would be analysed through the speaking tube, and if difficulties developed the pupil would first be invited to exhaust his own ideas before the instructor intervened.

When the basic manœuvres had been grasped, the cadet would be sent up for his first spell of solo flying. As the inventor of the programme put it: 'The object has not been to prevent fliers from getting into difficulties or dangers but to show them how to get out of them satisfactorily and having done so, to go and make them repeat the process alone. If the pupil considers this dangerous, let him find some other employment as whatever risks I ask him to run here, he will have to run a hundred times as much when he gets to France.' Nevertheless there was nothing of a kicking out of the nest about solo work. The instructor specified the exact

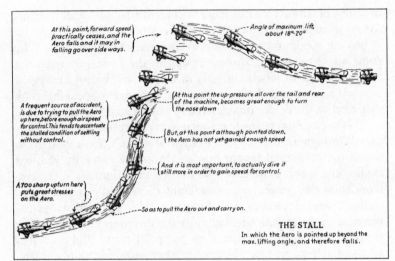

At this point, forward speed practically ceases, and the Aero falls and it may in falling go over side ways.

Angle of maximum lift, about 18°-20°

At this point the up-pressure all over the tail and rear of the machine, becomes great enough to turn the nose down

A frequent source of accident, is due to trying to pull the Aero up here, before enough airspeed for control. This tends to accentuate the stalled condition of settling without control.

But, at this point although pointed down, the Aero has not yet gained enough speed

And it is most important, to actually dive it still more in order to gain speed for control.

A too sharp upturn here puts great stresses on the Aero.

So as to pull the Aero out and carry on.

THE STALL

In which the Aero is pointed up beyond the max. lifting angle, and therefore falls.

FIGURE 5△   ▽FIGURE 6

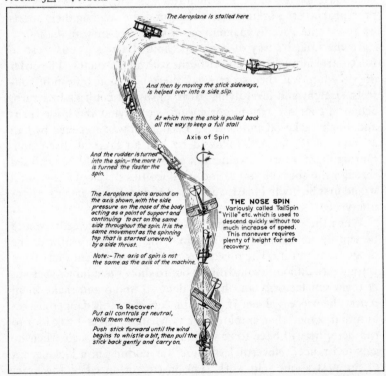

The Aeroplane is stalled here

And then by moving the stick sideways, is helped over into a side slip.

At which time the stick is pulled back all the way to keep a full stall

Axis of Spin

And the rudder is turned into the spin,— the more it is turned the faster the spin.

The Aeroplane spins around on the axis shown, with the side pressure on the nose of the body acting as a point of support and continuing to act on the same side throughout the spin. It is the same movement as the spinning top that is started unevenly by a side thrust.

Note:- The axis of spin is not the same as the axis of the machine.

THE NOSE SPIN

Variously called TailSpin "Vrille" etc. which is used to descend quickly without too much increase of speed. This maneuver requires plenty of height for safe recovery.

To Recover
Put all controls at neutral, Hold them there!

Push stick forward until the wind begins to whistle a bit, then pull the stick back gently and carry on.

manœuvres for each flight and discussed them after landing. This solo period was then followed by a final period of dual work, because: 'Unless a learner has practised doing a given thing in detail a good deal, he will not appreciate the details that are shown him. In this way, bad habits are corrected before they had time to become fixed.' Williams wrote of crashing on his first solo flight and of then being taken up again within minutes by his instructor.

The atmosphere on the training aerodrome was always one of calculated buoyancy, for, as Smith-Barry put it, 'half the battle is won when the pupil is instilled with the necessary confidence'. The ground behaviour of instructors typified this psychological approach. At Gosport, Vernon Castle instructed with a pet monkey on his shoulder. Gordon-Bell, with his off-white breeches, yellow leather strappings and massive stutter, always had two white Cairn terriers at his feet. Then there was Billy Williams:

> On one occasion Captain Williams, one of the greatest exponents of Avro flying, took up an Avro to practise completely stalled landings. At 500 feet he stalled until the engine and prop ceased to revolve. Then gliding down at a steep angle rather like the descent of an autogiro, he held his machine in balance by sheer piloting skill. In attempting to land from the stalled glide, he misjudged the final movement of the elevator and fell heavily

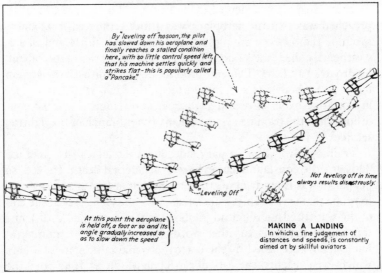

By "leveling off" too soon, the pilot has slowed down his aeroplane and finally reaches a stalled condition here, with so little control speed left, that his machine settles quickly and strikes flat – this is popularly called a "Pancake".

Not leveling off in time always results disastrously.

..."Leveling Off"

At this point the aeroplane is held off, a foot or so and its angle gradually increased so as to slow down the speed

MAKING A LANDING
In which a fine judgement of distances and speeds, is constantly aimed at by skillful aviators

FIGURE 7

the last few feet, crashing the undercarriage. Commanding officer Smith-Barry stood on the tarmac and without a word watched Williams jump out of the wrecked Avro and into another. The second Avro also stalled near the ground and crashed. Still the colonel stood, unspeaking. Williams went up in a third Avro and made an almost stationary landing right in front of his own hangar with the engine stopped. The colonel stepped forward. 'Good show, Williams. Good job for you you didn't stop trying at number two.'

Pupils' aerial confidence was made possible by Smith-Barry's success in getting the ban on stunt flying in the UK removed in August 1917. 'There have been too many prohibitions against reckless flying and too strong an emphasis upon death. This was against the very purpose of flying training, namely to make courageous fliers and aerial fighters.' Constraints removed, Smith-Barry made certain that, within the limits of his curriculum, machines were flown to their limits – and further when a pilot was proficient. Wings would be clipped, interplane struts removed and walking sticks poked through the fabric to simulate combat damage. Pilots would be ordered to use minimum landing space, to land on poor surfaces, to simulate sudden engine failure when flying low, or to take off and land in any direction. The aim was expressed simply by chief Gosport instructor Sidney Parker: 'The gospel which SB preached was that the aeroplane was a nice tempered, reasonable machine that obeyed simple, honest rules at all times and in any weather. By shedding a flood of light on the mysteries of its control, he drove away fear.' The end product of the Smith-Barry system taken as a whole was a training schedule which provided a more invigorating experience and gave truer knowledge of combat conditions than the training systems of any other branch of the fighting services in the Great War.

Training always had a dark side, however logical its conduct. This was the constant haemorrhage of accidental death. Indeed, so pervasive was the fear of death in training that few memoirs chose to probe that area deeply. Put statistically, official figures at the end of the war listed 14,166 dead pilots, of whom 8,000 had died while training in the UK. In other words more pilots died training at home than were killed by the enemy, a remarkable state of affairs which even reached the ears of Parliament. On 20 June 1918 the

Secretary of State was asked for an explanation. His answer naturally put the blame on the pilots themselves, since 'discipline after all was not the pre-eminent quality of youth'.

This was nonsense. German training deaths were only about one quarter those on active service, while official figures clearly show that as soon as the Smith-Barry programme was adopted deaths in training in the UK were cut from one per 90 hours to one per 192. Before adoption, 23 Wing reckoned on thirty-five deaths and seventy-five minor crashes monthly; after it, sixteen deaths monthly became the norm. The fact was that for three years the combination of a faulty philosophy and simple incompetence murdered many men, as the irrepressible backbencher Pemberton-Billing (later founder of Supermarines) never tired of pointing out during 1916. Director general of military aeronautics Sefton Brancker expressed the faulty philosophy when early in 1917 he told the Aeronautical Society that 'on the whole, flying itself is so easy that pupils suffer from over-confidence. Very few Englishmen won't make good pilots as long as they have sufficient experience.'

Incompetence found expression in the persistence of a rudimentary training system for three years, while the Blériot System was all the time available for comparison or adoption in France. Nevertheless for three years Farmans of one sort or another, with their top speed about 40 mph and stalling speed around 35 mph, were the chief training machines. The use of such machinery was laid down in a manual which devoted just six of its 141 pages to actual flying instructions and was administered by instructors chosen from men taking a break from active service for reasons of exhaustion or breakdown. Even Brancker reckoned that at best only 10 per cent of them were efficient teachers. Typical of such a 'system' was that, in Sidney Parker's first four hours of training, he had three different instructors and then went solo while they were all at lunch. McCudden later wrote that in his own training the best work had been done when two or three cadets gathered indoors and with their feet on the fender (rudder bar) and the poker (control column) in their hands combinations were devised and their probable effects worked out. Leigh-Mallory wrote that in his training he had learnt nothing except that low stunting was encouraged before men could fly well and that many accidents were the result of lax flying discipline.

Even when the Smith-Barry system took over, death remained

a constant fear, because many features of the day's aeroplanes made crashes unpredictable yet regular occurrences, and all men knew, if not exactly, that 10 per cent of all crashes meant death and a further 15 per cent produced severe injury.

In addition to these deficiencies in the training programme were flaws built into the actual aircraft.

Sopwiths were a well-respected and experienced firm, manufacturers of first-class war machines like the Pup, Strutter, Camel and Snipe. Their building process was nevertheless one of startling casualness to the modern eye. Sopwiths reckoned to conceive and construct a new fighter prototype in under eight weeks, with sketches converted into chalk lines on the floor and the walls of workshops without involvement of stress engineers at any stage. Even when systematic plans were produced, inexactness was so great that licensed builders in the USA found them completely unusable. Designers were by tradition after all the lowest-paid skilled men in Edwardian industry. The sort of qualities looked for in such men was suggested in a Short Brothers advertisement on the eve of the war: 'Draughtsmen wanted. Must be able to work out calculations.' Major defects were thus easily built into aeroplanes. Such were the unpinned centre-section wing struts of the Camel which Hurricane designer Sidney Camm later reckoned to be the cause – in combination with kiln-dried spars – of so many Camel deaths from wing collapse in a dive.

Another major defect was in petrol supply systems. Captain Hucks, an expert aeroplane tester, told the Aeronautical Society during the war: 'I think I have had to make more forced landings through the failure of the petrol supply than through all other troubles combined. This is due more often to the failure of the pressure feed than to a choke in supply pipes and very seldom to severed connections in the feed system. The present system of pressure feed is such a bugbear that it is high time something was substituted.' Nothing was.

When a new aeroplane came into service, Brancker reckoned that on average 400 modifications would be required. Even a fine machine like the SE5a needed over a hundred. Lower longerons would split along the length of the fuselage. Lewis guns had to be moved up five degrees since they shot the propellers off in the original design. Radiators leaked and oil-relief valves had to be reground and so on.

Engines suffered even more from these rule-of-thumb methods. A large-capacity rotary engine for the Avro 504K was the product of lengthy, precise manufacturing processes. The crankcase alone began as a one hundredweight steel block and ended fifty operations later weighing 28 pounds, each cylinder surface machined to a hundredth of a millimetre yet with all machining carried out individually on each crankcase. Even by the end of the war Rolls-Royce, makers of the only fully satisfactory British aero engines, had no machine tools or interchangeable parts.

Labour problems compounded such flaws. By 1918 manpower shortage meant that 44 per cent of aeroplane erectors were women and 10 per cent boys, while such was the War Office's mismanagement of conscription that in September 1917, when the Ministry of Munitions sought 203 skilled toolmakers for aero work, only three could be found in the whole of Great Britain, while 80 per cent of engine fitters then at work in the UK were men who started the war as unskilled labourers. Little wonder then that Hartney reckoned that a forced landing every two hours, most of them due to engine failure, was standard for most of the war.

Bad training methods, poor machinery and bad luck thus combined to make pilots build death and mutilation into their scheme of things at an early stage of their careers. Ward wrote of initiation the very moment he came to his training squadron: 'Going into the nearest hangar I asked a mechanic if he could direct me to the CO. At the far end of the hangar we approached a pile of wreckage. "Yuss," said my guide in a cheerful tone. "That is Captain Kane's Parasol. I was the fust to get 'im aht." Then, lowering his voice to a dramatic whisper, he added, "The top of 'is 'ead 'ad been tiken clean orff and there was 'is brains 'anging aht like a bunch o' grapes."'

Crashes thereafter formed punctuation marks during the course. Since men on solo had to be watched from the ground, these crashes were invariably within sight and sound of the aerodrome. 'From a distance we saw a column of dust rise and heard the sound of wood breaking into a thousand fragments – a sound that sends a cold shudder down the spine. And then that awful silence,' wrote Willy Coppens, with memories of his basic training at Hendon. All men would dash over to the pile of timber and cloth. Even if the pilot managed to survive the impact, the position of his seat next to the petrol tank was likely to give spectators experience of that other great fear of pilots. Burns on the palm of hands and lower part of face indicated first-degree burning. If the eye area was scorched, treatment had to be for second-degree burns. Third-degree burns took the skin off ears, nose and hand backs and would require the full apparatus of morphine, transfused blood and glucose drip immediately, for experience had shown that third-degree cases could not survive the preliminary journey to the burns centre. Observers would stand silent and reflective meanwhile.

In all these matters training was typical of the whole experience of war flying, with its mixture of short flying hours and lengthy stretches of relaxation; its mixture of gentlemanly routines and rakish individualism with death constant, utterly unpredictable, stunningly quick. When Hall, a war later, did his basic training in Spitfires at Ayr, seven men died during the first week of the course. According to rumour all deaths had been preceded by the sighting of a ghostly RFC machine. In the Great War, Ayr too had been a training aerodrome.

4
LEARNING TO SHOOT

During his work in the training squadron, the pilot would not have seen mounted machine guns. Landing, after all, represented the most difficult skill in learning to fly, and gun butts at eye level just a few inches from the face would have been too dangerous. Only when landing techniques became predictable were trainees sent to the special school of aerial gunnery, initially at Hythe on the Kent coast.

This course gave the fighter pilot of the future his first, indirect savour of war, since from Hythe the guns of the Ypres salient could be distinctly heard when the wind blew from the east; and when high cloud covered Ypres, field glasses could even detect distant aeroplanes pinpointed in combat. The period at Hythe was therefore a time of quietness and subdued behaviour. Time off was spent walking the adjacent golf course or sitting among the ruins of the old Roman coastal fort directly under the flight path of the main runway, adding new scope to the complex, introverted skills slowly being acquired.

Hythe specialized in two weapons. The Lewis gun, the more straightforward of the two, had been the RFC's original weapon, mounted on the top wing over the pilot's head so as to shoot over the propeller in the days before interrupter gears slotted bullets between the rotating propeller blades. Lewis guns seldom jammed or froze. Their problem was one of loading, for even the largest double-capacity ammunition drum held only ninety-seven rounds to the 500 for each Vickers. Re-loading was therefore a frequent exercise and a difficult one. The safety catch had first to be released and the gun slid down over a virtual right-angle bend in the aluminium mounting quadrant before the spent drum was lifted off its spike and another fitted against a slipstream of over 100 mph. At best, the operation required three separate movements in five seconds, during which time the machine had to be flown with the hands off the controls and the eyes disengaged from enemy activity. The final stage of moving the gun up and forward was scarcely within the physical capacity of most pilots, or so Fry thought. Though the Lewis in the hands of a skilled man was a killing instrument of the highest order – aeroplane designer Lanchester wrote of once seeing the forty-seven rounds of a single drum fired from an altitude of 600 feet at 1,000 yards distance all enter a ground target measuring three by twenty yards – the basic killer of nearly all pilots was the Vickers gun and it was on that gun that most time at Hythe was spent.

The Vickers, 43 inches long and 31 pounds in weight, was about the same length and weight as the second war Browning. Compared with the army version, the RAF muzzle cup of 1918 speeded firing from 600 to 1,000 rounds a minute. In addition, the aerial Vickers was fitted with an instrument like a car milometer which noted the exact number of rounds remaining at any moment. As a counter to freezing at height, a heater of nickochrome wire, wound round mica and powered from the machine's 12-volt power supply, was cased in copper and placed round the breech.

The chief problem with the Vickers was its tendency to jam, so the first task of all trainees was to understand the twenty-five possible causes for stoppages in flight. As the manual put it: 'Every pilot who is called upon to use a machine gun must have such an intimate knowledge of its mechanism as to know instinctively what is wrong when a stoppage occurs and must be able to rectify defects whilst flying.' Such work would always be done in a cockpit placed securely on the ground, the pilot in full flying kit and wearing several pairs of gloves. Blindfolded to simulate working without taking his eye off the gunsight, the student would have first to find the hammer clipped inside every cockpit, then wield it with his right hand after his fingers had assessed from the position of the gun's lever just what the particular reason for stoppage was.

Then came firing. The two problems to be faced were posed by aeroplane vibration and the moving target, which in practice merged to form the single greatest problem of aerial gunnery.

In the hands of even the steadiest fliers, it was reckoned that engine vibration in high-speed combat produced a bullet cone 30 feet in diameter at 500 yards. Such dispersion, combined with the small calibre of the bullets (0.303 inches) coming from just two machine guns, demanded that shooting should commence at short distances: 100 yards was thought about right. Even with eight such machine guns, the Battle of Britain wizards maintained similar Great War distances; thus 'Sailor' Malan and Deere specified 250 yards as the distance at which their bullets should converge. Blood on a victor's windscreen or fabric damaged from debris shot off an opponent were ace trademarks in both wars.

Such distances magnified the second problem of a moving target. An opponent, if aware of his situation, would always be turning away from his chaser and moving at about 70 yards a second. Even though bullets travelled at about 800 yards a second, such evasion meant that the bullet stream would have to be aimed ahead of the target. The difference between the straight-ahead shot and the actual aiming point was known as the deflection angle. On the one hand, the closer a pilot got to his target, the more likely he was to concentrate his bullets and score; on the other hand, the closer he got, the greater the deflection angles became and the more suddenly they would be created by evasion movements.

Until 1917 these problems were attacked with emphasis upon ground targets. Lieutenant Knocker wrote of strafing reservoirs and diving on to a target set in a chalkpit near Turnberry school. He recalled that the neighbouring market gardener was a frequent visitor to the squadron, with spent cartridges in one hand and broken cucumber frames in the other. But ground shooting could only be a poor substitute for aerial combat, since no ground target could move like a German aeroplane or induce realistic levels of vibration in the pilot's own aeroplane.

The breakthrough came with the adoption of two devices pioneered in Canada. The first was the deflection teacher, a one-eighth-sized wooden model placed at 25 yards and mounted on a trolley which could change quickly from forward to sideways motion. This would be used until a pilot became so handy with his gun sight that, as the 1918 manual laid down, 'placing an enemy in the sight became so natural that no effort of mind is required'.

The sights so used were of two types. Some men always remained faithful to the original ring and bead sights, in both wars. The theory was that at 400 yards an enemy machine overlapped the bead, at 300 the inner ring, at 200 it half filled the outer ring. When the ring was completely filled, indicating a target at 100 yards, action began. The problems were that the ring was easily knocked out of alignment and the bead was not easy to see in poor light.

Most pilots therefore switched to the Aldis sight when it was introduced late in 1916. Twenty-five inches long and two in diameter, the Aldis had two non-magnifying lenses and a ground-glass screen imprinted with lines and circles with a fitted rubber eyepiece fitting the instrument directly to the pilot's eye without him having to lean forward.

The other Canadian invention was the camera gun, which looked like a Lewis with a large box for breech. In this breech was a roll of film which registered the destination of each 'bullet' when the trigger was pulled. One roll of film per man per gun each day was the aim. The film would be developed within the hour and results posted in the mess 'in order to foster a competitive spirit among the pupils', as the manual put it.

Despite these developments, aerial shooting remained for the majority of pilots a baffling thing. There were always a handful of men like Princeton student George Vaughan, who hit a German machine and brought it down on his first flight with a single shot at an impossible deflection angle and then went on to knock down another six with his favourite shot – a vertical one with his SE5a hanging on its propeller. For most, basic skill with guns came only with long practice on active service. Fifth highest-scoring RAF man Beauchamp-Proctor hit nothing for five months. McElroy, who finally registered forty-nine Germans, likewise went five months without opening his account. When Ira Jones fought sixteen actions without result, he asked Mannock's opinion and was told to make less allowance for deflection. He then began to score. Mannock spoke from experience. The British ace of aces was forty hours in the air during Bloody April in 1917 before scoring. Similarly, in the second war, Hartman, who ended with a score of 352 killings to his credit, made little impact during his first six months. Aerial shooting was therefore an altogether more difficult business than the novels of W. E. Johns or the frames of post-war aerial combat films would have us believe. Calculation of distance and angle, synchronization of throttle and control column, counter-action against the distortions generated by fear and blood excitement, made killing in the air always a nice combination of geometry and experience.

Indeed, for most men it remained to the end an impossible business. One experienced pilot reckoned that vibration and deflection angles gave just five seconds of clear shooting per combat.

During that time, bullets would form a cone on the target about 20 feet square. To be sure of putting one bullet into a particular square foot – the enemy pilot's head or petrol tank – required a machine gun capable of 5,000 rounds a minute and in the Great War no British gun got above 1,000. Faced with such a task in coordination, Ira Jones reckoned that only one man in twenty reached the ace score of five. In his own crack squadron of fifty-six, which got more than its fair share of good pilots, just ten men got 246 of the squadron's final bag of 427. Of these, two men got ninety-four between them. So it remained in the second war. The Germans calculated that the average pilot would hit one of our night bombers with only 2 per cent of his cannon shells, in spite of having an elephantine target, gyroscopic sights and ammunition of massive calibre and with radar fair compensation for night shooting.

5
FINISHING SCHOOL

Up to the summer of 1915, fighting in the air involved few tactics. Aeroplanes just flew towards each other or turned away on the same plane with no thought of gaining height to convert into extra speed or of adopting defensive formations. At most, two or three machines might cooperate in a rough and ready way, circling endlessly for the chance of a straight-ahead shot. Combat was therefore a leisurely manœuvring which might take up to an hour. Even when Max Immelmann began to invent the basic tactics of all future fighter combat and create havoc among reconnoitring BE2cs, Smith-Barry's chief instructor Sid Parker noted that the RFC actively discouraged quick turning or evasion. Men never discussed defence, he thought, though all were developing a secret fear of being pounced on.

Then in May 1916 came official recognition of changing conditions. 'As the number of combats in the air is constantly increasing, it has been decided that pilots under instruction should be trained as far as practicable in fighting in the air.' To this end, schools of special flying were laid down at Turnberry, Marske, Sedgeford, Freiston, East Fortune and Ayr. There, finished pilots would simulate combat flying under the supervision of veterans. Ira Jones wrote of 74 Squadron doing this spell at Ayr in March 1918 under Colonel Rees, VC, instructed by aces McCudden and Maxwell, encouraged to throw their machines about and told verbally what to do and what not to do.

The basic mode of attack which had to be worked on was always the dive. Diving meant a reserve of speed which could be converted into manœuvre and gave the right to select the moment of combat by achieving surprise. It also enabled the attacker to anticipate his opponent's manœuvres more quickly and to guard himself from rear attack after a sudden turn on his opponent's part. A gunnery memorandum in 1916 laid down that height was half of success.

Most practising pilots would have put the figure much higher. 'Always above, seldom on the same level and never beneath,' was Mannock's cardinal piece of advice for any pilot asking for tips.

There were two problems to be worked on in the dive. First was control, because, as a Ministry pamphlet admonished, 'Inexperienced pilots are too apt to be content with diving and pointing their machines at a target and ignoring everything. Mere noise and fright will not bring down an opponent. It is necessary to hit him in a vital spot.' The possibility of such a shot followed only on holding a dive well in hand. 'By holding the right arm firmly against the body,' wrote one pilot, 'the machine can be held much steadier in a dive. It is essential to have plenty of engine power in hand so as to keep the means of climbing above the enemy throughout the fight and thus retain the advantage of height.'

The second problem was to calculate and then maintain optimum trajectory. The aim was to place the machine in the right position at the right speed for shooting. Against a single-seater, this position was reckoned by most to be above and behind for the straight-ahead shot. Against a two-seater, with its rear gun, 100 yards behind and 20 yards below, zigzagging to hinder the rear gunner, who would have to fight weight and wind resistance in moving his gun on its mounting.

Counter-measures against such diving attacks from enemy aeroplanes would have to be worked on at the same time. The most favoured was to wait until the last moment and then make a hard climbing turn for an attack of one's own above and behind the attacker. In other words, when the opponent was levelling for his shooting pass and losing his power of manœuvre, try to reverse positions. If the attack came from below and behind, then hard right or left and down into the firing pass. In both evasive movements, timing was the crux. Too early and the attacker could alter his angle of attack smoothly, still shooting. Too late and the attacker would have a simple straight-ahead shot at close range as if he were holding the twin machine guns to his shoulder like a single high-powered shotgun.

The official pamphlet also indicated the only other ways of escaping from an enemy closing in from the rear. 'If time permits, it should be the invariable rule to turn and attack before he comes to close quarters. If however he succeeds in doing so, the best chance lies in sideslip or a fall out of control.' Sideslipping could certainly be effective. McLanachan described an occasion when a sideslipping German dived from him in such a way that he never once got his guns to bear. Noble too wrote of an enemy sideslipping to within 100 feet of the ground and getting away with a ground-level dash. Sideslipping was nevertheless second-best, since it gave an attacker the permanent advantage of height and involved loss of speed.

Diving had as little to recommend it, since it meant playing to the main strength of the enemy throughout the war – his heavier and more robustly rigged aeroplanes. If a German managed to stay close in the dive, at some point the escaping dive would have to be levelled out with consequent slowing, presenting an easy target. It was crucial therefore to initiate a dive as fast as possible while the enemy was expecting a turning fight. To achieve this abruptness, the classic manœuvre was the 'wing-over', otherwise called the 'split-S'. The stick was pushed forward with the bottom rudder to achieve an outside loop; then the machine was rolled on to its back and the stick pulled fiercely towards the stomach, gravity forces

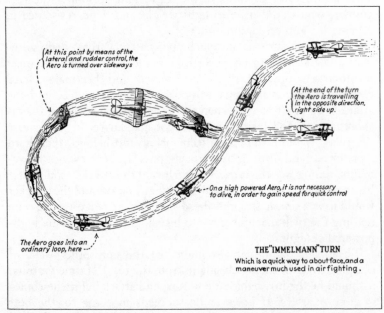

At this point by means of the lateral and rudder control, the Aero is turned over sideways

At the end of the turn the Aero is travelling in the opposite direction, right side up.

On a high powered Aero, it is not necessary to dive, in order to gain speed for quick control

The Aero goes into an ordinary loop, here

THE "IMMELMANN" TURN

Which is a quick way to about face, and a maneuver much used in air fighting.

FIGURE 8

pressing the pilot back into his seat throughout the manœuvre. Thus the diver not only avoided dangerous negative gravity forces but was also able to keep his eyes on his pursuer throughout the initiation of the dive. Rickenbacker wrote of once being forced into a split-S escape and diving his Nieuport at 200 mph. All the way he eyed the Nieuport's absurdly frail lower wing, then heard a crash like the crack of doom when he zoomed. His right wing collapsed but against the odds he survived, seeing clear scenes from his childhood and feeling a strong desire to meet his mother. Fry survived a similar dive away from a German Albatross with his radiator boiling. His machine needed a complete re-rigging on landing.

Diving or being dived on, men at the special schools spent their time flying one against one or in loosely threaded dogfights, close to the ground or using cloud cover to put combat theory into practice until it became almost a physical reflex. As a taster, the experience was valuable. Its practical value though was always desperately limited, since the demands of the west front for men meant that pilots seldom simulated combat for longer than a fortnight. There were moreover no live bullets, no anti-aircraft shells to produce those explosions of adrenalin or the drenching sweat of desperate fear which erased so much of the teaching of the schools above the actual battlefield. There was after all no way that home training could simulate the constant unreasons of men impelled to search for killings yet always intensely determined to live themselves. Therefore even more important perhaps than the shadow boxing of the finishing schools was the fact, never noted in the manuals or in memoirs, that such 'split-arse' flying was done in active service machines. The Avro 504K of the training squadrons, whatever the torque of its rotary engine, was a large aeroplane without the hair-trigger character of the service machine. Most squadrons had the odd Camel or SE5a, but the queue for them was always substantially longer than the experience of flying them. Only at the special school could a pilot get the feel of the real thing in combat-type manœuvre by flying at the full range of heights for longer periods than the Smith-Barry system ever allowed.

Such experience was crucial, because the machines of the intensive air combat period – late 1916 onwards – were unlike any fighter aeroplanes which followed. Hand-made by rule-of-thumb methods, their designers only just beginning to understand the characteristics which fighter pilots required, the early fighters were astonishingly individual. The DH2 was one-sided, the Camel super-sensitive, the Nieuport beautiful and responsive but liable to lose its wings, and so on. Further, each machine was personalized in rigging tune and engine character, so that it would fly harmoniously only for its regular owner. To these owners, such machines were looked upon as extensions of their own hands and feet. Pilots would absent-mindedly stroke the patched fabric of one particular machine and instinctively cock an ear in the mess when one particular distant engine began to work on test, like blind shepherds naming unseen sheep. One French ace called his machine '*Je*' and so too did all pilots of that period.

In another sense, besides the acquisition of 'hands', the special school finishing period was critical, for according to the machine allocation made by the commander the future pattern of a pilot's war flying was determined. In the first war there were only two types of fighter aeroplane. One sort hunted in tight circles like a dragonfly. The other dived like a kingfisher. The difference derived from engine type, for with the body of a moth and wings as fragile, the power unit imposed its own personality. Turners were rotary-powered and air-cooled; pouncers were water-cooled, with cylinders set either in line or V-paired in a massive cylinder block. Allocation therefore to the rotary Camel meant the high-adrenalin world of ground strafing, combat higher up being invariably initiated by an enemy whose machines were nearly all better equipped in height and speed than the Camel. In contrast, allocation to the water-cooled SE5a meant the safer world of top cover and stalking, of diving attack and diving disengagement.

The Sopwith Camel was always the principal rotary scout machine: 2,582 were in service by the end of the war, making up 40 per cent of our west front fighter strength.

Seen today from close to, museum Camels appear the most beautiful of our Great War fighters. Stitches and rivets are few, while the aluminium cowling has that dull sheen and smoothness which only hand-valeting can produce. Typically Camel are the butterfly nuts holding down the engine inspection panel to the cowling and making a sharp contrast with the legion of nuts and bolts bespattering other marques. Here is a machine with the simplicity of inspiration, compact as a hawk and with the hunched shoulders of a dart. Under these shoulders, on top of the cowling, are the twin Vickers guns, the butts just six inches from the pilot's face, the priming levers framing his vision like spectacles. Only six paces in length and nine from wing tip to wing tip, there is yet a feeling of space in the cockpit. The top wing is high and the bottom wing well back, giving a generous downward view. The centre wing section too has no cross-wiring and, since the pilot is able almost to reach forward and touch the propeller with his gloves, there is a sensation of freedom rare among the compact little single-seaters of the age. Within the cockpit, the pilot even has space to turn his shoulders, since the fuselage tapering from the fat rotary engine nose gave width unknown to the pilots of water-cooled machines. Here was both engine power and killing power, space and lack of distraction happily combined. Photographs of Camel pilots are different from any others. Invariably the pilots stand more jauntily and have that relaxed smile which goes with owner-ship of a classic – and anachronistic – machine.

On paper, the Camel's specification was not remarkable. Test pilot Carr at Martlesham, flying a standard 130 hp Clerget engine, reached 10,000 feet in twelve minutes and 20,000 in thirty-six, attaining a top speed of 125 mph. Its French Spad contemporary reached 10,000 feet in eight minutes, could touch 138 mph and could fly 3,000 feet higher. Camels delivered to the front, moreover, performed well below expectation for some time. Lambe, in charge of RNAS machinery at Dunkirk, wrote to the Ministry in June 1917 that Sopwith's 'need a damn good shaking up. They are simply out for profit and don't give a damn about the war pilots.' Logbooks were faked, finished products not inspected and Camels at best were reaching 10,000 feet six minutes slower than had the model originally demonstrated.

It was not speed or climb or ceiling which separated the Camel from other fighters and made their owners so jaunty. None was exceptional by the standards of the time. Responsiveness, that was the Camel trademark. Outside today's custom-built aerobatic machines, it was probably the most manœuvrable piston-engined aeroplane ever made. In official tests, the Camel would turn twice for every one turn of an SE5a and to the end of the war it could out-turn any machine in the sky except the Fokker triplane. Hartney, new to the type, was staggered by his first Camel flight when the machine seemed to go straight into the air and turn through 360 degrees in an instant. 'To make a swift right-hand turn without losing height,' he wrote,

one had to apply left rudder the instant the manœuvre began and push on the full rudder before full bank. Then the Camel turned very fast, far more swiftly than to the left. It was mainly on this ability that she won her fame in fight, for the heavier, stationary engined German scouts could not turn as quickly and when they were engaged at close quarters the Camel would make three turns to their two in a right-hand circle in spite of relatively inferior climb and speed at even moderate altitudes. But let the ham-handed or inexperienced pilot pull the stick back just a little too far while turning all out and the Camel would flick quickly into a spin. Never did I fly another aeroplane that spun so fast as a Camel for so little loss of height. She could complete one revolution of a spin in a drop of 100 feet. No wonder I was giddy after 25 rapid revolutions and needed the height loss of four more to restore my sense of equilibrium.

Put more simply and in war terms, here was a machine to win any turning fight, a machine to ground-strafe as easily as it could chase partridges and catch them on its wires; a machine to rise and fall sharply as a grouse, hitting the pilot with sods of earth shot up with its own machine guns.

There were penalties attached to these qualities. One was utter unpredictability. Whitehouse described the Camel as 'a moody, savage beast'. Some days it would perform all stunts, on others, none. Sometimes it would touch 120 mph, on others just 70 mph, and the pilot would return black as a pit pony, drenched in evil-smelling castor oil, the Camel's lubricant. Without throttle or carburettor, maintenance of optimum revs came only from constant blipping of the ignition button on top of the control column and movement of the fine adjustment control (choke). At any time, petrol vapour might be drawn through the exhausts and become flaming streamers which threatened to seize on the fabric covering the Camel.

The rotary movement of the engine cylinders around the fixed camshaft set another handful of problems. The torque of such a configuration combined with a very forward centre of gravity made the Camel, in Bridgman's judgement, 'one-sided, feverish and vicious'. Even more than with the 'spinning incinerator' (the DH2), take-off and turn were periods of danger. Taxiing for take-off, full right rudder had to be applied as counter to forces urging to a ground loop. Then, as soon as the tail fin rose, the rudder had to be straightened quickly to combat left circling and a crash on to a wing tip. The choke had to be cut immediately on take-off by moving the fine adjuster and the throttle continuously as the Camel rose. Once at a height at which change of direction could safely be attempted, torque would force the aeroplane nose down if a right-handed turn was attempted, and then, if the stick were pulled back too far to counter this, the Camel would stand up abruptly on end and stall. 'Wind up, tail up,' as the saying went. If a Camel was then dived, rotary torque tried to impose an outward loop. Tail-heavy in a climb, nose heavy in a dive and tending to stall in a climb and hunt in a dive, with inordinate vibration at all times, the Camel's rotary engine was to its pilot like a moody wife, loved perhaps for its sensitivity but punishing of the slightest lapse in affection.

Controls posed an additional battery of problems, as if the engine alone was an insufficient test of skill. Rigged tail-heavy, the stick had to be pressed forward in normal flight at lower altitudes, while the combination of ultra-responsive elevator with stiff ailerons could startle the unwary, as Hartney discovered:

The Sopwith Pup was smooth and stable, mellow like old wine. The Camel was a buzzing hornet, a wild thing, burning the air like raw spirit fires the throat. On the $1\frac{1}{2}$ Strutter we had to exert all our strength and skill to dive forward for they were very stable aircraft and resistant to any sudden change of flying position. We shoved the stick hard forward, simultaneously turning the tailplane wheel to increase tailplane incidence. In my keenness to follow the flight leader now, I inadvertently thrust my stick hard against the Camel's instrument board. B2314's response was instantaneous. Her tail rose like a bucking bronco and threw me head first out of the cockpit. I was shot out on to the top of my Vickers guns. There I lay with the windmill propeller blades almost grazing my nose until the terrific initial acceleration died down. Using all my strength, I forced myself backwards and upwards inch by inch to the cockpit until my right hand found the spade grip on the top of the stick.

With a back somersault I landed in my seat having fallen downwards for almost a mile.

Another pilot summarized: 'The Camel hated an inexperienced hand and flipped into a frantic spin at the least opportunity. They were quite unlike ordinary aeroplanes being quite unstable, immoderately tail-heavy and so light on the controls that the slightest inaccuracy would hurl them over the sky. Difficult to land, deadly to crash, the first flight in a Camel was a terrific ordeal.' Expressed in figures, Yeates reckoned three months' hard flying necessary to tame the Camel. Hence the value of the diving and stunting at the school of special flying. The period was never long enough to give instinctive control of a Sopwith Camel, but a single week still gave the novice a judiciously humble approach for his period of induction on the fighter aerodrome. Once 'hands' were acquired though the Camel was the chosen tool of the killers, the machine of Biggles and those other composite literary heroes who helped impose 'Camel vision' on the Battle of Britain generation of fighter pilots. It was, too, a machine good enough to survive into 1918, though 20 or 30 mph slower than its opponents.

The other type of aeroplane was the water-cooled, government-produced SE5a. Though Fokker and Sopwith, most prolific of the Great War aeroplane makers, remained by and large faithful to the rotary engine, the future lay with water-cooled, in-line engines because a heavy mass of rotating cylinders imposed a drastic limit on the possibility of increasing revs, and by 1918 it had become clear that speed rather than turn was the crucial element in combat. Fast in and fast out was the aim of 1918 fighters and remains so today.

Compared with its rivals, the SE5a was slower than the French Spad or German Fokker D7 and climbed more slowly than either. Its short, straight wings meant a long run to take-off, lack of lateral stability in the air and the need for an abrupt descent for a fast landing, with a strong urge to nose-tip on touch-down (during one week 40 Squadron reported twenty such nose-tippings). Henry Tizzard, testing the prototype, had nevertheless reported very favourably and most pilots agreed with the original verdict. Sholto Douglas, for example, gave a detailed analysis of the type in his unpublished memoirs. He pronounced it a singularly comfortable machine with a good all-round view, its Hispano Suiza engine very reliable, exceptionally silent and without the rotaries' nauseating smell of burnt castor oil. Performance at the combat height of 15,000 feet was vastly superior to the Camel's, its larger wing area permitting much easier handling than the Spad at such altitude. Heavy engine and low torque meant a fast, vibrationless dive without the varying angles of Camel and Dolphin, allowing both a stable gun platform in attack and an ideal means of escaping a Fokker D7. The one defect Douglas did remark on was heaviness in handling, but, as he pointed out, that mattered less in the formation fights of later 1917 and 1918. If a patrol were well led, he thought that SE5as should be seldom attacked by a cautious enemy. Looking back from today, German Great War veterans Schoenebeck and Jacobs were divided in their opinions of the SE5a and Camel as their stiffest opponents – a fitting tribute to the two classic British fighters.

Standing by museum SE5as today one is struck chiefly by the feeling of power. Cylinders project on either side of the nose like a boxer's pectorals, while twin exhaust pipes as thick as drainpipes flank the length of the massive engine unit, which in itself is about half the length of the aeroplane. Such a machine was clearly conceived as an aerial drag-racer, a sawn-off shotgun to the Camel's rapier. Even to get into an SE5a cockpit is a problem, as if the machine were reluctant to feel the weight of a man on its back. The left foot has to be placed on the foothole under the cockpit, the right on the wing base, with care to avoid the hot exhaust pipe. Then followed a twist of the shoulders, the buttocks resting momentarily on the fuselage top behind the cockpit, the feet reaching down and forward to the rudder bar loops, carefully avoiding the six control cables on the floor. Once in, the pilot was held firm, without even space to shrug his shoulders.

Closer examination of the bodywork reinforces the impression of purely functional, throwaway machinery. The long engine unit is covered on its top surface by three metal panels which fitted together as badly as they might in a mass-produced modern car. Rivets are everywhere. Many hand-made, ill-assorted panels or brackets seem to be added to the general shape almost as an afterthought. The cockpit area in particular gives an impression of hasty design by a team of designers working separately. The instruments are too deeply set for easy visibility despite the translucent panel above them. Dials, fitted into an ill-cut plywood panel, are of differing size and have a random assortment of numeral type and pointer shape. Some have lavish brass surrounds, others are in functional gun-metal. The airspeed indicator is tiny, the rev counter large. A crude and bulky hand pump for the petrol tank contrasts with a small control column which might be from a modern racing car. If an SE5a pilot wished to know his altitude, he would have to lean right forward, his head below the cockpit rim, to see a dial placed far to his right and set horizontally; the bubble likewise was set deep and recessed so that assessment of correct horizontal position in the gloom of a storm cloud must have been nearly impossible.

The overall impression is nevertheless of motorized thistledown, despite the army surplus store appearance of the detail. The fabric seems paper-thin, the unpainted underside translucent as a bubble. The wooden ribs of the skeleton press visibly, while the fabric is as tightly stretched as parchment overall. To the lightest flick of the finger anywhere, the machine answers with the unexpectedly loud boom of an African finger drum.

As long as such aeroplanes formed the basic trade tools of the fighter pilots, special flying schools were a necessity, since to a degree unknown to later pilots their handling was so different from any of the machines in which a pilot had learnt his scout flying that the week in the special school was like a completely new beginning. To the Camel or even the SE5a, the Avro seemed a parody in slow motion, a family saloon to a rally-tuned car. Great War veterans found it difficult later to explain these sensations, for even before the armistice the situation was changing. Machines like the later Martinsyde models, Dolphin and Snipe, needed no elaborate balancing act during flight. They were built to travel fast in straight lines and indicated the way ahead to the depersonalized machinery of later wars in which most things were done at second-hand through hydraulic intermediaries. But until such machines became the norm, each side had need of finishing schools before entry into the combat area – the French in their Réserve Générale on the Valois plains north-east of Paris, the Germans at Valenciennes and the British in their special flying schools.

6
OVER TO FRANCE

When training had been completed – after about seventeen hours of solo flying in 1917 or fifty in 1918 – pilots would be dispatched to France. In 1917, 3,400 of the 6,607 sent travelled with infantry drafts by train and steamer. The rest flew new aircraft, following the line of the London and South Eastern Railway to Dover before lining up the cross carved on the cliffs of Dover with a corresponding cross at Gris Nez. The common destination for both was the base depot at St Omer, until the smallness of that aerodrome precluded the faster machines of 1917 and Marquise took over.

Base was always a sort of limbo. While French pilots at the same stage would be on aerodromes and expected to fly daily within the looser disciplinary structure of active service conditions, British pilots at the pool just waited for the call individually to fill dead men's shoes on aerodromes at the front. This might well mean a wait of up to three weeks and, since no aeroplanes were made available, pilots meanwhile lost sharpness in their newly acquired skills.

A mood of sourness came to mark the void between the hard and anxious days of training and the certainty of tense and violent action to follow. 'My hat, what a place!' wrote Bewsher when he discovered that bacon and eggs, meat and veg, tea with milk and cakes were unknown at St Omer. Commoner were such denunciations as Lewis's:

> I must say, I think France is a bit of a hole. We are now at the best hotel in town but except for the food and a comfortable bed, it isn't in it with a comfortable inn at home. It is purely an eating house, nasty and untidy. Kitchen chairs and tables lie about in a mucky looking room with two funny looking wash basins in the corner. The streets are dirty and the people have a habit of

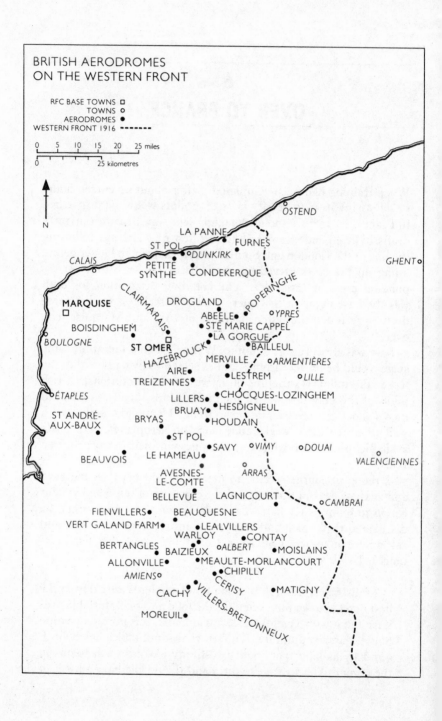

BRITISH AERODROMES
ON THE WESTERN FRONT

RFC BASE TOWNS □
TOWNS ○
AERODROMES ●
WESTERN FRONT 1916 ------

0 5 10 15 20 25 miles
0   25 kilometres

N

OSTEND

LA PANNE
ST POL   FURNES
         DUNKIRK
PETITE   CONDEKERQUE
SYNTHE
CALAIS   GHENT

         DROGLAND
CLAIRMARAIS   ABEELE   POPERINGHE
MARQUISE   STE MARIE CAPPEL   YPRES
BOISDINGHEM   LA GORGUE
BOULOGNE   ST OMER   BAILLEUL
         HAZEBROUCK   MERVILLE   ARMENTIÈRES
         AIRE
         TREIZENNES   LESTREM   LILLE
ÉTAPLES   LILLERS   CHOCQUES-LOZINGHEM
ST ANDRÉ-   BRUAY   HESDIGNEUL
AUX-BAUX   BRYAS   HOUDAIN
         ST POL
         SAVY   VIMY   DOUAI
BEAUVOIS   LE HAMEAU   VALENCIENNES
         AVESNES-   ARRAS
         LE-COMTE
         BELLEVUE   LAGNICOURT
FIENVILLERS   BEAUQUESNE   CAMBRAI
VERT GALAND FARM   LEALVILLERS
         WARLOY   CONTAY
BERTANGLES   BAIZIEUX   ALBERT   MOISLAINS
ALLONVILLE   MEAULTE-MORLANCOURT
AMIENS   CHIPILLY
         CERISY
CACHY   VILLERS-BRETONNEUX   MATIGNY
MOREUIL

throwing all refuse out into the streets to be taken away. The women are very slovenly and the whole place seems asleep.

Mannock commented in the same spirit on 'a nasty town full of dirty women and very dirty children with unmade roads glistening with their dirt', like the squalid villages he had seen when working as a telephone engineer in Turkey at the start of the war.

There was little to do. The straightness of the roads and featurelessness of unhedged and empty chalk landscape dulled the pleasure of walking, while no horses meant no hunting. Certainly there were many estaminets (or bars), but only infantry seemed able to relish the flat white wines of wartime. This left just gambling, and with each newcomer drawing 375 francs in three days from the field cashier as allowance for the next month and with the facility of being able to cash cheques in town to the value of £5 daily, Howsam's memoirs among many comment on the result. He recalled the large, bare rooms of the pilots' pool filled daily and all day with men in various stages of undress playing poker, blackjack and the bones, talking casually of death rates and crashes and speculating about new types of aeroplane. Type X was said to be supremely manœuvrable, with a tremendous rate of climb, but its ailerons were utterly useless. You could move the stick from side to side and nothing would happen. Another type was said to have no elevator. It stalled suddenly on a right-hand turn and spun on the least provocation. Yet another marque was said to be stable if inverted, so that it could not be righted if flown on its back.

The call to the front was therefore a relief from such nihilistic activity. It came as a list of names written in the ubiquitous indelible pencil of the Great War and on a squared army form held by a single drawing pin to the pool noticeboard. This board would be surrounded by a huddle of men each morning, talking in a serious, restrained way and comparing information. 24 Squadron meant the tradition of Hawker and Hazell. Wasn't 74 Mannock's squadron? And what of the aeroplanes? An acknowledged ace like Barker might be permitted to lead a Snipe squadron with a Camel but for everyone else 19 and 23 meant Dolphins, 4 and 43 Snipe. Overall, Camels constituted sixteen squadrons and SE5as the same number through the period of most intensive fighting. Pilots would therefore compare the machines to which they were allocated with the experience they themselves had had in the UK. They would know, too, the importance of aeroplane type in terms of survival or scoring. 24 Squadron's history set them out clearly:

8. 4.16 to 25. 5.17: DH2s flown with 44 killings in 774 combats
25. 5.17 to 25.12.17: DH5s flown with 3 killings in 205 combats
25.12.17 to 11.11.18: SE5as flown with 175 killings in 1,765 combats

Next morning a lorry would call for the pilots. Two men would join the driver in front, the rest climbing into the back, six men on each side with the floor a jumble of officers' Wolseley valises. Those who had made the journey before would have left unpacked the customized cushion intended for cockpit seating. Such men had previous knowledge of the combined effect of leather clutch soaked in castor oil and steel-studded tyres at 60-pounds pressure which gave a high-pitched whine on cobbled stretches of road.

On this journey new pilots entered 'no man's land', a country which made sense solely in terms of war and the atmosphere of war. This landscape through which the lorry drove conveyed only bewilderment to men who knew just the neat hedges and trim villages of England. Wrote Cecil Lewis:

God was painting a miniature when he filled in England. He brought a bigger brush to France. England can be mournful, dreary, damp, miserable but it is not melancholy. Melancholy implies a pensive sweetness and that is not an English quality. The wide, featureless landscape of north France, miles and miles of cultivated fields, brown from the plough receding to the horizon in immense vistas of peaceful fertility, is the sort of country that makes you understand why the French love their earth

– or conversely why the British could never accept the desolation of the Nord and perhaps the more so because they were travelling the same roads as the men and munition limbers of earlier battles. Today books delineate and give shape to these battles. At the time censorship and rumour gave a horrendous quality to words like 'Loos', 'Somme' and 'Passchendaele', which seemed to possess unlimited capacity to absorb, kill and dispose without trace. For newcomers, north France was therefore a landscape of death, a thing of vast views and emptiness, of skylarks and ominous peace in which men talked with hushed voices.

The people they saw reinforced the impact of the landscape. All seemed either directly related to the war or scarred by its passage:

> Everything is in khaki or blue. Every town is full of British soldiers either resting or doing work behind the lines. Hospital cars, transport and staff cars crowd the dusty roads. I admit that I never realized there was a war on until I came out here. Not a Frenchman to be seen. Women, boys or old men do all the work in the towns and in the fields. All the carts are driven by women – carts, blue smocks, sabots as in a Corot painting – and nine-tenths of the women are in black. I certainly never realized there was a war on in England. No one does. You can't help it out here.

The journey would be long and slow. In the war zone of France any journey was long, slow and apparently inconsequential, since routes and speed of travel were laid down with the most minute care by GHQ. Perhaps this might not be gathered from the calm of the driver, civilian for all his khaki, probably a city bus driver previously, since for him the route was instinct and his passengers the obverse of men now dead who had sat with him on previous journeys.

Under the influence of an alien landscape and taciturn driver, the journey would soon become a silent one, punctuated only by stops in the middle of desolate countryside, as Vee described:

> The passengers left at various points along the road where the squadrons had their headquarters until at length I was the only one remaining behind the silent driver. We came to a farm, turned off the main road and bumped over the ruts of a winding track. My head began to nod for the drive had been a long one and the evening warm. When after one exceptionally long doze I opened my eyes, I saw a line of poplars and thought myself back on the Lys. But there was no river here, just a wide expanse of open field. Then at a gate leading to an orchard we came to a halt. 'Here you are, sir,' the driver announced, speaking to me for the first time while with a stub of pencil he ticked off my name from his list. 'This is your squadron.'

Valise at his feet, the new pilot would first make a quick visual check on his aerodrome and have his worst fears confirmed. The smallness of service aerodromes was an enduring memory of the war and they had a reputation which earlier struck dismay into the expectations of trainees in the UK. A scout machine needed a minimum of 200 yards in which to land. France never allowed much margin of error.

Then came the matter of surface. Lee wrote of cinder runways under potato fields, Hartney of flags marking potholes on aerodromes shaped like saucers sloping the wrong way, Armstrong of runways flanked by woods or acres of hop poles with the hangars directly in the take-off line. Squadron cows whose job it was to keep grass down to a viable twelve inches might offer the sort of wandering obstacle which gave grateful pilots like Sholto Douglas welcome periods of injury leave. Some aerodromes had surfaces undermined by field mice; others required the attentions of marching infantry columns to flatten mud or press down sugar-beet roots. Only one feature linked such service aerodromes – none was as suitable for flying as the most unsatisfactorily sited training aerodrome in the UK.

Around a field perhaps 300 yards square, about thirty aeroplanes would be scattered. A dozen might be in a super Bessoneau hangar thirty yards square, its rain-soaked side billowing and sagging. The rest would be in small, portable canvas hangars holding three machines apiece and surrounded by hardstands of pitprops. The menace from German night bombing dictated such dispersal. Men, on the other hand, with a curious twist of military logic, were concentrated, the RFC manual prescribing an officers' compound 140 yards square, with Other Ranks adjacent in a space 142 yards square, despite being six times as numerous as the officers.

In 1916 many squadrons had slept in barns, used aeroplane wrecks as windbreaks and eaten breakfast on their aerodromes. By 1917 bleak rows of Armstrong huts registered the gradations and hierarchies of service life: officers' kitchen and Other Ranks' cookhouse. Officers' bathhouse and Other Ranks' ablutions hut. The squadron commander his own Nissen hut. Flight commanders a quarter of a hut apiece. Flying officers one sixth of a hut.

This hut settlement reflected something more than the fact that two separate Englands had gone to war. It stood too for the utter isolation of the air war, set between the war zone and rest zone of the infantry, remote from any army camp or headquarters. The only human settlement within reach would be the small village from which the aerodrome took its name, a single straggling street of tumbledown farm buildings and crumbling clay walls part concealed by piles of rank cow manure. Such a settlement seemed an almost prehistoric encrustation upon the dirt road, as ancient as the countryside within which it crouched. Up the road, past the aerodrome and over a wrinkle of low hills was the front line, perhaps fifteen miles distant. Awareness of it would be indirect, a constant thunderstorm by day, by night a horizon of stuttering arc lights which burnt the names of obscure villages into the memories of that first generation of fighter pilots.

Cut off from the mainstream of the war's movement, the aerodrome was a unit as independent and self-contained as a battleship. In the NCO huts would be six carpenters, two blacksmiths, four sailmakers, four electricians, four coppersmiths, fifteen riggers, twenty-four engine fitters, a welder, a vulcanizer and three instrument repairers. The presence of such craftsmen was the expression of a separateness and introversion which gave the fighter pilots' war its distinctiveness. Fifteen Leyland lorries and eight motor cycles, which consumed one third of the squadron's 180-gallon daily petrol allocation, linked the aerodrome with the periphery of the British Expeditionary Force's war.

After his silent survey, the new pilot would cross the field, pass the fire whose smoke indicated to returning pilots which limb of the airfield to land on and make for the largest of the huts – the mess.

The orderly officer then took me along to a Nissen hut. Five officers were playing poker at a table on the far side of the hut. 'Lieutenant Vee', said the Orderly Officer. They looked up as we entered but immediately returned to their game. Two more fellows were in bed, reading. 'You can put your bed up here,' said the Orderly Officer, indicating a space near the door. 'Good night.' And he went out. Nobody took the slightest notice of me. I pulled out a cigarette and sat down on one of the beds smoking it. Presently an ack-emma (air mechanic) came in and dropped my valise on the floor. He unrolled it, put up my bed and made it and then he too went out. The light in my corner of the hut was too poor to read by and I did not feel like asking my future comrades in arms for a candle so I went to bed. I was tired after the day travelling and soon dropped off.

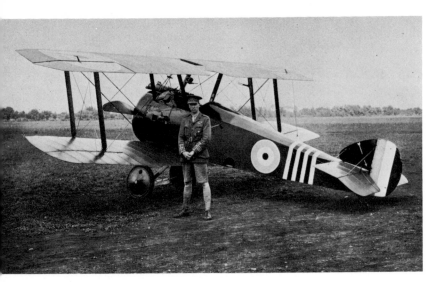

8. The Sopwith Camel made up 40 per cent of our west front fighter strength. Compared with a second war fighter like the American Thunderbolt, it had just a quarter the speed and a third the rate of climb, but with its fierce rotary engine set in such a light airframe, rigged tail-heavy and with hair-spring elevator controls, the Camels could turn twice as fast as most other Great War fighters or brush the grass with their wing tips, flick-rolling at 80 mph. With powers of turn and control like a polo pony – in skilled hands – Camels were rivalled only by triplanes in the turning dogfights. The pilot here is Canadian William Barker, termed by the man who was second in RAF scoring lists 'the greatest of all fighter pilots'. He led a Snipe squadron with a Camel and won a VC in combat against about sixty opponents.

9. The Dolphin was another Sopwith machine with a fine reputation, built specially for high-altitude work. The absence of a wing centre section was distinguishing mark. This gave fine upward visibility but made pilots uneasy about head injury in case they crashed. Bottom left are the fuel lever and magneto switches. The altimeter gauge is above. The twin Vickers guns with their priming levers and electrically heated butt ends are only about six inches from the pilot's face. Above them is the non-telescopic Aldis sight. To the right of the joystick, with its twin gun buttons, are fuel-tank pressure gauges and safety valves, with an oil temperature gauge above them. This is probably a test machine at Martlesham, hence the extra altimeter on the pilot's right. The number of instrument dials contrasts with the forty in a modern Lightning.

10. Pilots relax.

11. When the RAF was created in April 1918 from a fusion of the RFC and the Naval Air Service, authority produced the blue uniform to distinguish the new service. In this photo, taken at the RAF sports at St André in June 1918, the officer competitors are already wearing it. For all the easy-going equality of the service, it would have been unthinkable for NCOs to run against officers. The expressions of the NCOs and mechanics in their old-style maternity jackets suggest the novelty of this event.

2. Number 1 Fighter Squadron at Clairmarais. There seem to be three flights with six machines a piece. The squadron commander, recording officer and armaments officer are distinguished by the absence of flying helmet and goggles, the skipper standing out clearly because of his cap, cigarette and cane of office. Two fitters and two riggers stand by each machine at a respectful distance. The diversity of dress was peculiar to the service. Footwear ranges from Oxford brogues through ammunition boots to flying boots, trousers from cavalry breeches through putteed slacks to what look suspiciously like civilian trousers. Topwear varies from maternity jackets based on dragoon uniform to the all-in-one Sidcot suit of 1918. The scarves all the pilots wear served the dual purpose of eliminating cold air and protecting the neck against chafing during constant turns in flight to check the tail. The various stray dogs in the picture reflect the magnetic quality of aerodromes for dogs from miles around. The machines are SE5as, rated our best all-purpose fighter. In the photo, the top-wing Lewis on its quadrant and the marked wing dihedral to increase stability may be seen.

3. An informal picture of some men in 141 Squadron. Tinted triplex goggles stand out well. Many pilots – like Ball – preferred sore eyes to restricted peripheral vision. Even more would push their goggles up to check their Aldis sight more accurately if combat were imminent. Since fighter squadrons were months in the same location, egg- and milk-producing pets were common.

14. Edward Mannock began the war as a labourer, almost blind in one eye, and ended the war as British ace of aces. The critical time for him had been a leave in June 1917 when he worked out theoretically all the tactics of Circus fighting and returned to the front to win most of his victories, like Richthofen, in team fighting. As 85 Squadron wrote when they applied for Mannock to lead them after Bishop had been recalled: 'He plans every manœuvre like a chess player.' There was nothing daredevil about his tactics. 'My system was always to attack the Hun at disadvantage.' Killed in the Ypres salient, he was almost forgotten after the war.

7
INDUCTION

The new pilot's first full day on the fighter aerodrome invariably started in a low key. A fighting unit of just eighteen men, all officers, had no need at any time of those little ceremonies which elsewhere in the army re-asserted hierarchy and subordination. Nor would such slow-motion rituals have fitted easily a unit which fought every day, without rest. The fighter pilot's day had therefore a civilian beginning. Wrote Vee:

It was broad daylight when I woke again. Two or three fellows were stirring and one of them asked another for a gasper. A man near me was dressing. He looked across and seeing me awake said 'Morning'.

'Morning,' I answered. 'How long does the early patrol stay up?'

'Oh. A couple of hours.'

Presently they came in, walking clumsily in their Sidcot suits and thigh boots.

'See any EA this morning, Mac?' asked the man who was dressing.

'Ran into eight of them over Guise. Brooks got one and the rest of them cleared off.'

'Good egg.'

Our aerodrome of Guizancourt was only eight miles west of St Quentin and the intermittent gunfire could be heard very clearly. I was conscious of it all the time but no one else seemed to pay the least attention to it. When I had dressed and shaved, I went out and found Smiles smoking an early pipe. 'The OO told me last night that we had to report to the CO immediately after breakfast,' he said. So after breakfast, Smiles and I went along to the orderly room to report to Major Field. Smiles was called in first. He was in the orderly room for about ten minutes. Directly he came out, I was sent in.

The tone of this first official meeting with the commanding officer was likely to surprise the newcomer, whose initial impression of the squadron had been one of ease and informality, the CO lounging in the mess or joining a game of tennis on the squadron's improvised court. Now, in his office, the CO would be wearing the unsmiling face of a veteran pilot commanding a unit whose death rate was as high as any in the army. The CO knew too just how heavily the odds were stacked against the man now in front of him.

Without checking any records, he knew that about 80 per cent of air casualties were among pilots who had flown fewer than twenty missions and that, even if the pilot survived the twenty, odds would lessen only slowly because, if 70 per cent of losses amongst first-year fliers were directly attributable to faulty piloting rather than enemy virtuosity, so too were 30 per cent among second-year men and 12 per cent among third-year veterans. Acquiring survival techniques on active service was thus a slow business, but the CO probably quoted no statistics when he met newcomers. As keeper of the squadron book and the man whose task it was to cross through names and write to parents, faces and voices rather than numbers marked the passage of time for a squadron major.

In addition to such probabilities, the CO knew also that the attitudes of most new pilots reinforced a strong tendency towards death, because each newcomer had been preceded by a confidential report from his training squadron commander in the UK. A large sample survives today in the London Public Record Office suggesting that for every one cadet like Robert Saundby ('A very keen officer with good judgement and excellent hands') or Arthur Harris ('Keen and capable. A good organizer') there were a dozen like Lieutenant Shields ('A very confident pilot. Will need watching at first as he is inclined to be reckless') or Lieutenant Greig ('Has the makings of a very good pilot but inclined to be uppish and is of civilian aerodrome pilot type') or Lieutenant Chabot ('Very capable at looking after an aeroplane and engine. Lacks common sense with regard to flying. Qualities as an officer? Wants watching'). The high social status of many pilot cadets together with the absence of any awareness of the effect of Spandau machine guns or Krupp anti-aircraft shells in training seem to have generated a sporting attitude which in the war zone meant a quicker death whatever the basic flying skill.

The major wouldn't mention these things. Glancing through the squadron book for himself later, a new man would work out such statistical probabilities in due course. His attitude, too, would become more sober with time when set against the realities of war flying and the resonance of the mess – if he survived long enough. But what the major could check on was general level of basic skill, for this was a tangible thing capable of that concrete, brisk analysis which gave point to the squadron commander's authority.

In the early stages of the war the bulk of training had been left for France, so that Belgian ace Willy Coppens had been sent to the front from Hendon without once having banked an aeroplane in flight or landed into the wind. In the war's middle years, high mortality rates had cut short training to the point where the average pilot crossed the lines with just fifteen hours' solo work behind him – about half what was necessary. Lieutenant Williams, the last man to be gazetted from Sandhurst, was an example. Sent to France without having fired any machine guns, Williams discovered that only one flight commander in his squadron had had war experience, with the result that after four weeks he found himself the only survivor from the original squadron. Even when the Smith-Barry system improved such matters, the old regime of low morale, dirty machines and instructors living off the squadron survived in stations distant from Gosport. After the ten-minute interrogation, the new pilot would therefore be sent up on a test flight to probe this dark area and with instructions to fly within sight of the commander.

The mess would empty to watch this test flight. Loops, vertical banks, landing in particular, because on the pilot's lightness of throttle work and exactness in three-point landing would depend his strength of hold on life. As far as the new man was concerned, the squadron at that moment felt little concern for his future health and would watch in silence, for underneath the ritual friendliness was an ambivalent feeling towards the newcomer. On the one hand, an inexperienced pair of hands in a war in which survival depended above all on maintaining formation endangered the other five men in the flight. On the other hand, the very presence of a new man meant one squadron pilot dead. With this aspect in mind, Albert Ball once wrote in his diary of three topping chaps lost and of the bitter need always to have to get used to new faces belonging to young men straight from school, without ideas and foul of language, good only for ragging in the mess. McLanachan, with 65 Squadron, found himself sent up immediately on arrival in Jake Parry's Nieuport. He was only told later that the machine was due for a complete re-rigging and engine re-bore at depot. Commenting on the episode in his memoirs, McLanachan observed that it always took a long time for a new man to be accepted as a colleague even if the squadron was harmonious and had suffered no drastic losses.

If the newcomer were fortunate enough not to join the squadron during a major land battle when pressures on the squadron were extreme, the first stage of induction would be under the control of the squadron commander and involved daily flying within sight of the aerodrome. Robert Orr's logbook shows this period of flying behind the British lines to have lasted five weeks, while future ace Beauchamp-Proctor remained under his CO's eye for six weeks.

During this time, the new pilot came under Standing Orders, posted on the squadron noticeboard:

> Take a daily interest in your machine. Check it for half an hour before and after every flight. Sit in the cockpit on the ground and practise gun loading. Spare your engine all you can. Always. As soon as a pilot begins to know his work, the keenest offensive spirit is expected. At all times it is to be remembered that it is the squadron's duty always to fight well east of the lines and keep the enemy from approaching his own lines.

This last point was for the future. In the meantime the CO would be checking progress in the novice until he approached the point specified by Major William Bishop:

> To be able to fight well, a pilot must be able to have absolute control over his machine. He must know by the feel of it how the machine is, what position it is in and how it is flying so that he may manœuvre rapidly and at the same time watch his opponent. He must be able to loop, turn his machine over on to its back and do various other stunts – not that these are actually necessary during a combat but from the fact that he has done these things several times he gets absolute confidence and when the fight comes along, he is not worrying about how the machine will act. He can devote all his time to fighting. The flying part of it will come instinctively.

Once this point had been reached, the novice was handed over to another teacher, because it had been laid down early in 1917 that no squadron commander could lead his men across the lines. War zone training was thus the duty of flight commanders, who received an extra 7s. weekly for their responsibility.

Few flight commanders are mentioned in the pages of memoirs. Perhaps this was due to their proximity to the sharp end of war. As in the land war, such a position made authority quieter, graver. With competence in survival and killing measurable daily, a flight commander had no use for those little touches of flamboyance which, away from high explosive, asserted status. Boaker stuttered and suggested. Arthur Harris ordered with laconic bluntness. Grid Caldwell led his team without orders or tactics, like a man possessed. Mannock planned every manœuvre like a chess player. But whatever their personal style, such men were crucial. In his unpublished memoirs, Canadian ace Raymond Collishaw wrote that, since all practical matters were in the hands of flight commanders, the CO's job consisted just in being cheerful. If flight commanders were incapable, the squadron commander's job was hopeless – or so Collishaw thought.

The flight commander often seems to have taken pride in his responsibility, chivvying his flight to early bed if a dawn patrol was imminent or watching their smoking and drinking habits narrowly. William Barker comes down to us specifically as having taken much satisfaction from not losing a man on his patrols. A flight was after all the equivalent of a section or even a platoon in the ground war, units in which the relation of subaltern or senior NCO to men was often tinged with the passionate protectiveness which togetherness in battle gave. American ace of aces Rickenbacker gave an extreme example of such feeling. When a Fokker swooped on the rear man in White's flight,

> like a flash White zoomed up in half a turn, executing a renversement and came back at the Hun leader to protect his pilot. White was one of the finest pilots and best air fighters in our group. He had won seven victories. His pilots loved him and considered him a great leader. White's manœuvre occupied an instant. He came out of his swoop and made a direct plunge at the enemy machine which was just getting into line at the rear of the Spad's tail. Without firing a shot, the heroic White rammed the Fokker head on while the two machines were approaching each other at a rate of about 250 mph. It was a horrible

yet thrilling sight. The two machines actually telescoped together, so violent was the impact. Wings went through wings and at first sight both Fokker and Spad seemed to disintegrate. Fragments filled the air for a moment, then the two fuselages, bonded together by the terrific collision, fell swiftly and landed in one heap on the banks of the Meuse. For sheer bravery, I believe this heroic feat has never been surpassed. This was White's last flight before he was to leave us for the USA on a visit to his wife and two small children.

Formation flying was the first thing a flight commander had to teach his new men. Adopted systematically only in May 1916, formation work had formed no part of the UK training system, and even in France there was never an attempt to impose orthodoxy. Some flight commanders chose diamonds, others the stepped-up V with steps of 50 yards between pairs to counter anti-aircraft shells and slipstream. Basic second war formations like stepped-up pairs in echelon or two such pairs working together were certainly common in 1917, but it was no unusual thing to find each of the flights in a squadron adopting a different formation shape. But whatever the formation, one flight would cover about one square mile of sky, the leader distinguished by his rudder streamer and front position, which relieved him of the need to check his tail and made him the eyes of the whole flight. If he were eliminated from a patrol, his deputy, distinguished by streamers flying from each outer wing strut, would take over.

Formating was never easy even for experienced fliers. On calm days, turbulence would harass novices struggling with the rhythm of their throttle work ('Good formation work can only be carried out by pilots who know how to use their throttles', stated the manual) or failing to anticipate sudden changes of direction (wrote Bishop: 'Every time the formation turned, it took me two or three minutes to get back into my proper place'). Often a novice was so concerned with his instruments that he failed to notice the wing-rocking and inclined arm of his flight commander, the signal for the initiation of direction change. Or he might be catapulted backwards by slipstream blast before he had discovered the correct technique of flying nose down into it, using rudder pressure to counter distortion of the flight path.

While a newcomer struggled with these procedures, the flight commander would tuck him into a particular position. McCudden put novices at the rear so they could dive under the formation if threatened. Jacob wrote of placing them in the middle of his V with the best men at the back, while in Ellwood's formation new men flew next to the leader and any tendency to straggle was countered by machine-gun bursts over the offender's tail by the next man astern. Wherever they were placed, their capacity to keep formation was perhaps the single most necessary skill in war flying. Wortley reckoned that 80 per cent of war deaths were the direct result of losing formation. When position could be kept, therefore, a novice was reckoned ready for his first flight over the line.

This first flight was never forgotten. Wrote Bishop: 'The way I clung to my companions that day reminded me of some little child hanging to its mother's skirts while crossing a crowded street. I remember also I felt like a child when it goes up a dark flight of stairs and is sure something is going to reach out of somewhere and grab it. I was so intent on my clinging part that I paid very little attention to anything else.' Ira Jones recalled 'a very trying flight' and thought it a tenser experience than receiving a first ball from Larwood. Mannock described his feelings on first going over the lines as 'very funny'. Meanwhile the self-absorbed novice would be watched most closely on this flight. Any sign of hesitation or of losing flying skills under pressure and the newcomer would, in Macmillan's experience, be very quickly sent to a two-seater squadron – for a single weak link endangered the whole flight.

During his first flights, there was little else the novice could do but concentrate on keeping formation. As to the sky, all beginners were as good as blind. When Rickenbacker began his war flying, his friend Lufberry ragged him for failing to see a single machine on a flight which passed 500 yards away from two separate formations of five Spads apiece, with a flight of four enemy Albatrosses at two miles and a German two-seater just 5,000 feet below. In his first dogfight, Ellwood likewise saw just two of the fifteen enemy involved, while McLanachan drily commented on Wolff's first dogfight: fighting seven Albatrosses, he had seen only one and had thought the stunt-flying of his formation simply an expression of good feelings. On returning to ground, Wolff's mechanics counted fifty bullet holes in his fabric, eight within a foot of his head.

In part, this problem was a mechanical one, for biplane configuration created many blind spots, while engine noise, cold and air rush, which always vibrated the goggles, conspired to confuse concentration. The basic problem was a simpler one though – the fact of an empty visual field focusing eyes at one or two yards. To counter this, partial remedies were passed on by the experienced. Best was the figure-of-eight scanning of the sky, which would be divided into three sections by means of top-wing and centre-section struts. The crossing point at each figure of eight was the wing tip, which allowed the eye to re-focus. The sequence might be: first, a straight-ahead search from port wing tip to struts; second, from the centre section to the starboard wing tip; third, a steady sweep from wing tip to wing tip, with a check behind by swinging the machine from side to side; finally, a check of the area round the sun, the thumb acting as a shield. Such movements were usually set in a slow corkscrew of the machine, which allowed the whole sky to be searched every thirty seconds. Other men preferred a flight path made up of a sequence of 45-degree tacks to cover blind spots, but under no circumstances did any machine ever fly straight for over half a minute. Blind machine, dead pilot.

Looking back after the war, Rickenbacker thought vision in the air was gained only by experience and that no beginner was gifted with it. Ira Jones reckoned such experience meant the capacity to see the enemy at one mile, though the hostile aeroplane would seem no bigger than a wood splinter taken from a man's thumb at that distance. Yeates wrote that even after a couple of months an experienced pilot could still be surprised as aeroplanes seemed to appear or disappear mysteriously.

Wild shooting was the little publicized result of persistent difficulties in seeing. Crundall wrote of once seeing a 'friendly' machine 1,000 feet above him on dawn patrol. Unseen, it got on to his tail and began shooting. For several minutes he thought the noise was just lose wires flapping. Ira Jones had a similar experience. His 'French' aeroplane turned out to be a Rumpler which put nine bullet holes in his seat cushion and caused a wing strut to collapse when he landed. Errors were made the other way round as well. Twice Rickenbacker recorded nearly firing on French machines and once was chased home by a pair of American aircraft. On another occasion he was met head on by a French Spad which tried to get on his tail. Since his own Nieuport was faster in climb and turn, he was able to show his colours, but drew the necessary moral – never trust any machine in the sky. These were not just problems of the Great War. German ace Balthasar in the second war all but shot down Galland's 'Spitfire' 3,000 feet below him. On our side, Blenheims would be intercepted as Junker 88s while 'the battle of Barking Creek' turned on the likeness of the Hurricane to the Messerschmitt 109.

In the end, experience and rules of thumb were the only counter. Top wing extensions were characteristically German. The V struts of an Albatross stood out at a great distance. Monocoque plywood fuselages with the appearance of aerial cigars could only be German. Allied camouflage tended towards khaki-green; German camouflage to black dotted grey or blotchy green purple with octagonal lozenges. But, if in doubt, pilots tended to shoot before checking. During Third Ypres, the RFC had to make automatic court martial the penalty for shooting down a French machine.

Keeping formation, seeing the enemy – these were the basics. In the absence of aerial intercommunication by wireless in the Great War, whatever else was learnt was acquired in those informal de-briefing sessions with which a good flight commander ended a patrol.

Mannock gave lots of useful advice. He explained how to effect surprise by approaching the enemy from the east or how to utilize the sun's glare or clouds to achieve the same end. Pilots, he said, must be kept physically fit by exercise and by the moderate use of stimulants. Pilots must sight their own guns and practise as much as possible as targets are usually fleeting. His fighting tactics, he told us, varied with circumstances. There were rarely two identical situations. Enemy personnel, type of aircraft, meteorological conditions and the position of the enemy constantly varied and, consequently, adjustment of tactics had to be made to suit the occasion. However the main principle of his tactics remained the same – the enemy must be surprised and attacked at disadvantage, if possible with superior numbers so that the initiative was with his patrol. To achieve this objective, it was sometimes necessary to spend over half the time of a patrol manœuvring the enemy formation into an unfavourable position . . .

In all memoirs which touch on this spate of verbal advice, there is invariably a striking absence. What of the enemy? How good were his pilots or their machines? How much were they to be feared? How did they work together? Why did an RFC aerodrome have no hut with information on enemy aerodromes or aeroplane types, as French aerodromes did? Why did the Air Ministry pamphlet of 1918 follow its first point – 'The pilots in the German flying corps are bad. Also their morale is poor' – with the caution that they should never be attacked unless the British had more machines in hand? The intelligent novice guessed quickly enough. Knowledge so damaging to morale was only to be picked up slowly, privately, by each individual pilot.

The novice's first experience would be gained in manoeuvring against enemy aeroplanes. There he quickly found that only Spads or SE5as were a match for German Albatrosses and Fokkers. When Sholto Douglas was given the opportunity of flying a captured Fokker D7, mainstay of the German force in 1918, he was impressed. As fast as a Camel in a left turn, it had twice the Camel's rate of climb, while in mock combat with an F3 Martinsyde (185 hp BMW against 275 hp Rolls-Royce) the Fokker won comprehensively. Like most German machines, too, the higher the better. Flying an SE5a, Springs was saved several times only by the intervention of purpose-built Sopwith Dolphins above 20,000 feet. The year 1918 saw too the beginning of mass production of the Siemens Schuckert D4, with a double rotary engine which gave a faster turn than a Camel in both directions, a faster climb than an SE5a and a ceiling 2,000 feet higher than any RAF machine.

When he reached the stage of fighting, the RFC pilot acquired similar respect for German pilots. 'The German aviator', wrote McCudden,

> is disciplined, resolute and brave and is a foeman worthy of our best. Although I have seen some cases where a German aviator has on occasion been a coward yet I have seen on the other hand many incidents which have given me food for thought and have caused me to respect the German. The more I fight them, the more I respect their fighting qualities. I have on many occasions had German machines at my mercy over the lines and they have had the choice of landing and being taken prisoner or being shot down. With one exception, they chose the latter path.

French ace of aces René Fonck similarly found only one German willing to surrender, while ace pilot Claxton, who favoured the head-on attack, several times had to give way to fighting enemy who came straight at him.

After establishing for himself the strength of the enemy in terms of machinery and personnel, an RFC man slowly began to realize that he was fighting a force altogether more precise and professional than the RFC/RAF. In contrast with the gung-ho policy of dispatching scouts across the whole length of the line throughout each day and at regular times to patrol a predictable front of about thirty miles, the enemy picked his punches. Indeed, with only one third the number of aircraft, his options were limited.

If the Germans required information which could not be got from balloon observation, solitary two-seaters were sent across the line, usually too high to be reached and too heavily armed to be attacked if they were reached. René Fonck rated fighting enemy two-seaters the most dangerous way to gain experience. Springs reckoned that two fighters were needed to take on a single German two-seater; Porter preferred odds of three to one on. Even pinning them down proved a problem. Lewis described Rolands running rings round DH2s on the Somme, while Ira Jones found the Rumpler faster than SE5as above 18,000 feet. Little wonder then, as Long noted, that the enemy's two-seaters were the only aeroplanes which always flew straight and took no evasive action.

German fighters meanwhile flew no regular patrols. Richthofen laid it down that such regularity reduced a pilot's appetite for blood. Enemy scout pilots would therefore be waiting on the ground in deck chairs, looking for prey through field glasses or waiting for phoned information from front-line observation stations. When German fighters flew and attacked it would only be with superiority in numbers and height, and they would be guided by their own AA guns, which would use shell bursts to indicate danger. Fighting just over their own lines, the enemy had in addition a permanent advantage in fuel capacity and the direction of the prevailing wind. As strategists, therefore, the Germans came to be respected by all British pilots. Wrote Bishop: 'Almost every evening we would find well-laid traps set for us. It required careful manœuvring to avoid falling into them. Several times we did and it took a lot of trouble to get out safely. Four or five Huns would come along and we would engage them. Then suddenly as many as fifteen or twenty would appear from all angles and join in the fight. This happened every day and the Huns were evidently out to get us.' And so it remained in the second war. In the *News of the World* (21 March 1943) veteran Ira Jones wrote that the Hun had not changed. He gloried in ruse and decoy as much as he had done in the first war and deserved a little credit for some of the stratagems he had conceived.

A final element of unease might be added when a German pilot was shot down and entertained in the officers' mess before being sent into captivity. Talking shop, RFC men would discover that no German could become a single-seater man unless he had demonstrated above-average capacity in two-seater machines. That, of those chosen, 30 per cent would then be rejected on medical grounds. That no German scout pilot was sent to the front without six months' overall training, which had to include three weeks at Valenciennes under the eye of men like Richthofen or Udet. That a strict check was kept on all flying through a barograph in the cockpit, while electrically heated suits, parachutes and liquid oxygen were standard equipment by early 1917. Such differences between the two services were perhaps even more disturbing than the strategical and tactical, for the latter might be countered by superior individual skill and knowledge. Differences in training and equipment, however, seemed to give a permanent built-in advantage in every situation.

The overall result of this greater professionalism was reflected in the casualty figures. According to official figures issued to the press in February 1919 and repeated exactly in the official history, the relative statistics were:

Dead: 6,166 British to 5,853 German
Missing and prisoners: 3,212 British to 2,751 German

Even if these figures were correct, they were alarming enough, because British figures related chiefly to the west front while the German covered both east and west fronts, and on both the British and French sections of the latter. There is the suggestion, more-over, that official British figures were as unreliable as those supplied for ground war losses, for when official British air historian Jones contacted the Potsdam archive, the figures he received relating just to the west front were:

1915: 50 British dead to 27 German
1916: 357 to 67

1917: 1,811 to 296
1918: 2,508 to 662

A competent and critical historian with a huge mass of information available to him which has since been mislaid, Jones thought that the figures may well have been correct and in his official history was prepared to accept the possibility that the British had lost men at about four times the enemy's rate.

Official British figures certainly contain puzzling features in their support of equality in loss. When statistics for the whole war were published in the HMSO volume of 1922, the dead, missing and prisoners after April 1918 were listed at 1,922. Figures given in the press briefing in early 1919 however, though agreeing with the overall figure of 6,166 dead, with 3,212 prisoners and missing, set the post-April 1918 figure at 4,517 – more than double the figure given three years later. In addition to this discrepancy, it seems rather hard to accept that 44 per cent of all fliers dead, missing or taken prisoner could have been concentrated just into the last seven months of the war, bearing in mind the constant activity throughout 1917 and German advantage throughout that year.

But such figures would have meant little to the pilots of the time. They wanted just a general trend and that was always clear enough. Officially, the constant offensive was achieving moral superiority over the Germans – the enemy reluctance to cross the line was given as proof. Fighting men seldom thought in such broad GHQ fashion, and, if they had, would have been able to give it the lie. What concerned pilots was the selection and processing of those pieces of information about the enemy which might have immediate personal relevance in combat. Seen in such a way, the skill and danger of the enemy made him a constant, invisible presence on our fighter aerodromes, as unpredictable and dangerous as those chilling fogs which in north France would suddenly seep from the earth and blot out all sight of the ground. Fighter pilots never had illusions about moral superiority.

8
THE RHYTHMS OF WAR FLYING

The image of the RFC held by most outsiders during the Great War was of a service which lived as safely and luxuriously as châteaux-bound generals and fought as it chose.

Pilots who transferred from the infantry – as about half of all pilots did – would certainly find the image reinforced by first impressions. Wrote Fry:

> It was a wonderful life we pilots led. We were not bothered with parades nor with rules about uniform nor were we expected to look after the welfare of the men in the flight – they could look after themselves better than we could. We were burdened with no responsibilities whatsoever. No senior officers in the Mess were bent on keeping junior officers in their place. Those of us who had come from the regiments could hardly believe our luck.

As for flying, one pilot on arrival at his aerodrome overheard what he took to be a typical RFC dialogue:

> 'Is that you, Dowsing?'
> 'Yes sir.'
> 'I'm off for a raid. Fill my hot water bottle about a quarter past nine and put it right at the bottom of my bed. If you think the fire too hot, move my pyjamas back.'
> 'Good luck sir.'

It came as a surprise to many pilots therefore, as it did to Belgian ace Willy Coppens when half an RFC squadron was stationed at Les Mœurs, to discover that the RFC held to a schedule of 'highly intensive work strictly according to detailed instructions and co-ordinated with neighbours'. That a fighter squadron was characterized in fact by routine procedures no less stringent than an infantry unit.

First of these was location. In the ground war, infantry divisions were shuffled round at such pace that corps commander Claud Jacob reckoned that by the end of the war every single division of the British army had passed through his hands. RFC squadrons by contrast, attached to armies, took root for much longer periods. The fact is clearly recorded in the papers of 24 Squadron, the original fighter squadron:

St Omer	7. 2.16
Bertangles	10. 2.16
Chipilly	17.12.16
Flez	19. 4.17
Baizieux	10. 7.17
Teteghem	23. 9.17
Marieux	24.11.17
Villers-Bretonneux	1. 1.18

Such a contrast was maintained too in patterns of fighting. A typical infantryman might expect to be under fire for one week in a month, in reserve for another and then in rest for a fortnight. A fighter pilot on the other hand was expected to fly daily or as often as weather permitted. The log of Maxwell, in 65 Squadron, shows eighty-four patrols flown between 7 April and 21 October in 1917 – at about a flight every second day Maxwell seems to have been about the average.

In his period under fire, the infantryman might be holding the line, raiding or taking part in a battle in one of many waves of attack. Again, the fighter pilot fought a simpler, more uniformly aggressive war, for in the air every flight had the same function as an infantryman in the first wave of an attack. As Trenchard put it in a speech in April 1918, 'British and American pilots have only one policy, one method of fighting – to go and find the Hun and to make him fight.'

If the fighter pilot thus fought a more constant war than the infantryman he could at least look forward to a more finite end. Whereas the foot soldier might expect to fight until he was injured or killed, with at best ten days leave in a year, the pilot flew about 200 hours, which would take usually around six months, and could then look forward to a break of perhaps three months. Fry, for example, in the spring of 1917 flew 118 sorties, totalling 170 flying hours, between 23 April and 21 June and then had a lengthy period of leave, the demands of the battle of Arras accounting for shortening of the usual six months.

The fighter pilot's war was thus fought according to a basic rhythm as regular as that of a Benedictine monk, with the unpleasant business of being shot at concentrated into a short period – or so it might seem at wing or corps headquarters. For pilots who had to do the flying, the only enduring impression was that of an experience which refused to remain in focus and of which irregularity seemed the only significant ingredient.

Weather was the most tangible dislocating factor. On 5 May 1918, for example, GHQ weather reports noted low cloud and rain, and on that day along the whole front allocated to the RAF there were just two low reconnaissances, no reported single combat and only 7½ tons of bombs dropped. In contrast 6 June 1918 was fine and sunny. On that day 134 balloons were engaged and sixteen of them shot down. Artillery fire directed from the air produced eighty-one explosions and thirty-one fires, while twenty-eight tons of bombs were dropped on enemy rail towns. In addition there were seventeen reconnaissance flights reported and fourteen enemy machines destroyed in combat.

Not until dawn each day would a pilot know which of these patterns awaited him or whether the orders given the night before by the CO would take effect. The response would then be ambivalent. On the surface, the huge relief generated by sound of rain on hut roofs at dawn seemed indisputable. German fighter pilots made a distinction between *Fliegerwetter* (pilots' weather) and *Flugwetter* (flying weather), just like the French, who spoke of '*temps mauvais pour l'aviation, excellent pour les aviateurs*'. Rain and low cloud after all meant not just the certainty of another day's life but also 10 o'clock reveille followed by a warm bath, bacon and eggs and the choice between sleeping all day or wandering in the squadron orchard wearing silk pyjamas and savouring the rich feelings of men reprieved. Yet such acts of God made the return to duty only the more painful and disturbed the pilots' mental adjustment to anticipated danger. With their semblance of leave, rainy days broke the inevitability and regularity which made it easier to accept the daily possibility of death yet without giving that compensating relaxation which longer periods of leave offered. An RFC poem of the time put the matter briefly:

I left the mess room early
before the break of dawn
and greatly to my horror
the weather promised fair.

Even if, in a sustained spell of fine weather, patrols could take
off daily, there was never any pattern to the degree of activity or
level of danger which might be anticipated, for with fewer aeroplanes the enemy husbanded his resources. He had the advantage
too in greater flexibility, since he was not bound to the absurd
British practice of allocating fixed numbers of squadrons per army
and so could send circuses along the front by train to appear at a
particular point suddenly and in overwhelming force before dis-
appearing again for weeks.

The logbook of Beauchamp-Proctor suggests the result of these
German practices:

1 June 1918: Got a balloon down in flames. Forced another
down. Archie broke water pipe.
2 June 1918: Nothing doing.
3 June 1918: Dawn patrol nothing doing. Archie damn good.
Second patrol scrapped four triplanes. Nearly
done in.

The logbook of RNAS ace Rochford shows the same thing. Fighting seventy combats in nineteen months, Rochford found six concentrated into the last week of March 1918 and another thirteen in
a five-week period of May–June 1918. Over a longer period and
wider front 24 Squadron records reflect the same pattern:

February 1918:	Fired 300 rounds
March 1918:	25,405
April 1918:	7,765
May 1918:	50
June 1918:	0
July 1918:	8,260
August 1918:	15,507
September 1918:	5,400
October 1918:	20,260
November 1918:	9,775

Finally, perhaps most confusing of all, came the daily pattern of combat. Intense fear was first of all concentrated in just a two-hour spasm. The effect was noted by Oliver in the summer of 1917:

> No one can imagine the strain of two hours over the line. First one has to keep one's place in the formation. This necessitates waggling the throttle and petrol supply continuously. Then one has to watch the leader who does all the scientific work of dodging the archies. There is nothing more nerve wracking than getting really badly archied for a long time. Then there's every machine in the sky to be suspicious of. As a matter of fact, with all this wretched aerial activity we get a dogfight now nearly every time we go up – too often for my liking. It is extraordinary how warlike one feels before one gets to the line. Then suddenly it conks out when you cross it. As a matter of fact I suppose most people live in a perpetual state of wind up during a patrol, a most unhealthy state of mind.

Yet so much fear and anxiety compacted into such a short time seemed impossible to understand however long a man flew. On landing, many pilots would stare in disbelief at their cockpit watches, quite unable to reconcile quantity of emotion with quantity of time. One pilot specifically wrote later of his total bewilderment on a day when he started his soup, bombed Ostend, then returned in time for the fish course with only the vague memory of a disturbed dinner.

Another aspect of this two-hour concentration was the total contrast with the time which preceded and followed it. Cecil Lewis wrote of his personal bewilderment at 'the extraordinary double life', with drinks in the mess and sheets on sprung mattresses just fifteen miles from the front line and within sound of the guns. In the ground war infantry soldiers all noticed how much more difficult it was to face the return to the battle zone after each leave and how each leave or rest period seemed to cut into a man's supply of courage by suggesting too strongly the delights of survival. For fighter pilots there were periods of leave and going over the top perhaps each day.

The basic structure of the fighter war was thus one of daily fluctuation between the most violent combat and total idleness, between the depths of terror and the most generous of ease, yet with periods of being grounded by bad weather or of flying without meeting the enemy mixing predictability and confusion in a Russian roulette. Such a rhythm was unlike that of any other branch of the fighting services and made air a war apart in mind as well as medium. When pilots met infantrymen relaxing in back area towns like Amiens or Doullens they therefore seldom spoke of their trade, for to a pilot all other servicemen were as alien and uncomprehending as the civilians they met on home leave.

9
ROUTINE WORK – THE PILOT'S VIEW

The basic task of any fighting squadron was the maintenance of constant patrol work on the German side of the line. Such flights took two distinct forms. Boldest were the offensive patrols which penetrated up to fifteen miles into enemy airspace, with an aerodrome or railway station as target. By 1917 such patrols involved whole squadrons or even two squadrons, SE5as going in first with 25-pound bombs, followed by Bristol two-seaters, which would add 112-pound bombs and with rear gunners who had saved their ammunition for the return journey.

Much more frequent were the ordinary patrols, which flew perhaps thirty miles of line, about three or four miles on the German side. The purpose and style were sketched in a letter from Blaxland to Mannock's mother in 1917:

> He is stationed at present at Bruay which is south west of Bethune and about ten miles from the line. The work our squadron chiefly does consists of patrols on the other side of the line somewhere between Arras and La Bassee. A patrol generally lasts $1\frac{1}{2}$ hours and we fly at 11,000 to 18,000 feet. It consists of three to six machines according to circumstances. The whole idea of the patrol is to find the hun and shoot or drive him down. The latter is generally the case as they very rarely stop to fight unless they are in vastly superior numbers – except of course their specially good pilots. Your son is very good at his job and is very much liked in the mess. No more now.

The squadron's whole day was fitted round such work so as to maintain an unbroken succession of patrols over enemy territory. In high summer the day would begin with reveille for the dawn patrol men at about 2.45 am and end at 9.15 pm when darkness chased back the last patrol. Into this framework, meals would be slotted – breakfast from dawn until midday, lunch of cold meat at noon, tea at 4 and dinner between 8 and 9 pm.

More realistically, the squadron day began with evening dinner in the mess. During this formal meal a dispatch rider would usually enter with a sealed envelope, delivered personally to the squadron commander and containing orders for the next day from wing headquarters. Convention prescribed that conversations should be continued. Men drew into themselves nevertheless, keeping an eye on the CO, waiting for the quiet voice with stomachs clenched.

The envelope would contain only the broadest outline of the areas to be patrolled, the timing of corps reconnaissance machines needing escort or perhaps the targets for bombs on an offensive patrol. All details of the flight sequence were left to the squadron major, who would probably pull a battered service notebook from his pocket to check flight hours against his own observations on estimated states of morale. Combining need with suitability, the skipper would draw reflectively on his pipe, aware that decisions could be death warrants. The reception of his decisions was as painful. Memoirs later recalled such scenes with that brevity given to important moments in the individual's war experience – 'Sorry Voss, you're for the high jump tomorrow', and a cold shudder the length of the writer's body would start from the commander's hand on his shoulder.

Men selected for the dawn patrol would leave the mess quickly, hurried by their flight commander, though hurrying carefully. Custom prescribed that there be no impression of unease. Time to light a cigarette, pass a quiet self-deprecating comment, leave the mess in a lounging amble, hands in pockets as if going down the road to buy a paper. Above all, no flinching. Servants meanwhile would be arranging flying clothing around the central stove in the hut set aside for pre-flight dressing, as pilots went to that troubled sleep marked by the pinpoints of cigarettes in the darkness, glances at luminous watch hands, both hands clasped on the pillow under the pilot's head as his eyes stared upwards into the darkness. Sleep often came only at about 2 am, when a sergeant mechanic would rouse his team to prepare the machines for action.

' "Quarter to four, sir. You're on patrol in half an hour and its fine weather." The orderly batman, himself called by the night-guard five minutes earlier, shakes me gently and speaks in a murmur so as not to disturb the other pilots asleep in the hut.' A bad time now. A time of foul temper and bad language, of misbuttoned shirts and grit scratching the back of the eyes. Seasoned men would have devised a routine to quieten themselves. Thus Vincent always had a hot bath whatever the hour, using the water his Irish batman had heated over the CO's oil lamp. Mannock invariably put the Londonderry Air on his wind-up gramophone while dressing. But for most, silence and sourness better fitted the hour and prospect. Washing was once over with a hot sponge and a mouth rinse – shaving was omitted because the destruction of the skin's dermis layer could lead to frostbite. Lee describes breakfast:

> As we make for the mess in the near darkness, we are joined by two other muffled figures. We grunt our good mornings but say nothing else. As we move along, I momentarily shiver for the air is chilly after the rain but it is sweet and fragrant and the damp ground smells of the richness of the soil. In the mess, the orderly cook has prepared a snack breakfast of tea, hard boiled eggs, bread and margarine. He puts everything before us without a word. We don't speak either. This is no hour for light chat. We gulp the food down not because we're hungry but because we have to have it inside for nobody can fly and fight on an empty stomach; when we come down from a patrol we shall have a real breakfast at leisure. Maybe coffee, bacon and sausage. Something to look forward to.

More precisely, dawn patrol on an empty stomach meant air sickness with nausea, projectile vomiting and lengthy spasms of retching with clammy skin and racing pulse. Ten per cent of fighter pilots often experienced air sickness anyway. Even the eating, which was the best prophylactic, had to be done with care since, at height, intestinal gas expanded to push up the diaphragm and distend the abdomen to give acute colicky pains. At the common fighting altitude of 18,000 feet, intestinal gas would have swelled up to double its ground volume. Without the second war's special K rations, pilots had to discover by trial and error that tinned food, suet or biscuits had to be consumed with discretion. Tea also, for the intense cold at height induced an urgent bladder, and taking the gloves off for a fumbled excavation through layers of clothing meant not just the danger of frostbite but also a period of distraction exploitable by an enemy with the advantage of height.

Breakfasted, pilots walked slowly over to the dressing hut. Further distanced from sleep, they would be reacting more keenly to imminent flight, checking wind strength and direction on their faces while evaluating humidity and cloud type. On the ground, all detail would be lost in darkness, though trees would be suggesting a shape against the faint glow on the eastern horizon. But only the sky concerned the pilot. Upward glances would be constructing an approximate three-dimensional map of the forces which would be progressively impinging on aircraft. In particular, the movement of those great circulating systems which came in from the Atlantic at a rate of about 300 miles daily, invisible whirlpools which spelt icing-up, rain belts, thickening cloud, rising or falling air currents. No one ever bothered to gather such information into a book or pamphlet, for like so much in Great War flying the most important information was acquired only with experience.

The brightly lit dressing hut was an invention of 1917. By that time flying kit had become standard issue, based on the fact that dry stationary air had been found a poor conductor of heat. Clothing had therefore to be put on just before flying, otherwise the body would give out moisture which would freeze again at altitude. Dressing would then be in a strict sequence. Silk underwear. Close-woven woollen underwear duplicating the silk and worn loose. Cellular two-inch-squared vest. Silk inner shirt. Army khaki shirt. Two pullovers. Tight-woven gaberdine Sidcot suit lined with lamb's wool. Muskrat-lined gauntlets with silk inners. Thus dressed, the pilot could withstand temperatures of minus fifty degrees centigrade – though high wind, poor fit, sweat before dressing or the poor circulation of an unfit man could chill him to the point of tears at ten degrees fahrenheit. One final military touch before leaving the hut – the presentation for signature of an army form, FS20. 'Date. Time. Pilot's name. Thigh boots, furlined boots, gauntlets, furlined goggles with triplex glasses, Sidcot suit and oversleeves. These are the property of the public. Losses due to the exigencies of campaign must be certified by the officer commanding.'

The final adjustment would be to the head area. A silk scarf would be wound carefully round the throat to prevent air entering the vulnerable neck area and getting inside the flying suit as well as preventing skin chafing from that constant turning round in flight to check for enemy behind the tailplane. The face would then be smeared in whale-oil, surrounded by a balaclava helmet and covered with a non-absorbent face mask, ideally of Nuchwang dog-skin from China. If dogskin was unobtainable, the mask would be of wolverine fur, favoured anyway by Canadian fliers since breath would not freeze on it. The triplex goggles which covered the single gap in the mask (32s. 6d. over a London shop counter) were of fur-lined moulded-sponge rubber with sage-green-tinted glass to absorb ultraviolet rays. Various preparations would finally be rubbed on to the glass to counter fogging below ten degrees Fahrenheit and frosting at minus ten, with perhaps a touch of ointment on the lips, though pilots philosophically accepted the fact that all lips cracked at altitude whatever specifics were used.

Fully dressed, the flight would walk together to the CO's hut, stumping as noisily and heavily as lunar astronauts. The major would have phoned for a 'meteor' weather report and would probably have taken a flip to check it, but that would be about the limit of his briefing. In the Great War there were no Intelligence reports or checks on aerial photos before the flight. Chance comments overheard in the mess or personal experience gave a pilot all he ever knew about his enemy. Thus the only real purpose of the CO's meeting was to fill individual boxes with personal belongs topped by a signed form: 'I swear on my honour that I do not have on my person or on my machine any letters or papers of use to the enemy.'

There was never much talk or noise, since dawn was the one patrol in the day not summoned by klaxon so that the rest of the squadron might rest. The dawn men would next shuffle towards their machines like files of London policemen setting out for the beat, separating as they walked because their aeroplanes would have been widely dispersed around the aerodrome as a precaution against German night bombing. A glance, a touch on the elbow, and the men who slept together in pairs and fought together in pairs separated to begin the first stage of that progressive introversion which became total for all men as they approached the battlefield.

Next to each aeroplane fitters, riggers and armourers would be morosely gathered. In both wars, no machine ever took off – or returned – without a cross-section of ground crew watching.

The 'into machines' order was given by the squadron commander with a Verey flare. Then pilots would climb on to the petrol tank hump just behind the cockpit and slide forward and down into the seat, ducking their heads below the upper wing. As they eased down into the cushion on their wicker seats and slid their feet under the loops of the rudder bar, the mechanics would wish a quiet 'Good luck, sir' and assist the pilot into his Sutton safety harness. This consisted of four separate straps for shoulders and thighs, each strap twelve inches wide and a quarter inch thick which came together over a large-diameter central conical pin held down by a spring clip. The mechanic's job was to select the correct hole alignment, combining ease of release with tightness sufficient to sustain the pilot in inverted flight.

The pilot meanwhile would be checking the machine with the absorbed, anxious air of a housewife checking a shopping list, yet not too anxiously or critically, for the ground crew would be quick to detect lack of confidence. First the basic controls. Rudder bar working? The right hand would move the control column with a turn of the head to check tail response. The left hand would reach for the throttle. Sufficient friction to maintain position when the hand was removed? Similarly the adjacent fine-adjustment lever? The right hand felt for the wooden pump handle which pumped up petrol pressure in an emergency. Then an eye-check of the rigging. Once, Springs noticed a broken elevator turnbuckle and immediately aborted, for flight commanders insisted that each man must be perfectly satisfied before take-off. The discovery of faults in the air meant a cumbersome change to an unfamiliar formation, with all its dangers.

Next was the instrument check. The facia in which the instruments were set was of polished hardwood, neat as the control panel of a modern racing yacht but compacted into the area of a small modern car's dashboard. First the engine instruments – radiator thermometer, oil pressure and temperature gauge. Then speed and direction indicators. Was the compass moving freely? Was the height indicator set at zero? Was the bubble central in the lateral indicator? Such a check was quickly done, for the mechanics would have switched on the lighting and instruments were few, for example an SE5a had just seven dials to the Spitfire's nineteen, the Hunter's twenty-five and the Lightning's forty.

So to odds and ends. Was the watch wound up? Were the map boards in their flaps? Mirror clean (that small, circular thing fixed to the rear starboard centre-section strut and made quite useless by vibration and air blast for its purpose of spotting the hun coming up from behind)? Aldis gunsight lens free from oil smears? The $2\frac{1}{2}$-pound hammer for rectifying machine gun jams in its socket?

Automatic pistol? Fire extinguisher? Prisoner of war haversack with silk pyjamas, shaving and toothbrushing gear, spare socks and pack of Turkish cigarettes?

Satisfied with his life support system, the pilot would check quickly on the positions of the other machines of his flight, quietly sitting and chewing boiled sweets in readiness for the changes in air pressure during ascent. Pre-dawn shadow would obscure any detail apart from the black shapes set above the ground mist which cut off mechanics below the shoulders, so the pilot's glance would not be for seeing and comparing but more of a reflex jerk, slowed down, showing that he had completed the check on his own machine. The mind would be shifting towards the void of coming flight, the more abruptly for the previous concentration on an elaborate checking routine. This would therefore be a moment of relaxation as the pilot perhaps savoured the personal touches on his own machine. Already in December 1915 RFC notes had laid down that 'the personal comfort and feeling of homeliness in the machine' were the first priority. It was absolutely essential, the notes went on, for every pilot to have his own aeroplane since no two men arranged in the same way 'those little details which were so important', like windscreen or belt adjustment or instrument positioning. A pilot was thus free to transfer instruments from one machine to another, add shelves for spare goggles or cigarettes or replace his seat with a cut-down armchair. Gravity tanks might be removed from wing centre sections, Lewis guns placed to fire through the floor, Avro windscreens fitted to SE5as.

The pilot would check too upon those things which reminded him of past survivals and linked him with ground certainties – dice, playing cards, powder puffs on the struts or teddy bears in the upper wing sections. Roberts thought that 90 per cent of service machines had such mystical ballast and that length of service could be estimated from their number. Others turned round three times before entering an aeroplane, or were wished '*Hals und Beinbruch*' rather than '*Glück auf*', Bewsher whistling continuously during a flight the cobbler's tune from *Chu Chin Chow*. The repetition of previous pre-flight mannerisms associated with a safe return was a ritual which put a pilot in tune with life forces. It was too risky anyway not to repeat anything which might contribute to future security.

The squadron commander would then check on readiness with another Verey and if all pilots raised their arms, 'Start up' would be ordered. 'Before starting the engine, turn it over once or twice,' advised the official manual. 'Note that the valves are not sticking and that compression is normal.' The next stage was to replace air and inert gas in the cylinders with an explosive charge. 'In stationary engines this is done by turning the engine with the air intake closed and petrol on when a rich mixture will be drawn into the cylinders and the inert gas expelled. In rotary engines this is not practicable owing to the large volume of the crank case through which the mixture passes on its way to the cylinders. In engines of this class it is usual before starting to dope the cylinders by injecting petrol through the exhaust valves.'

'Ready, sir?' the mechanic would inquire.

'Ready.'

'Switch off, sir?'

'Switch off.'

'Suck in, sir?'

'Suck in.'

At this point the mechanic would be moving the propeller to the accompaniment of a slow 'clonk, clonk, clonkety' noise as the petrol was sucked into the rotary's cylinders to combine with air drawn in through the suction valve on the cylinder head. The mixture was critical, so the mechanic needed to know the exact character of each engine, moving the prop against its natural direction to weaken the mixture, the other way to strengthen it. When the mechanic sensed that he had the precise mix of eighteen volumes of air to one of petrol vapour he would probably glance quickly up at the pilot's fingers, double-checking their position on the cockpit's rim and that ignition was indeed off. Then he would step back, wipe his hands on his overalls and kick the mud off his boots. Leaning forward with his fingers round the top edge of the prop, close to the boss, weight on the left foot, he would shout 'Contact, sir?'. With the reply 'Contact' the pilot would flick both switches, push the fine adjustment lever (equivalent to a car choke) right back and open the throttle halfway as the mechanic swung the propeller hard against compression, anticlockwise for rotary, clockwise for stationary. One jerk usually sufficed, though perhaps with the odd backfire of pre-ignition.

The engine would start with a jet of thick blue smoke and a gale-force slipstream, forcing the grass flat for about fifty yards back behind the tailplane. Castor oil lubricant, which fed directly into a rotary's crankcase, would spray from the cylinder heads, burning with a bitter, nutty tang like the after-taste of racing fuel in a modern motor bike. The pilot advanced his throttle slowly to reach 800 revs a minute, then eased through to 1,500 for perhaps two minutes in summer or twenty on a cold winter's day, until the oil reached 70 Fahrenheit and had circulated to all bearings. Meanwhile there would be a mechanic holding down each wing tip and a third draped across the fuselage just in front of the tailplane, hair almost torn from his head by the propeller blast.

When the instrument read correctly, the pilot gave a side-to-side hand wave for the chocs to be removed. The senior mechanic then checked the sky and taxiing path, saluting the pilot to indicate that all was clear. The pilot's reply was a fore-and-aft handwave before taxiing slowly to the cinder runway in a series of brr-rrrps as he blipped the button switch on the control column.

The usual procedure was for machines to take off at minute intervals, the leader going first, the rest following in a series of left-handed circuits. The greatest care was needed because about half of all flying accidents occurred in take-off. As taxiing speed increased, vigorous and coarse movement was needed with sluggish controls so as to counter cross-winds and the tendency of engine torque to throw the machine on to its wing tip in a ground loop. As the speed increased, the pilot would also have to counter an increasingly responsive elevator as the machine tried to leave the ground prematurely. The nose had therefore to be forced down until the airspeed indicator reached a predetermined speed, when the stick would be flicked back. Airborne to those with an acute sense of touch meant controls immediately responsive and control column trembling like a thing alive. But most pilots, like Lee, didn't realize they were off the ground until about 500 feet, which represented an insensitivity not without danger if the controls were still handled with the vigour of the ground and the fine adjustment lever was not eased back to maintain constant revs. A choked engine spelt a stall just after take-off, with insufficient altitude for correction.

Formating became first priority. The six machines of a flight got into approximate formation during the first ten minutes of climbing. After another five minutes the flight commander would fire a

Verey and fly straight and slow until all machines had tightened into the formation. If a machine lagged, the commander would indicate with his arm a right or left turn to enable the laggard to cut a corner and catch up. Then came the final Verey from far below as the squadron commander ordered the start of the patrol. The line was crossed at about 15,000 feet.

During this initial period, all pilots would be glancing frequently downwards to fix their bearings, for otherwise no pilot would be aware of speed or distance. 'It was not always easy to find your way or to read a map,' wrote Cecil Lewis. 'You could get lost in the air as easily as in a forest. One or two sharp turns to pick up a landmark and you lost all sense of direction.' This explained how a seasoned flier like Lewis could miss Amiens though flying at 10,000 feet just twenty miles from it. Or why the Germans consistently delivered Fokkers to RFC aerodromes just as the RFC delivered the prototypes of Sopwith Triplane and Handley Page bomber to the Germans. A downward fix was therefore important should a sudden pounce by enemy fighters split the formation. At first, little would be clear. The ground was still dark, but white mist patches lay in hollows or blue veils of smoke hung becalmed around villages. Against this sombre background, occasional flashes from windows or firing artillery pieces would start like laser bursts. All the while, and imperceptibly, intensifying light would seep from the east, fixing golden haloes to hill tops, dispersing mists, blinding the pilots.

Even with morning light, the landscape required a seaman's eye for interpretation, since above 2,000 feet objects lost their colour and uprightness. Bartlett describes a typical scene:

> The flat country stretched to the four horizons. The real thing had a bewildering amount of extra detail, a wealth of soft colour, of light and shade that made it at first difficult to reconcile with its map-printed counterpart. Main roads, so importantly marked in red, turned out to be grey, unobtrusive and hard to distinguish from other roads. Railways were not clear black lines but winding threads even less well defined. Woods were not patches of green except in high summer. They were dark browns and blacks merging sometimes imperceptibly into the ploughed fields which surrounded them. Then there were cloud shadows darkening patches of landscape and throwing others into high relief; or

ground mists blurring the horizon and sometimes closing in around you for a few miles.

The lateral panorama was vast. On a clear day, a pilot at 10,000 feet saw clearly the curvature of the earth, while at 20,000 feet the Alps were visible from any point on the west front. Wrote Lee:

> We were flying east of Ypres. Straight below lay the ruins of the town. So close that it was preposterous was Ostend. England's white cliffs stood out and to the left lay the Isle of Wight. To the right the land ran into a sweeping curve around the Foreland before nestling back into the Thames estuary where it was lost in the haze which extended from Gravesend to London backwards. In the Channel, a convoy of ships moved over the sea, a tiny destroyer foaming ahead in white curves. The crack of a shell close behind us made me turn quickly. Near Soissons the smoke of a continuous barrage mingled with the dark haze which lay below the sun line. We were around 10,000 feet and must have viewed the limits of vision – the distance at which a straight line made a tangent with the round earth. It struck me as curious how the more distant places – the islands of Borkum and North Foreland – appeared tilted up at an angle while the shipping in the Channel looked as though it were sailing in the sky. We felt as if we were flying in the centre of a huge balloon with the sky, sea and earth painted on the outside of its transparent but all-enclosing sphere.

Such views were usually well broken by the cloud of an almost unbroken sequence of depressions which moved from the Atlantic over the battle area. 'Struck cloud at 4,000 feet,' wrote Bartlett.

> Never saw such magnificent ones. For sometime we succeeded in threading a path through the gaps and valleys with enormous masses towering up on either side and almost brushing our wingtips. Finally, a huge mass barred our way and for five or six minutes we were buffetted by terrific bumps. With no horizon to guide on, the airspeed indicator rushed up and then fell most alarmingly. At one time we were hanging by our belts. At length I managed to get her level and climbed hard, emerging into dazzling sunshine again with a gorgeous cloud panorama at 9,000 feet, huge white masses towering up thousands of feet above us and many gaps showing villages and woods below while far out

to the north lay the deep blue of the Channel and all Thanet
stretching away on the horizon. Quite the most beautiful view
I have ever had.

Such clouds were always a hazard to the fighter pilot. Collishaw
once described spinning down for ten minutes in unbroken cloud,
while Ball wrote of coming from a cloud upside down, totally
disorientated and with petrol flowing into his air intake. During
the long glide necessary for re-starting his engine, he remembered
glancing back anxiously many times. Even if there were no such
convection currents, cloud flying always meant saturation and
moisture droplets covering everything in the cockpit, as the engine
boomed like a drum with deafening echoes. Emerging from clouds
therefore induced a feeling of relaxation as though a blindfold had
been dropped.

Crossing the lines for the first time, Hartney recorded 'a powerful
experience'. Jotting his own feelings down at greater length,
Grinnell-Milne wrote of amazement at the vast length of trench
lines in each direction and of the resemblance to a Doré engraving
of Dante's Inferno when a battle was on, smoke rising soundlessly
to 5,000 feet. But usually all would seem peaceful down below,
with just a brown smear visible as if a painter had drawn a finger
over a painting still wet. Perhaps the odd shell puff or gun flash
might show against this landscape apparently devoid of people and
these the pilots would watch with the calm curiosity of uninvolved
tourists.

Anti-aircraft shells represented the first contact with the enemy
when the line was passed. First would come the range-finding
shells with phosphorus in their base, like giant tracer bullets, sliding
up fast from the ground like strings of pearls. These would burst
to leave an area two hundred yards square filled with falling fire-
balls. Such white smoke trails would then float like a gossamer
curtain before the arrival of the killers - high-explosive shells which
sent metal splinters through 360 degrees. Their danger could be
judged by the noise of the burst, thought Lannoe Hawker. Visible
but inaudible meant harmless. Visible and audible created appre-
hension. Noisy coughs were dangerous. Close bursts were different
in kind, like giant hammers hitting galvanized iron sheets to deafen
pilots for a minute, while huge hands seized his machine, jerked it
upwards and bombarded it with fragments of metal sounding like

rattling shingle when a wave sweeps back to the sea. Courtney likened it to being kicked vertically upwards 300 feet by a hundred horses inside dirty brown smoke reeking of cordite, to leave the fabric flapping, wires slackened, blood smeared over the face and hands, and a severe headache.

Shrapnel seemed altogether less dangerous. Its burst was a subdued fizz sounding like an epidemic of coughing during a dull sermon. The danger was in the upward burst, which produced an altogether more concentrated metal burst than high explosive, with a smear of black smoke which stayed in position even through the strongest winds for up to fifteen minutes.

Many pilots took anti-aircraft fire lightly at first. Springs wrote of it as the most useless thing in the war and would yawn under fire, turning only when he was knocked up 100 feet by percussion. In such anti-aircraft storms, Bert Hall would loop, barrel roll, sideslip and spin, while Macmillan would deliberately turn just before the end of an anti-aircraft fire path, his sharp eyes picking out the gun flashes and calculating that there would be 400 yards of space to alter position in before the shell reached him. An official pamphlet in 1918 seemed to support such a flippant approach. It suggested that to an anti-aircraft gun crew, horizontal range was immaterial because deflection was easily calculated. What did puzzle gunners though was variation of vertical height with consequent problems in fuse setting. Steps of 500 feet by a machine would therefore beat the calculations of most gunners, since even on a perfect day it took a flight of shells thirty seconds to reach even 8,000 feet. On a windy day, quick turns and drift alone would suffice to beat German anti-aircraft. But were the Ministry the best judges? Between September 1917 and May 1918 British anti-aircraft batteries defending London calculated that it was necessary to fire 14,540 shells for a single killing. The enemy orchestrated himself more professionally, so that even at the start of the war Krupp's triangular ranging system fixed a target within three seconds. Such a speed was beyond the scope of our National Physical Laboratory for another two years, by which time German central observation posts would be reading altitude instantly from an electric volt meter, predict firing path and lay down fuse settings for a pre-arranged barrage line. Quick-firing 77s would then blast off fifteen shells per minute per battery accurately up to 16,000 feet. Positioned in groups of four just two miles from the front line,

5. A few pilots in the Great War risked the additional weight of a camera gun to get authentic air photos, among them the great French ace Guynemer. This shot shows graphically in what a small area the slow, tight-turning aircraft of the day fought their actions. According to the photographer, the German machine in the foreground had just flown through his Aldis sight and was about to drop in flames from a burst through the petrol tank located under the pilot's seat. The positions of the other aircraft suggest the violence of manœuvre in a turning fight.

16. The Caquot observation balloon represented a formidable spying device. From a quarter its maximum height, the observer in his basket could see sixty miles on a clear day. His normal duties would be the direction of artillery fire by wireless and the reporting of enemy activity. This balloon on the Somme battlefield near Fricourt is being hauled down by a mechanical winch mounted on a motor lorry. Horse lines are behind the balloonists, a communication trench on the right.

17. In such a setting as this, combat reports would be made out if machine guns had been fired on a patrol. A recording officer casually dressed, pilots still helmeted and dictating notes while their minds were still fresh, a pilot's cockpit seat mounted on an ammunition box – all hint at the improvisation of active service.

18. A balloon observer parachutes to safety as an enemy aeroplane fires incendiary bullets into his gasbag. Such parachutes had been demonstrated by a Captain Maitland, who jumped safely from an airship in 1913. Only the Germans issued them to pilots in the war, however. The kindest explanation for the British omission is perhaps that the additional weight, equivalent to an extra Vickers gun, would have further slowed fighter aeroplanes which for most of the war were already slower than their German rivals. Not until 1935 did the RAF do the basic research into parachute jumping from crippled fighters.

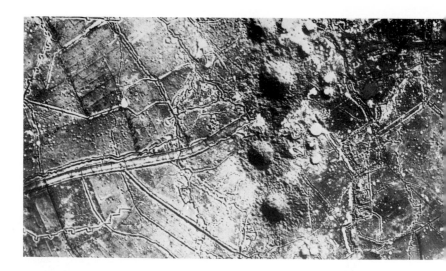

19. The astonishing amount of detail seen by the human eye – on a clear day – from an observation balloon at 2,000 feet. The scene is St Éloi, crucial high ground at the eastern end of the Ypres salient and much fought over. Both front lines and the mine craters between them are clearly visible.

20. By the end of the war about one quarter of all British aeroplanes were photographic machines which produced about 6 million prints in all for the army. For a battle like the tank offensive of 8 August 1918, pre-planning required 88,000 separate negatives of the enemy position, low-flying aeroplanes taking oblique photos from 1,000 feet to give infantry the feel of battlefield topography. Most photos would be taken from about 16,000 feet, each exposure covering an area two miles by three with pin-sharp accuracy and complete area coverage being achieved by the jigsaw puzzle assembling by staff officers as in this photo.

screened from balloon observation and 6,000 yards apart, German batteries had no blind spots and could coordinate their fire, while the shells they fired did not need to hit directly. To be within twenty yards of an explosive burst or within 100 yards of shrapnel could be fatal to a machine dependent on a few wires and with an unarmoured engine and petrol tank.

The longer a pilot flew, the more he came to fear anti-aircraft fire, as evidence accumulated of its effectiveness. Roberts once counted ninety-six shrapnel holes in his fabric from a single flight, after which he no longer joked when the shrapnel came to greet him like a boisterous dog. On one occasion Hartney got 416 holes from a single shell while both Crundall and Collishaw wrote of losing cylinders and engine cowling before being spun down to a pancake landing by high-explosive bursts. Even the imperturbable René Fonck received a burst which took two wooden ribs with it just one metre from his body and left him with a prolonged fit of uncontrollable trembling. Whitehouse wrote of being in tears when he saw his friend Bert Warren's machine disintegrate like a shot duck from a direct hit. At that very moment he had in his pocket a photo of Warren's sister.

Accuracy, quantity and certainty, together with the fact that each shell was aimed by a man the size of a pinpoint, gave the anti-aircraft burst a peculiarly personal quality, the more worrying because the eyes which aimed were so far away, so impersonal. An enemy pilot could at least be seen and would give the sporting chance of counter-action. Cecil Lewis wrote of himself as petrified each time he heard anti-aircraft bursts, while Belgian ace Willy Coppens described them as the most worrying thing in a fighter pilot's war – and with justification. By the end of the war, German anti-aircraft had downed 1,588 allied machines, the bag rising from fifty-one in 1915 to 748 in 1918.

Once across the anti-aircraft fire zone, the pilot entered the most dangerous part of the patrol. German fighters seldom flew over the British line, so the danger from air attack entered a pilot's calculations at a precise moment marked by a tightening in the stomach, a new urgency in checking the sky. Yeates described the sensation:

We had to train our eyes to serve our senses of smell and hearing for the continuous sound and smell of our own engines and exhaust filled all our immediate presence to the exclusion of more distant smells and sounds, except the dull woof of an archie burst. It was the pre-hearing vision that meant so much for it was the keenness of eyesight in spotting the Hun afar that enabled his eventual attack to be prepared for and met. The chief danger was to be surprised, to be shot down before one realized that an attack was in being.

There were thoughts of hunting too:

Sometimes we played hide and seek with the enemy in and around large cloud formations towering in an otherwise clear sky, diving into the clouds when things got too hot while the enemy would do the same. For the first few seconds coming out of a cloud one was vulnerable, being blinded by the sudden light and having to pick up one's bearings. It makes me shudder to think now how gaily we flew into these clouds in formations, not thinking about chances of collision. We came out of them in all directions, sometimes in a spin, but never together. We would also fly around the outside of a cloud formation, looking for enemy patrols, not knowing what we would come upon round the next corner where there might always be an enemy formation doing the same thing.

To fighting airmen, clouds always gave the best possibility of stalking and trapping, of taking by surprise.

More often, particularly in the last year of the war, when the air was tightly organized, patrols flew with the awareness of dangerous stalemate. Wrote Yeates:

Every day the sky between 10,000 and 20,000 feet was infested with three or four layers of aeroplanes, colourless dots. Perhaps 30 to 50 in all. These German circuses were not collectively aggressive, keeping to their own side of the line and waiting to be attacked. If the circus could split up a hostile formation, its more enterprising members would chase scattered individuals. As a rule though, the circus waited to be attacked. Camels could not outclimb Fokkers to attack the top layer and when they dived on a lower formation, they put themselves into a dangerous position. The only thing to do therefore was to watch carefully, dodge at the right moment and keep determinedly with one's formation; the strain was tremendous.

During all such sparring, chief watcher was the flight commander, zigzagging his machine every few seconds.

If the skipper did spot a group which he judged might be safely attacked, he would give the flight the sign. Waggled wings, crossed index fingers, arm pointing to the target, or perhaps a red Verey.

At such a moment, individuals reacted violently. Sholto Douglas drily noted: 'Whenever I went into a scrap I knew a tightening of nerves, an awareness of anxiety that caused some fear.' Balfour wrote more bluntly of his terror when combat was announced. He likened the feeling to that of plunging into a cold bath. Voss just shivered uncontrollably. The body prepared anyway for a display of violence with deeper, slower breathing, rapid heart beat, increased arterial blood pressure and cessation of digestion, the pilot being made aware of such metabolic change by a foul taste in a mouth as hot as a lime kiln and sweat trickling from his scalp to cut runnels through whale-oil smeared on his face.

The next phase was practical. Ammunition drum full? Petrol gauge? Wind and weather? A downward fix was made to get landmarks ready for that confused moment when a pilot emerged from combat. The pilot would work the gun priming levers, flick up the synchronizer gear lever, uncap the Aldis sight and glance round the whole sky to fix relative positions and select lines of retreat. Perhaps the target looked too easy. The sun area would be checked carefully from behind an upheld thumb.

During this basic check, the pilot's feelings would have changed. Wrote Roberts:

> My mental attitude became detached from all emotions so that I felt a feeling almost as of boredom creeping over me. This sense at such times was a strange one but I suppose it emanates from strangulation of the emotions into an intensity of concentration upon one definite object. It may be the outcome of a mental state which is called upon to encompass a great deal in a swift passage of time akin to the emotionless impression one forms when the ultra high speed camera reproduces a subject in slow motion. It was probably enhanced by our total inability to communicate with anyone while flying in the aircraft of that time.

Balfour also noted such a feeling of impersonality and calm, describing it as if a secondary person were taking over, leaving the self to become detached, as a kind of impersonal observer.

An Air Ministry pamphlet of 1918 suggested possible ways of conducting the attack.

Important as self-control and courage in action, attacks to be successful must be thoroughly thought out. The actual attack should be carried out by two machines, the third remaining above to protect them from surprise. The two attacking machines may converge on the enemy from different directions on the same level but the attacks must be simultaneous so they cannot be engaged separately. Another method is to attack echelonned in height, the lower machines diving to attack the enemy from behind while the upper wait an opportunity to swoop down when the enemy turns to engage the machine that first attacked him.

Such was theory. Beauchamp-Proctor, with 84 Squadron, did manage to achieve formation attack in 1917, but the majority, like Mannock, desisted when they found their men more frightened of collision and machine-gun noise than by what the enemy might do.

Most attacks therefore took the form of an all-out dive, each pilot concentrating just on his own action. The sensation of power diving almost precluded any other approach. All pilots took an instinctive deep breath before throwing the stick forward. Many gripped the side of the fuselage to counter the feeling of being crushed. Excitable men might throw the Aldis sight back and pull up their goggles, using just tracers for aiming. But old hands kept steady, the left hand on the throttle, the right on the stick, two fingers lightly touching the gun buttons. Black vapour would be pouring from engines working close to 200 mph so that German pilots, glancing up, would have the impression of some devil's trident about to strike. Then came a check to an approach speed around 90 mph, so as to eliminate vibration, gliding into the attack on a slower machine, diving behind with a climbing turn onto the tail of a faster aeroplane until the target filled the whole Aldis screen. Then the right hand from the stick, stretched out slowly with the thumb brought back to the mouth before pressing the firing buttons in a succession of one- or two-second bursts.

During combat, pilots were too desperately involved to be able to think beyond immediate need. Looking back though, most reckoned that aerial combat lasted a surprisingly short time. Long thought that three minutes was about average. Hall and Coppens both believed twenty seconds nearer the mark, while Lee wrote of his first fight having been too fast to remember anything at all of what had happened and leaving him quite breathless. On mood in combat all agreed. Mannock would howl like a dervish. Ira Jones swore at the top of his voice throughout. Even Sholto Douglas wrote of screaming abuse at his target and feeling exhilarated as in a dangerous game of rugby. 'The bastard. What the devil does he think he's doing? My God, he's trying to kill me. I'd better bloody well try and kill him first.' Roberts wrote of shaking with excitement, deafened by the noise of machine guns jumping on their mountings, and black gunpowder smearing his face.

Most combat was indeed a desultory, skirmishing type, its course determined by uncertainty and unease in participants or by an early sighting on the part of the prey. Yeates wrote about one of many such indeterminate skirmishes:

> Mac wiggled his wings and turned southwards. Tom could not see what he was after. Mac had the most marvellous eyesight. Then he made out a group of moving dots hardly visible against the grey world. They were perhaps three miles away and below to the south east. When he had gained enough height, Mac put his nose down to 130 mph in order to catch them. They were ten Albatross scouts and seeing the attack coming, they turned east to avoid it but the Camels had enough height to make a final dive at 160 mph. This enabled us to get a shot at them. Tom did not hit anything but he saw Mac's victim go spinning down out of sight. He spun at least 10,000 feet and he would hardly have spun so far intentionally when he was not being followed down. The Albatri vanished into the east and stopped there. The Camels resumed patrolling their beat and saw nothing more of them or any other Huns. Archie barked; the sun climbed and brightened. The earth looked more real. Guns and shells puffed. A fleet of DH9s and Bristols came back from a distant raid. Some Dolphins appeared higher up. There were no Huns.

Such a typical Great War fight was endlessly repeated, the description true even to the total uncertainty whether a target had been hit or not.

Occasionally, combat might resolve itself into one against one, a format which most ground soldiers or civilians assumed to be the basic fighting pattern. Again, Yeates described such a simplified confrontation:

Just as I opened fire, the enemy machine turned sharply to the left and I was doing about 200 mph so couldn't turn but had to overshoot and half roll back. As I half rolled on top of him, he half rolled too and when I did an Immelmann, he turned to the right and forced me on to the outside arc and gave his observer a good shot at me as I turned back the other way to cut him off. I fired a burst from my turn but the shots went wild so I pulled up and half rolled on top of him again and opened fire from immediately above and behind. He stalled before I could get a burst in and sideslipped away from me but gave me a no-deflection shot at him when he straightened out. The observer dropped down into his cockpit so I suppose I killed him. But I couldn't get the pilot. He put his machine into a tight spiral and I couldn't seem to get into position properly. Cal and Tiny Dixon came in at about the same time and everybody was shooting at him from all angles. I knew he didn't have any motor because he came down very slowly and didn't attempt to man-œuvre. But we couldn't seem to hit the tank or the pilot and every now and then he'd take a crack at me when I tried him head on. He was a stout fellow. If his observer had been any good I wouldn't be writing this now. He hit one of my front spars and that was all. I left him at 100 feet as my engine was overheating and was sputtering and I'd had enough machine gun fire from the ground to last me for a while and I didn't like field guns from directly in the rear. Accidents will happen so I started back and joined the patrol. Archie went simply mad.

Such Biggles-like scenes were never typical of the second part of the Great War though. By then the Germans had turned protective top cover into an art, and solo machines were usually too dangerous to approach.

The years 1917 and 1918 were necessarily ones of generalized engagement. With ground strafers at 1,500 feet, photographic machines at 7,000 feet, corps observation at 10,000 feet, bombers at 12,000 feet and high scouts up to 20,000 feet, combat was sel-dom allowed to remain a private matter. Slow closing speeds and the capacity of biplanes for violent evasive movement prolonged most skirmishes to the point where anti-aircraft bursts and tracer streamers hanging in the sky would draw reinforcements from both sides like sharks to blood. Dogfighting was thus a natural development.

Official communiqués first used the word 'dogfight' in November 1916 to describe thirty British machines engaging forty German. McCudden always reckoned that thirty machines had to be involved to justify the word. Whitehouse preferred a bottom limit of fifty. But whatever the specification, the phenomenon was a Great War one, for only then did low speed combine with high turning capability to allow fifty machines to be fitted into an aerial box of three square miles. A modern jet fighter would need seven miles just to turn.

To a watching pilot held in reserve, the dogfight might well seem a confused whirlpool, like a cluster of bees swirling round a honey jar and losing height gradually as they turned. The whole mass would drift with the wind leaving in its track plumes of tracer and exhaust fumes which would hang in the air like corbels and combine with anti-aircraft puffs to trace a delicate grid which recorded every manœuvre and every shot. Just occasionally a machine would leave the fight with a defective engine or jammed gun to make ideal prey for those specialists in peripheral hovering like Mannock and Richthofen.

HQ pamphlets suggested what an observer might judge – that there were no rules in a dogfight. Hartney agreed, reckoning that team work counted for only 10 per cent. There seems to have been system nevertheless. Wingmen fought inwards towards their leader with the characteristic circular motion resulting from the standard combat manœuvre to counter the straight-ahead shot. In such a fight McCudden wrote of chasing a machine which nipped in front of him only to find his prey's wingman on his tail, twin Spandaus sounding like a vast canvas being ripped by a giant. There was system too on the periphery. General Staff notes in 1917 advised that surplus machines should be gathered as a reserve to give top cover, adding egregiously that dogfighters should always fight to the end.

Whatever the degree of system in dogfights, the emotions experienced by the pilots involved were as extreme as those of infantry going over the top. Most pilots, like Ira Jones, confided to their diaries that they could never again be so frightened:

Mick spotted a dozen Huns coming from the direction of Roubaix. We were then over Lille. As we had not much time for a fight, he decided to go straight at them. We had already been up for over an hour and had the slight advantage of height. The Huns, who were Albatross scouts, were of the stout variety and they accepted the head-on challenge. Both Mick and the Hun leader opened fire at each other as they approached from about 300 yards range but nothing happened. This burst of fire was the signal for a glorious dogfight – as fine and frightening a dogfight as I've ever been in. Friend and foe fired at and whistled past one another at tornado pace. It was a real stunner. Of late I've been able to keep very cool in an actual fight but now I became so flustered that occasionally I fired at my own pals in an effort not to miss a chance. Thank God my shooting was erratic.

As Cecil Lewis laconically observed, 'The concentrated violence of aerial dogfights has to be experienced to be known.'

Such fights had a limited life. If there was no spontaneous break-up as the circle became too tight it would disintegrate into a number of individual combats with 'the same rules applying throughout the war' as Immelmann tersely put it. Often, though, the ending would be sudden. If there was a collision, combatants would separate spontaneously, converting bedlam to an empty sky within seconds, as described by Lee:

We waltzed round one another as if in a vicious, unbreakable circle. First Giles, then Begbie, then a scarlet and black Hun would rush in mad confusion, each sweeping through the stringy mass of tracer bullets, making it curl up as if in a whirlpool. The barking of the machine guns was obliterated by imminence of a terrifying collision. It was an awe-inspiring sight of hurtling machines smashing through the sky at one another which developed into a game of snap-shooting. There was no time to take aim. Try as I would, I could not bring down a single bird. Through the corner of my eye I could see my comrades taking pot shots. Suddenly I spotted a machine commencing to smoke, then burst into flames. I wondered if it was a comrade. It was. I recognized by the marking that it was poor old Begbie. A sudden feeling of sickness overcame me. Fascinated with horror I momentarily forgot to fight. Poor old Begbie had to leave us without a wave of farewell. I had a final peep at him as I flew nearby. Thank God he looked as if he were dead. There was a void in my stomach as I looked over my shoulder and saw the long black trail of smoke which marked the last fight of a beloved companion.

At the end of a group fight, or when the patrol's allocated time-span expired, the flight commander would fire a green Verey to end the patrol. The descent would then take one of two forms. If there had been no contact with the enemy, an overwhelming sense of relief would be given expression. Some flight commanders demanded return in formation to a point above the aerodrome and then, with a hand signal, there would be a race to earth in a series of vertical sideslips as a final touch of battle practice. More often the commander allowed an expression of the mood.

Mick wagged his wings once asking us to take our wingtip to wingtip formation and without giving the second waggle that would have indicated the presence of an enemy, dived slowly towards the clouds. He flattened out just above them and began contour chasing among the steep, feathery mountains and valleys, round one peak, down the slopes into a hollow, zooming up to avoid the next mountain. All the time, silent rainbow spectres followed us or proceeded us as we turned and twisted over the arctic expanse. In the thrilling excitement of flying in such exceptionally magnificent conditions, we entered into the spirit of the chase, forgetting the war in our enjoyment. On and on we went, six dark shapes skimming heedlessly of whither we were going. It was cold. Not a shivering damp cold but a clear empty chill that made my bones feel light and as each successive plunge through the edge of a cloud left another rough layer of ice on the front of my wings and on the ailerons, I began to fear that if we continued much longer, our controls would freeze altogether. Then we dived and leaving our sunlit world we descended into the dull region between the two layers.

The beauty of the sky on a day of sunshine with fear of the enemy removed seems often to have left the most powerful impression of all experiences on a fighter pilot's mind. Few articulate memoirs omit the feeling, unknown since childhood, of total absorption and exhilaration removed from all human associations.

Dropping into glens, zooming up slopes, leaping over ridges, wheeling round tors, sometimes he (Yeates) could not avoid a sudden escarpment and hurtled against its solid seeming wall. He would hit it with a shockless crash that expunged the universe. But in a flash it was re-created after a second of engulfing greyness. Then he would land on a cloud. He throttled down and glided into the wind on the cloud surface, pulling the stick back to hold off and get his tail down. He settled down on the surface that looked solid enough to support him. But it engulfed him as he stalled and the nose dropped with a lurch into the darkness and almost at once he was looking at the world of fields and trees and roads. It was like a bowl coming up round him.

Once near the ground there came the contour chase home. 'Nothing could be more exhilarating,' wrote Ira Jones, 'than flying at full throttle just ten feet up.' Yeates agreed: 'There is no fun in flying comparable. All sensation of speed was lost a few hundred feet up but the nearer objects were, the more dizzy the feeling of speed as they whizzed by.' Diving lunges at troops drilling or wandering brasshats dawdling were considered fair sport, so Lee was able to describe strafing a staff officer, wheels within two feet of his red tabs, before circling inside the mine craters of the Messines ridge. In the spring of 1918 a curt letter from the battery commander of an artillery position demanded an apology from a pilot of 24 Squadron responsible for skimming within six inches of his hut roof. More often, wrote Yeates, 'it was taken in good part, for there was still a certain glamour surrounding the RFC and most people seemed to feel slightly honoured by its cock snooking.'

Rather more dangerous than peppery brasshats were telegraph or balloon cables. Collishaw once hit such an obstruction and was lucky enough to avoid serious injury from the aerial cheese wire as his aeroplane slid down a cable to finish on top of an officer's tea table.

The second type of patrol return was different. This was after combat, for then pilots would return without celebration or stunting in case a machine had sustained unsuspected damage. Often the delayed action of shock resulted in botched landings, so that during May 1918, for example, the RAF were averaging seven crash landings weekly, despite HQ threatenings. Landing after all was the most exacting and precise of common manœuvres. When

a new pilot first came to the aerodrome it was the landing in his
test flight which received the most careful scrutiny. So now, too,
the squadron commander visually judged the work of a returning
patrol and the wear on each of its members.

Some pilots were almost hysterical when their machines came
to rest. Caldwell noted that Mannock would often return shouting
jokes 'in tremendous form'. 'Daddy' Kiddie too was another
laugher, keyed up by the strain of battle. Most were quieter. Some
wept. A few sat quite still, smoking a cigarette to the butt while a
mechanic silently waited before releasing the harness pin and helping the pilot to the ground. On one occasion Ira Jones had to break
through a line of six German machines by crazy ground-level flying
and noted in his diary five minutes of uncontrollable shivering
when he landed. Chased down from 16,000 to 3,000 feet on one
patrol, Mannock found himself unable to stand when he climbed
from his cockpit. Returning after a similar escape, Parsons remembered swallowing half a glass of neat brandy yet still shaking for an
hour. Perhaps it was seeing such things that supplied power to the
driving force behind ground crews. Certainly they gave point to
that deceptive appearance of languor and ease on a fighter aerodrome between patrols.

If the guns had been fired, the first point of call would have to
be the recording officer's hut so as to piece together a combat
report for wing headquarters. For all the violent emotions of combat, such a finished documentary record was a desiccated thing:

> Sopwith BR number 7270. 21 April 1918. Time 10.45 am.
> Locality 62DQ2. Duty OP. At 10.35 I observed two Albatrosses
> burst into flames and crash. Dived on large formation of 15-20
> Albatrosses and D5 scouts and Fokker triplanes. Two got on my
> tail and I came out. Went back again and dived on a pure red
> triplane which was firing on lieutenant May. I got a long burst
> into him and he went down vertical and was observed to crash
> by Lt Mellish and Lt May. I fired on two more but did not get
> them.

With such brevity was the killing of Richthofen recorded.
Ball was invariably as laconic:

> 3 pm. 15 September 1916. Albatross seen going south over Ba-
> paume. Nieuport dived and fired one drum within fifty yards

after which the gun of the Nieuport came down and hit me on the head preventing me from following the EA down.

Or again:

5.30 pm. 23 September 1916. From fifteen yards under a Roland. 90 rounds of 1 in 3 Buckingham fired. On fire after 15.

On such reports Yeates observed in his classic book: 'Tom was always interested in the great difference between the queer, exotic reality and the terse official narrative which recorded that reality for the practical world. It was typically human. The reduction of cloudy magnitudes to formal succinctness. The rejection of all experience that was not for the practical mind essential.' In a sense, perhaps, such treatment coincided with the recollections of most pilots, for, as one wrote, 'The impression I brought back from jobs was usually intermittent with blurred edges where observation had been so mechanical as to leave no impression on the fear-occupied mind.'

If victory were claimed, accountancy was careful. HQs of infantry, artillery and balloon units would be phoned up for a cross-check, since killing in the air was seldom certain. Dead pilots tended to fall forwards and take their machines down in a nose dive, but this was one of the standard enemy escape routines anyway so, in the absence of such demands as the French made for three eye-witnesses, British scores tended to reflect the enthusiasm of particular pilots or squadrons. With such haphazard accountancy, typical of British GHQ whenever the killing of men rather than the consumption of bullets or shells was the matter in hand, notches cut into walking sticks always represented hope and prayer rather than Germans burnt or boxed.

Once a combat had been described and combat report completed, an episode was finalized and mind emptied of fear for a time. In this way, the members of the patrol would then often join colleagues lounging in the mess and share drinks. 'When a man had been in an exceedingly tight corner and had managed to squeeze out of it, it was later related as a very amusing episode,' wrote McCudden. 'As the narrator told his story, the others would shriek with laughter at the tale of how nearly he had been hit and how scared he had been.' Perhaps someone would collect the cash pool awaiting the pilot who at the end of the week had collected the most bullet holes in his fabric. But quietness was the norm after an active patrol. Some men would go straight for a bathe in the squadron pool; others spend a quiet hour unwinding in the armoury by filling ammunition belts. Few in the mess would talk of their experiences in the face of such an urgent need for rest. Second war Russian ace Kojedoub later reckoned that the physical energy expended in one combat was equivalent to a week's effort on the ground, with up to five pounds of weight sweated off in a single fight. In this respect, the parsimony of the combat report represented a true record of what men wanted to recall after a fight. In 65 Squadron McLanachan reckoned that victories seldom became known unless the scorer was a hut mate or else someone happened to see a combat report. Only involuntarily and in sleep would each moment of the overwhelming experience be re-played.

10
ROUTINE WORK – THE MECHANIC'S VIEW

No sooner did a returning patrol touch down than each machine would be approached by a group of serious men in overalls who had been waiting round each of the hangars, listening for a particular exhaust tone. They would seize hold of the wing tips and flick the chocs into position, the senior mechanic helping the pilot from his cockpit.

As the pilots walked slowly and heavily towards the mess or to the recording officer's hut, the cockpit watch would be carefully removed and guns unloaded under the eye of the gunnery officer. The two fitters and two riggers likewise would move straight into a servicing routine.

While the engine was still warm, valve tappet clearances would be checked, followed by a slow turning of the propeller to check compression. As the prop turned so sparking plugs would be taken out in turn and a thumb stuffed into the hole. The force with which the thumb was ejected gave the quickest check on compression. An ear was turned at the same time towards the cowling to listen for the squeak of dryness or grind of wear in the valve mechanism. The distributor would next be cleaned with metal polish and a soft cloth, the carburettor jets and filters removed for a petrol bath and the main oil filter doused in paraffin. Finally the whole engine would be thoroughly wiped down with cotton waste after the oil and water had been drained out and stored carefully for the next flight. If the weather was cold, the engine would be covered with a quilted cloth and a notice hung on the propeller forbidding anyone to touch it until the pump had been checked for possible icing-up.

Simultaneously the riggers would be at work, moistening mud before easing it off and wiping oil and grease with Castile soap on a dry rag. In this massage of fabric, all flaws would be noted. Bullet or shrapnel holes always meant a check on the soundness of the control cables before sewing on patches of unbleached linen, over-lapping the holes by at least two inches and secured with stitches every half inch. Then struts would have to be hand-checked for signs of crushing from compression forces or bending at the centre. Finally, threading fastenings and pins would be tested for signs of loosening.

If the flight had been uneventful, such routine maintenance might last under the hour. But if there had been contact with the enemy, servicing would have to be more intensive. During January 1918 at Farnborough, a mock fight was staged between an SE5a and an RE8 with accelerometer attached to wings measuring lifting forces. It was discovered that stresses up to three times the normal wing loading were common and up to four possible. Such forces, applied to machinery designed and assembled by rule of thumb formulae and to engines worked at all angles and full throttle, produced results visible in any pilot's logbook. Lieutenant Gates flew an SE5a in 1918. In nine months he made 104 patrols, engaging the enemy six times without opening his account. Even such unremarkable flying produced engine trouble on roughly one flight in six – cylinder lining broken, disintegrating tappets, dud magneto and so on. Rigging problems were so commonplace as to receive no mention in the log.

Chief fitters and riggers would therefore walk away from the machine with the pilot, questioning him quietly and noting down his answers in a pocket notebook.

Had there been a suggestion of roughness in the engine? If so, a check would have to be made on valve clearances or cleanliness of distributor. Popping in the carburettors could mean an air leak in the induction system or choked jets. Periodic roughness might be a contact-breaker arm sticking. If linked with misfiring, the exhaust valve would have to be checked for freedom of movement, together with an examination of the tightness of the plug leads. The engine would also need to be turned over, since black exhaust smoke would pinpoint a punctured carburettor float.

Overheating meant a search for water leaks or an inefficient pump. Perhaps the engine was approaching its decarbonization point, so the technical sergeant major's machine logbook would be checked – though the cause might just be pre-ignition, with the vibration from an engine specially tuned for high-altitude work.

A knocking could mean slack bearings, a loose propeller or even the whole engine loose in its mountings of Canadian elm.

In this way the fitter built up by stages the surgical operation on his charge according to accumulated experience of a type of machinery new in war and with few manuals to assist in diagnosis. The chief rigger meanwhile was as quietly eager for information, because the air test was the only one which could reveal the competence of his work. A nose diving tendency meant checking on the stagger of the wings or the incidence of tailplane. A tendency to drift meant that the straightness of the wing leading edges or of the fuselage spars must be checked. A tendency to turn right meant checking the verticality of the rudder or warping on the wing trailing edges. A tendency to fly wing down meant that the wing incidence angle would then have to be measured.

In some ways fitters had an easier time, for lengthier jobs were done off the aerodrome, stationary engines every hundred flying hours and rotary engines every forty being sent to the central workshops at Pont de l'Arche near Rouen for decoking – perhaps more often if metal particles were discovered in the oil filter, which might suggest excessive wear or partial seizure. Routine work for fitters consisted largely of cleaning and grinding the inlet and exhaust valves or cleaning the plugs and piston heads every five hours of flying time, recording all work done in their logbooks.

Rigging work, in contrast, was all done on the aerodrome. After combat or at the end of a week's flying, the machine would be pulled from its hangar by the tops of the undercarriage struts and set in its flying position on top of padded trestles for a two-day check. The truth of the wings would first be checked with a steel tape and the truth of the fuselage by a string from the centre of the engine to the rudder post. If there was any doubt, the whole team would get out templates, protractors, plumb lines and straight edges or invoke the skilled glance of the master rigger. If there were still doubt, the fabric would be unstitched and the machine reduced to its skeleton for re-rigging.

Seen in such a state of undress, the fighter aeroplane might seem a flimsy structure of wood and wire. Certainly if the stressed metal skin construction of Rohrbach and Messerschmidt had been available a few years earlier, it would have been seized on for its advantages in terms of accurate workmanship and mass production potential using machine tools. But in the absence of easily worked metal, engineers constructed machines of deceptive strength using the materials and skills most readily available – those of coach builder and farm machinery manufacturer. Rigid and resilient, wooden airframes could absorb more punishment and be more easily repaired than metal ones. They required fewer tools in the making, and strength for weight were a match for duralumin, being weaker only in torsion. Great War aeroplanes, like Nelson's ships, represented the greatest achievement of an age-old technology whose abrupt death was imminent – hand-shaping of wood in large structures with the emphasis on feel, eye and experience.

The basic materials were wood and wire. By 1916 the various problems associated with the using of seasoned timber had been sorted out and by elimination ash and silver spruce had been found the perfect blend. Easily bent without splitting, yet able to resist sudden shock, ash proved as useful to the aeroplane makers as it had been to medieval bowyers. In the fighter aeroplane it became the four longerons which ran the length of the fuselage, making the four corners of the box fuselage. Careful selection was always needed, since straight grain was uncommon and without careful seasoning ash could snap. Even the best ash was weak in compression and here silver spruce was found the perfect support. Its tubular bundle structure of fibres could withstand compression forces up to 5,000 pounds per square inch – but only by eliminating all spars whose grain deviated by more than 2 per cent and seasoning what remained with such care that an autographic record was kept daily until moisture content was just 15 per cent by weight of the dry timber. With a propeller of Spanish mahogany or black walnut, no other types of timber were necessary.

The sinews which held the timber in place were of high-tensile Swedish wire. Basic or acid process home-produced steel could never pass the Ministry of Munitions test which required it to be bent through 180 degrees in a vice five to thirty times according to gauge, let alone the pressure test of 120 tons per square inch. Two types were produced bearing the Ministry stamp – control wires of seven-strand cord, each strand of nineteen separate wires, and solid fuselage wire, stronger than cord by diameter but less so by weight.

About a hundred such wires held the aeroplane in shape. If the machine were to be re-built, each wire had to be tuned by turning its individual turn-buckle, the riggers adhering to a strict system and sequence. The principle was simple. An aeroplane, both fuselage and wings, was made of a succession of boxes, each box held in shape by cross-braced wires. One by one, each box had to be tuned to geometrical truth, starting with the engine-bearing wires and concluding with tailplane wires.

Truing-up was done for the upwards and sideways planes separately as riggers turned the thumbscrew fitment with which each wire terminated until the diagonals of each section were equal. This equality would be measured with a trammel – a wooden rod with two separately adjustable pegs on it. Then a plumb line would be used to establish verticality. When the whole system seemed about right, a string would be stretched from the centre point of the engine bearings to a marked point on the rudder post. If all was in order, the string would be perfectly horizontal – a straight edge and spirit level were used to double-check the eye's judgement. The rule was that, if any slight adjustments were needed, diametrically opposite wires should be loosened in proportion as analogues were tightened, the final test being an ear twang before the turn-buckles were locked to establish rigor mortis. The fuselage was complete.

Like the fuselage, the wings were creatures of struts and wires. Leading and trailing edges took no load, so that steel tubes in simple sockets kept the edges parallel and firm. Between these rods and eighteen inches apart was a sequence of H-section plywood ribs whose job was to support the wing fabric tacked to rib centre. Since these ribs were compressed in flight, they were built with a bulge in the centre and, like the fuselage, made of spruce toughened with spliced-in ash. Cross-braced internal wires balanced forces on the upper and lower spars, while visible cross-braced wires between the wings cancelled rival forces on the two planes, all such wires being duplicated for safety and sandpapered and painted against rust. If correctly tensioned, wing wires never sang whatever the pressure of flight.

Once they were attached to the fuselage, the angle of the wings was known to be critical, so wing adjustments took longer than the construction of the whole fuselage. Firstly, they had to be true relative to the fuselage. Plumb lines were dropped from four points on the leading edge of the upper wing and various wires adjusted until the plumb lines were as one, viewed from the side. Then came the dihedral, that slight upward tilt of the wings away from the fuselage which made for greater stability and checked a tendency to slither in a cross-wind. The angle was commonly about three degrees and on the top wing only. To achieve this, a straight edge would be placed against the leading and trailing edges, and the angle read off on an inclinometer. Once correct, the front landing wires would be locked. By placing the upper wing in advance of the lower (stagger), lift could be increased. A stagger of about half the wing's width increased lift by about 10 per cent. Such a distance would be set by measuring with a rule the distances either side of a plumb line dropped from the upper wing. Finally came the setting of incidence. The leading edge always had a slight downward tilt, reinforced by the slightly hollowed underside. By tinkering with incidence, the side profile was inclined to the line of flight, a low angle of incidence giving a higher speed and a higher angle giving a better lift and a slower landing speed. Adjustment was by checking straight edges placed under the ribs with an inclinometer or Abney level, care being taken that incidence was not greater at the tip than the root (wash-in) or conversely (wash-out).

Similar checks had finally to be made on the tailplane unit. The Abney level measured incidence to flight direction (never vertical so as to counter the spiralling air stream from the revolving propeller) and the spirit level checked that the front spar and hinged tube were horizontal before the fin was bolted on and the rudder hinged to fin and stern post. The elevators, similarly checked, were then hinged to the rear spar of the tailplane and rigidly connected, so that if controls on one side were damaged, the elevators could still be operated from the other side alone.

The whole machine was now ready for benediction by the master rigger, whose skills were related more to a cooper or freestone cutter than to any mechanic of the present day. Indeed, even the humblest rigger used craftsman's tools. Only his pliers would have surprised a medieval carpenter. The master would first run his hands over the frame like a horse-buyer at Tattersalls. Did the parts fit snugly or had they been hammered into position? He would stand about twenty feet in front of the skeleton, head steady and eyes alone moving to test incidence. From a position ten feet behind the machine he could see if all struts were parallel and in line. This was critical, since the slightest leaning caused disproportionate flying problems. A cranky machine might fly, but only perfect balance made machine and pilot one unit. The master rigger therefore used his skill to make a simple decision – did it feel right? Perhaps he might double-check, moving slowly from nose to tail, flicking each wire and judging truth with the instinctive skill – or so it seemed to an outsider – of a Suffolk horseman laying his furrow. In the same way, a blipped throttle was all the chief fitter required to check the work of his juniors, his ear the equivalent of the rigger's eye.

A final stage remained – clothing the skeleton. For this, about 250 square yards of fabric was required for a small fighter. The best material was unbleached flax linen of F1 British Standard, with eighty ends in the warp and ninety picks per inch in the weft. Such fabric weighed 4 ounces per square yard and could withstand pressure of up to 90 pounds per square inch, stouter threads being woven in at intervals to check any tendency from tearing forces. Aeroplane makers always argued fiercely whether the fabric should be attached to the timbers diagonally or with warp in a fore and aft position. But however fastened, this fabric was never the cloth or canvas some modern writers have held it to have been. Rather it was a material of great organic strength, skilfully adapted to extract every natural quality. Towards the end of the war, when linen ran short, long staple American cotton took over. It was much cheaper, slightly lighter, but only half as strong as the original fabric. There was never an acceptable substitute for aeroplane linen.

Hide glue fastened the fabric to the wooden ribs, with sewed kite cord as doubling security, each stitch at three-inch intervals and knotted with a Flemish slipknot with exposed portions taped. When this had been done, the whole skin would be washed with dope. This was of two kinds. Nitrate cellulose with wood chemical solvent, though faster to burn in the air, was easier to obtain than acetate, for which shell makers competed, with results a fighter pilot might have guessed. Five coats of this dope would be applied, time for drying being allowed between each application and painting done with care, since sandpaper could not be used to eliminate error. It was reckoned that the first two coats tightened the fabric and the third filled it, proofing it against petrol or oil splashes as well as giving a good base for camouflage. The final coat of varnish smoothed and reduced water absorption by 1,000 per cent. Such varnish was of lacquer or shellac and, since resin dissolved in oil took three days to dry, turpentine was the usual solvent, with the addition of a camouflage paint, chocolate or olive green above and blue beneath. The effect of these liquid additions was to increase the strength of the fabric by 25 per cent and the weight by 100 per cent.

The clothed aeroplane would finally be handed over to the nineteen-strong armoury section. They would meanwhile have been spending most of their time with bullets, carefully examining each of the 50,000 (three days' supply in battle conditions) which were in stock. A hangfire by a single bullet of just 1/250th of a second could shoot off a propeller blade and shake an aeroplane to pieces in the sky, so that by 1918 the checks on each bullet were such that an accident due to faulty ammunition was reckoned just once per 35,000 shots and the disintegrating props of the Hawker-Immelmann period were rarities. Then came the equally time-consuming routine of belt filling. Just fitting bullets of a single type into the magazine of a Lewis took ten minutes for ninety-seven rounds. The Vickers needed 500 per belt, each fitted into the metal linkage and each belt varied by the requirements of individual pilots. The choice was between the standard nickel-coated lead bullet, the armour-piercer with a steel core, the tracer, the Buckingham or the Pomeroy. The tracer, with one part of magnesium to eight of barium peroxide in the base, made accurate shooting at close range easier, but it also burnt itself out of shape, making trajectory unreliable. The blunt nose of the Buckingham was ideal for balloon busting and did greater damage if it hit any target. On the other hand, lack of streamlining made its trajectory as quixotic as the tracer's, quite apart from the reactions of Germans if they captured a prisoner with such blunt-nosed ammunition in his belts. The heavy punch of the Pomeroy also had its drawbacks. The nipping of the explosive mixture between bullet core and envelope made it liable to premature explosion in the gun barrel. Each pilot had therefore to work out his own balance between reliability, heavy impact and projectile visibility. For Hartney this meant a sequence of tracer, standard, Pomeroy and armour-piercer. Douglas, on the other hand, specified four standard to one tracer and Porter, one to five. Spring's sequence was tracer, Buckingham, standard. When the war ended, Buckingham's Coventry factory was employing 500 men who had produced 26 million bullets for the air force during the war at a cost to the service of 2 shillings per bullet.

With the aeroplane in their hands, the armourers would first replace the Lewis, which had been removed and boxed as soon as the aeroplane landed. The twin Vickers would usually be left on the machine and just cleaned on the outside with an oily rag after the dry oil had been removed with spirit of turpentine and the innards purged with boiling water poured down the barrel, followed by cleaning rods and flannelette. The fitting of these guns had been left to each aeroplane manufacturer, but with the obligation to permit the movement *in situ* to a vertical position for this crucial cleaning process.

The aeroplane would then be pushed to the armourers' ground target and set up in its flying positon so that sample ammunition belts could be fired at the target. Each of these belts would have been loaded to the owner's specification and sights adjusted and harmonized so that bullet flow came together at the point required by the pilot.

The work of all ground crew finally came together before a patrol. Then fitters and riggers combined to pull the machine from its hangar under the eye of the disciplinary sergeant major, 'strictly and smartly as a drill – as if a gun were being brought into action', or so the manual laid down. Last rites belonged to the fitters. The old water of the radiator would be boiled and carefully decanted, the oil gently heated and poured back into the engine through a gauze of density 25 strands per inch and petrol of 80-octane rating (Castrol mixture for a rotary) filtered through a chamois leather which had been scrupulously checked for pin holes. If there was time, one of the fitters would start to warm up the engine. More often the pilot himself liked to perform the exercise, partly to re-assure himself about engine reliability, partly to give extra time for concentration.

The amount of work entailed by all these processes was considerable. During the sustained fighting of August 1918, Sholto Douglas reckoned that mechanics worked from 3 am to 9 pm and thought it was common for them to get just two hours' sleep each night. Such devotion and care was taken for granted throughout the war. Fry wrote that he never found a bad rigger or careless fitter, and all pilots who comment agree with Fry. Such an attitude was after all in the tradition of the service. Even before the war the RFC had been sending foremen to poach from the Midland metal towns, instructing them to recruit skilled and 'specially steady men', because such mechanics, authority pointed out, would hold the whip hand over their officers in mechanical knowledge – 'they know about the explosive engine and were used to thinking in terms of 1/10,000th of an inch tolerance'. The sort of men expected by the RFC was suggested by the salary they were offered – 45s. weekly against the 7s. of the infantry soldier. Mechanical faults were therefore most often the result of faulty design or faulty assembling rather than of slipshod maintenance. Status and proximity to the war zone meant that mechanics' devotion would be registered in time and care as well as in the bullets mounted on wire which they fashioned into models of the machines they worked on.

Devotion would certainly not be based on a personal relationship with the pilot, for peacetime conventions of caste proved stronger than any new unit formulation in war. Macmillan noted that apologies from pilot to mechanic were rare and Baker that visits to hangars were very infrequent. At best, the relation was expressed on the mechanics' side by those hand-made things which befitted a relation based on little else besides a common passionate relation to common machinery. Propeller blades might be used as a 'canvas' for combat scenes or bosses turned into tobacco jars. Most valued of all by the pilot, and something which by strict convention no pilot could ask for, was the walking stick made of the leather washers of petrol tin tops mounted on rigging wire, turned on a lathe, with one end tapped to take a nut as handle. In so far as there was further communication, it would only be with stiffest formality. Leslie Tupping wrote to Captain Garland:

> May I congratulate you on your well earned promotion. Perhaps I am not quite in order here as there is such a vast gap between an ordinary corporal and a captain but in civilian life, I believe, we are not so far apart ... you have been a sport and a gentleman to me since I first had the honour to be your mechanic ... asking you to overlook any statement in this letter which you may think too familiar. Jolly good luck, I remain your faithful mechanic ...

The worlds of mechanics and officers thus remained distinct in the air service throughout the Great War and not just because of the social distinction between gentleman and labourer. Tupping was after all aware that in civilian terms he and his pilot were close.

The real distinction was that Tupping was involved directly with something that was both mechanical and novel and therefore personified in miniature one of the tragedies of the British army in the first war – its inability to make full use of new technology or even recognize that new weapon systems were available. On the aerodrome this showed itself in the separation of pilots and mechanics; at Corps headquarters level it was seen in the complete failure to devise a policy which would support the army in some way other than a blind and constant hammering. At GHQ level it found expression in Haig's personal draft of his final dispatch: 'Mechanical contrivances have been greatly exaggerated in comparison with the value of infantry. There must also be artillery and cavalry as well! ... Each war has certain special conditions so some modification of organization will be necessary but if our principles are sound, these will be few and unimportant. The longer the war has gone on, the more satisfactory do the principles of our training manuals appear!' Even with their limited knowledge of casualty rates and tactical possibilities, many mechanics at the time would have been very doubtful of such conclusions.

II
BATTLE WORK

Major ground battles always made a break in the rhythm of incessant patrol work at high altitude. For the duration of such battles, fighter pilots were committed to a period of more frequent flying and at lower altitudes, their purpose being first to blind the enemy by shooting down his observation balloons, then to ease the infantry attack forward by harassing ground targets.

Observation balloons were the initial target. Given military birth in the 1870s as spherically inflated ox intestines, by 1914 they had become sausages of fabric measuring 70 yards by 20 and stabilized by three elephant ears squatting together at one end, filled by air through a scoop in the balloon's double bottom. By 1917 the Germans had 170 such balloons, grazing at two-mile intervals the length of the west front.

What made the balloon a tactical factor of critical importance was the human observer floating beneath the sausage in a tiny wicker basket. If German, he was a specially trained man with six months' theoretical work behind him. Dressed in camelhair vest, oilskin waistcoat, lined tunic, leather flying coat and fleece-lined high boots worn over assorted underwear layered, with his telescope he surveyed a horizon twenty-eight miles away from a height of just 600 feet. In practice, the customary height was 7,000 feet about four miles from the front line. The wicker basket was stable in winds gusting up to 50 mph. A film of haze or dead spaces covered by hills or woods could all blind the balloon's eye, but for the purpose of battle preparation balloons had to be blinded and the telephone link to the gunpit via the balloon's cable silenced before battle concentration began. Since during the whole war the artillery never managed to shoot down one of these balloons, the task was necessarily passed to the RFC.

For all their vaguely absurd appearance, observation balloons proved formidable targets. Flying from semi-permanent sites 300 yards square, these OBs were flanked by gun batteries positioned for maximum saturation of the airspace around the balloon: 20-mm machine guns firing bullets two inches long shot accurately up to 6,000 feet. Then there were the feared 'flaming onions', fired from rocket guns to become green glowing balls which twisted about like live things and seemed to chase an aeroplane, turning over end on end in a leisurely way yet, as Bishop observed, terrifying because moving just too fast for an aeroplane to take evasive action. Part of their terror was that no one knew what they were, or has found out even today. Some men thought them linked by wire or chain like phosphorescent Napoleonic cannon balls; others guessed them to have been ranging mechanisms like tracers. Bartlett probably came nearest to discovering how they worked through his experience of 'Nigger chasers' on 4 July celebrations in the USA, when such explosive fireworks shot out balls corkscrewing in a circular motion. Bartlett was even hit by one, later finding severe scorch marks on the fabric of his wing. In addition to these aimed missiles was the fear in the back of the mind that the balloon being attacked might have its basket packed with explosive, to be electrically detonated when the attacking aeroplane approached. Since Brock incendiary bullets burnt out of shape within 150 yards, they certainly had no choice in the matter of close approach.

Even when he had run the gauntlet of integrated artillery fire, it was not certain that the pilot would find his balloon: 60 hp winches could wind down the pencil-thin balloon cable at a rate of about 500 yards a minute. In an emergency the lorry holding the winch might even accelerate along a prepared getaway road.

Nor if the balloon were hit did destruction invariably follow. Rain or mist could make ignition of the gas problematical and in cold weather both helium and argon burnt with difficulty. Even in perfect conditions, penetration of the balloon fabric might be too fast to cause ignition. Even assuming that the balloon did catch fire, it did so in slow motion. The jet of fire would only slowly spread in a huge cloud of oily black smoke. This very slowness often meant that the observer had time to escape. With three separate parachutes attached by a springhook to his harness, he would probably have jumped at the first sight of an approaching aeroplane. Balloons were cheap and easily replaced, so it was always the trained eye of the observer that was the real object of the attack or, put another way, though a balloon shot down might mean a couple of days' extra breathing space, a dead observer represented plunder of a scarce enemy asset.

All these dangers and problems were officially recognized. British authorities rated a balloon equal to three enemy aeroplanes in the calculation of pilot scores, while the Germans made two balloons the equal of three aeroplanes, suggesting perhaps that the defences of British balloons were rather more pregnable than their own. Even so, few men voluntarily chose the hazards of balloon busting and fewer still became adepts. Of the high-scoring men, only Beauchamp-Proctor with sixteen and Willy Coppens with twenty-six went with equal relish and success for balloon and aeroplane targets. More were like the German Roth (seventeen balloons) or Frenchman Coiffard (twenty-eight balloons), who found the skills of balloon shooting so different from those of hitting a moving target that they kept to the former.

Balloon aces had no single technique. Some went high. For Bishop, this meant flying above the clouds on a compass course before diving hard. The method gave him an advantage in surprising ground defences, but gave little time to adjust trajectory of the dive, quite apart from threatening to detach his wings in levelling out from the power dive and blacking him out as he came away with a zoom. Sholto Douglas was likewise a diver, but his chosen aiming point was always about half a mile from the balloon to give him the benefit of a straight run in, his Vickers opening at 200 yards and his Lewis at 50 yards.

Low men included Mannock and Coppens. Both went in at about 20 feet, giving pom-poms a hard target, and for preference at dawn or dusk, taking their chance with telegraph wires and poles. To escape such hazards, Ira Jones and his flight commander Bond chose the height of 2,000 feet but often found their machines turned over by massive anti-aircraft bursts. The simplicity of their methods of flying straight at a balloon at the same height as the target seems to have been inversely proportional to the massive relief experienced by the pair when they got home safely.

What both the high and low fliers did have in common was knowledge of the importance of planning. Fritz Roth would use his telescope for hours to piece together the defensive patterns of allied aircraft and would then study weather charts so as to pick up a wind parallel to the front before making his dive along a line of balloons. In the same spirit of cautious research Rickenbacker wrote:

> First we obtained photographs of the five German balloons in their lairs from a French observation squadron. We then studied a map to ascertain the precise positions each occupied, the nature of the land, the relative positions of mountains and rivers, trees and villages in the vicinity of each. Then, one by one, we visited these balloons, studying from above the nature of the roadway on which the mother trucks must operate and where the anti-aircraft defences had been posted around each Drachen balloon. In the end I decided to fly eight to ten miles behind the front and then turn and come back from an unexpected quarter, trusting to the discipline of the German army to have its balloons ascending just as we reached them. I would cut off my engine at 15,000 feet and by gliding quietly with silent engine I would gradually lose altitude and turn to gain the balloon line with comparatively little noise.

The upshot of such care on this occasion was an unexpectedly early sighting by the enemy – 'I was in the midst of a fiery furnace' – and jammed machine guns.

Quite apart from all the physical hazards which balloon busters like Rickenbacker described were the mental obstacles which accompanied them. Wrote McLanachan:

> No pilot in 74 Squadron was expected to undertake a second balloon strafe, this work being done by the junior members of the squadron. There had been much chafing about these strafes and as the possibility of another becoming necessary made it probable that each new batch of pilots would have to undertake it, the prospect hung like a cloud over every junior fighter. The real dangers were never discussed and the strafes were surrounded with an ominous secrecy which induced the experienced pilots to reproach the more boisterous youths by saying 'What you need is a balloon strafe to knock the stuffing out of you.' Participation in one was regarded as a baptism. On the evening of 8 August 1918, the atmosphere at dinner was constrained and excited and on retiring to my hut, Mannock and Hall joined me. Mick stood leaning against the doorpost and grinned jeeringly at me. 'You're for the high jump tomorrow.'

'How?' I asked, wondering what escapade of mine had come to the ears of the CO. Each glanced at the other significantly.

'It's quite true, Mac,' Hall said. 'There's a balloon strafe tomorrow.'

They came into the hut and sat on Hall's bed, telling me what a strafe involved. I was very grateful for Mick's and Hall's advice. 'Keep as close to the ground as possible; five or six feet if you can.' 'Don't get rattled and fire at the machine gun emplacements that pepper you.' 'For God's sake mind the telegraph wires. They're all over the place, their side and ours.' Hall told me that the news was not to be imparted to the others until next morning as their thoughts of what they might have to face might disturb their sleep.

'We know you're all right,' Hall said. 'It would be mean of us not to tell you.'

'It won't worry old Mac,' Mick added. And to me, 'I promise I'll count every bullet hole when you get back.'

Hall departed to join a game of poker and Mick decided that we might as well have a drink together at 'Odettes'. The balloon strafe seemed to worry him more than it did me for on return to the camp having said nothing about it till then, he whispered, 'You'll be all right'.

Of his experience of that flight McLanachan went on:

My machine was only nine or ten feet above the trenches when it seemed to me that my lonely Nieuport suddenly became the target for every machine gun on the front. I imagined every Fritz in the trenches grabbing for his rifle and actually saw one or two firing at me. With no conscious volition on my part, I began crazy flying first on one wing tip then on the other, squirming and dodging to escape the hail of bullets that was being fired, yet all the time keeping a wary eye open for telephone lines. They were really breathless moments for any stray shot might have hit my machine and flying at that height I should have had no chance to land properly. But as long as I continued to twist and turn, refusing to fly straight for more than a second, no one could have fair chance to get his sights on me. The main danger lay in flying too high or remaining in line with a MG battery sufficiently long to let them fire along my line of flight. To my intense relief, my engine was growling away savagely and after only half a minute of severe firing, the shots tailed off and ceased finally. Flying low and hopping over the crude telephone cables for over a mile, I found myself above green fields. There was a village ahead and curious to see what it was like, I flew directly over the housetops. The street had a peaceful, countrified appearance and a few surprised German soldiers and peasants stared up at me. The sight of my red, white and blue circles made one soldier drop a bucket he was carrying and dash for cover – or to fetch a rifle.

After these moments of terror, the mood which followed surprised the writer.

As I flew at forty or fifty feet from the ground, three or four miles behind the German lines, a feeling of great serenity came over me. The balloon was still at 1,500 feet and feeling quite confident, I made up my mind to wait until they had pulled it down to two or three hundred feet. It was then that a good idea came to me. The two batteries were to the west of the balloon and if I attacked from the east, they would not be able to fire at me for fear of hitting the gasbag themselves. With this in view I flew a mile to the east of them where I saw a column of mounted German officers. Possibly because the last thing they expected to see was a British machine flying low down so far behind their lines, they made no attempt to scatter to the side of the road. Undecided what to do, I zoomed up to three or four hundred feet and in a spirit of devilment, dived hell for leather at the leaders. The sight of a friendly machine diving with full engine is a disconcerting one but the sight of my hostile circles must have caused consternation among the Germans. The horses stampeded and on circling round I saw several of them, riderless, tearing across the adjoining fields. The men and officers were sprawled across the road in ridiculous attitudes into which they had thrown themselves to escape my wheel.

Mission accomplished and dripping with sweat, McLanachan took off his flying helmet and opened his coat for the return flight.

Every machine had returned and there was great excitement. We went to the mess to have a proper breakfast. On the way Mick overtook us. 'What do you think?' he said, pointing an accusing finger at me. 'That blighter's only got one bullet hole in his machine - in the tailplane.' Several of the others had had an exciting time. Harrie's machine was riddled. Herbert's and Pettigrew's were also damaged. Kennedy's had bullet holes in every section except the tank (and the pilot) while Tudhope as usual had the worst of it. He had flown into a German telephone cable and miraculously returned.

Balloon busting was thus an ordeal. It meant a shapeless fear, a thing of so many variables that fighter pilots who managed to keep a precarious balance by compartmentalizing the phases of routine patrol work might find themselves destroyed by contemplation of the random odds of a balloon flight. The history of 40 as well as 74 Squadron therefore records that its pilots were called upon to make only one strafe each. William Barker, rated by Bishop the finest pilot in the RAF, shot down one balloon and never went for another. There was anyway enough battle flying left to occupy fully the men who had passed the test of a balloon strafe.

When the infantry battle began and the men advanced, the task of low fliers was to harass enemy ground troops and soften up strongpoints. The job was always called 'ground strafing' and was thought to have been invented by Major Thompson of 16 Squadron, who had been first winner of the title 'the mad major' for his low attacks with the antique Farman pusher in 1915. As a systematic form of activity, May 1917 saw the beginning, Cambrai later in that year being the first coordination of low-flying aeroplanes with artillery.

One participant described the experience thus:

The battle of Poelkapelle was on 9 October, with the first battle of Passchendaele beginning three days later. On each of these battle days we were engaged on ground strafing when we always flew in pairs. Our Camels did not carry bombs but our twin machine guns rattled out against troops and transport in the trenches and in the open, on guns and gunners and all objects that offered us a target. These low flying jobs offered excitement. Things flashed in view, were fired at, passed behind and were forgotten with the next target that loomed up. I have seen the field-grey German troops throw themselves down into open shell holes and dig feverishly with clawing fingers as we swooped in pairs upon them with our fire enfilading their position; gunners drop their occupations to scatter into shelter; horses turn and gallop away in terror, dragging swaying waggons along the shell-holed roads until they turned them over; marching troops run in confusion to avoid our bullets. The whole month of October was occupied with days of pushes, big and little. British pushes that nibbled into the enemy system of trenches. They looked insignificant enough perhaps on the map. To the man in the trenches and in the air who carried them through, they were big enough to fill the whole of life's horizon.

Put more technically, the aim was to fly in at about 1,500 feet so as to be below anti-aircraft fire and above effective machine-gun range; then to operate in a series of dives and zooms with short, rapid climbing turns, fitting the gun firing in between. This dive had to be at about 150 mph and down to 200 feet to beat ground fire before zooming back to 1,000 feet 'with the wires screaming triumphantly like the blare of brass in the ride of the Valkyries'. The same heights and methods would be used for dropping the two 25-pound bombs often carried, the Aldis again being used for sighting.

Some men enjoyed the work. Immediately after the war, Lee recalled it as 'exciting and sometimes enjoyable'. Rickenbacker wrote of 'the time of my life' while being tossed about by high ground winds like a wood chip in a whirlpool. On hitting an enemy gunpit he wrote of 'the most amusing little party I ever attended'. Another pilot thought the destruction of a machine-gun nest from the air the ideal method of killing. Men toppled over in the ring sight while the pilot felt no contact, heard no shriek, saw no blood. It added up to a delightfully impersonal killing and a serene sleep.

Some pilots even thought the work relatively safe. Rickenbacker reckoned that enemy soldiers were too busy running for cover to retaliate. Lewis too thought them pre-occupied with what was happening on the ground. Anyway, though an upward rifle shot might make calculation of gyroscopic deviation unnecessary, hitting a ground strafer meant aiming about fifty yards ahead of the machine, and General Jeudwine, in a report in January 1918, wrote of two enemy ground strafers working for two hours over a small area with impunity, despite intensive ground fire from machine guns of all types.

Most ground strafers would have disagreed though. Yeates was typical in writing of long gaps in his visual recall during which he

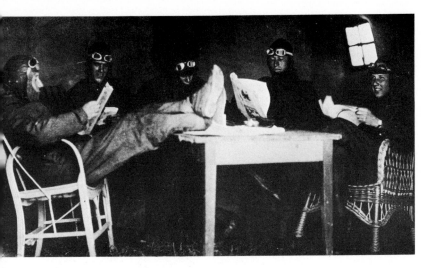

Newspapers sent from home were a favourite means of relaxation. Certainly the men would not
reading studies of enemy tactics and machinery, for very little of such literature was produced in
first war. It always surprised our men when they visited French aerodromes to find maps and
otos of enemy terrain, with models and specifications of their opponents' machines.

Albert Ball was the first of our widely known aces. He became a symbol of RFC work over the
mme. Living alone on the aerodrome and fighting alone in the sky, his method of attack was
ique – underneath so as to rake his opponents belly with upward Lewis fire. Later in the war, Ball's
other found these relics, after he had been shot down and killed in mysterious circumstances by the
emy. The cigarette case and tunic were returned, as was customary during that war. The fragments
aeroplane may or may not have been Ball's.

23. A fighter is prepared for battle. Oil is poured into its tank through a gauze, 80-octane petrol through a chamois leather. The engine would have been recently overhauled and de-carbonized – and the fabric cleaned with Castile soap. This machine carries the leader's twin streamers in its tailplane. In the background the canvas hangars threaten to sag on to the planes or blow down in high wind – which they often did.

24. Salvaged aeroplanes are restored at a depot by air mechanics. In the foreground is a two-seater with a rotating mounting for the rear Lewis gun, giving the rear gunner a wide field of fire except to attack from the front and above or to the rear and below. Camels are behind, with the hump for the twin Vickers clearly defined.

5. Weaponry and ammunition of all types were stored in the squadron armoury when not in use. Servicing the guns and filling ammunition belts was the full-time work of skilled specialists. In this photo, Webleys and Verey pistols are hung on the roof with Lewis guns and cartridge case bags in cupboards. The armoury is for a two-seater squadron. Two rear gunners select their artillery.

6. The business end of a Sopwith fighter before the addition of cowling and wing centre section. The pilot's personal seat would be fitted on top of the petrol tank, the petrol mixing with the castor oil (tank below guns) to propel the rotary engine. The engine cylinders whirled round a stationary cam shaft. The twin Vickers machine guns are synchronized with the engine so as to fire through prop blades at about 1,000 bullets per minute. Sopwith's spade joystick is clearly visible.

27. Edward Rickenbacker, American ace of aces. Veteran racing driver and personal chauffeur to US commander Pershing, Rickenbacker only took up flying at an age when most fighting officers would have been looking for a comfortable staff job.

had been too afraid to notice anything. Weather was the first ingredient of such terror:

Frew and I went on a low flying patrol over Broodseinde. A gale blew from the south west driving low cloud before it. Our light Camels were cruelly tossed about in the bumps, sometimes thrown up to the fringe of the clouds at 800 feet then again falling to 200 feet above the ground. We had very little control over them. The air conditions made the shell-pocked battlefields look even worse to the eyes of airmen bumping through the wind-torn air among the hurtling shells between the clouds and the ground.

Shells made up the second danger. Noble thought the possibility of flying a machine unscathed through a barrage very slight

and for that reason we were always informed of the areas of the massed guns and their barrage targets together with the maximum height of flights of shells. The different types of shells were fired at different angles and rose to different heights, thus creating a series of superimposed tunnels through which at certain definite levels we could fly in comparative safety. The lowest tunnel was the worst and our rocking flight through it was accompanied by torn wings from fragments of exploding shells and lumps of mud which bespattered our lower surfaces. The terrific buffets of shock waves from the concussion of exploding shells threw our little Camels about in almost uncontrollable fashion. There was always an element of uncertainty when the artillery barrage was intense. If caught in the aerial tunnel of a barrage, safe exit could only be secured by flying along the centre of the tunnel. Any attempt to fly through the shell-wall sides of the tunnel either towards the guns which threw the shells or towards the side where they fell to earth was folly.

The third, and most feared, danger came from bullets. A low-flying aeroplane might appear to present an almost impossible target in view of the huge deflection angle involved for the rifleman, yet a small bullet leaving a rifle muzzle at 2,500 feet a second and effective up to 7,000 feet could kill nevertheless. Sholto Douglas once saw a British soldier pick up a rifle lying on a road and shoot down a low flier, completing the capture with a flying rugby tackle when the pilot started to run from his cockpit. Voss too wrote of an army clerk bringing down a low Albatross. Even the great Richthofen may have been shot down by the ground Lewis fire of army cooks, though both army doctors who first examined the body agreed that angle of entry meant that another aeroplane had almost certainly been the executant. It was therefore with good reason that most ground strafers flew with flattened steel helmets on their seats.

Statistics can be provided for this combination of weather, explosive and chance. Casualties among British ground strafers during the Cambrai offensive in November 1917 were listed officially at 30 per cent daily, while Lee was shot down three times in a single week by ground fire.

Did the results justify such figures? Speaking as an infantryman, Cloete thought air attack the most terrifying thing in his war and the sight of an inhuman goggled figure as bewildering as the deafening engine noise. Dugdale rated low-flying German aeroplanes in the Cambrai counter-attack as the chief demoralizer. He wanted only to run away or dig into the ground when the enemy swooped low. Tactically, too, strafers may have played a crucial part in halting the Germans in their great thrust towards Amiens in March 1918, since so few roads ran with the axis of the attack in the area covered by it, so that advancing German supplies became vulnerable to air strafing. Just how close to success the enemy's March thrust had been is suggested by the fact that British plans were to withdraw towards the Channel ports and re-embark if necessary if the enemy reached Amiens. As it was, their thrust stopped within sight of Amiens cathedral spire, with the British Commander in Chief in such a state of collapse that War Minister Milner had to give control of the battle to Foch. Just what would have happened if the Germans in their turn had flown in mass against the congested roads occupied by Gough's broken army in that attack Lee would only speculate.

On the other hand, a special report on low flying published by 22 Wing in August 1918 concluded that all machines should be used while the enemy was in a state of shock, but that indiscriminate low flying thereafter led only to excessive casualties as well as greatly straining the pilots. Even in the initial phase, the report pleaded for detailed particularization in orders and indications of the likely development of the battle which might give the pilots some insight into the changing human map seen through their Aldis sights. Orders like 'squadrons will bomb and shoot up everything they can see on the enemy side of the line. Very low flying is essential. All risks to be taken. Urgent' were criticized as being both tactically futile and unduly costly in men. When the enemy had re-organized himself, flights should then take off sparingly and against specific positions about which there was reliable information. Even if the air was used in such a professional manner, Lee remarked tartly that there was always a distinction between shooting at men in ground strafing and hitting them. And just who the dead men were was not easily established, for, as Sholto Douglas noted, at high speed all uniforms looked khaki.

The German solution to the particular problem of low-level target shooting was to create specially trained battle squadrons equipped with machines whose engines and petrol tanks had been armoured. The British never did this, even though the RFC had spare men available. Just five days before the battle of Third Ypres, Trenchard had written to Haig offering to return 50 per cent of his pilots and 60 per cent of his observers to ground duty if they were required in the land battle. Third Ypres was also the first battle in which RFC machines ground strafed on any scale. Neither was the development of the purpose-designed Sopwith Salamander speeded up. In the end, therefore, just as every novice was called upon for the difficult and specialized work of balloon busting, so any squadron might suddenly be called upon for the equally specialized and dangerous work of ground strafing. Writing much later of his own experience of war flying, Smith-Barry's chief instructor remarked that 'an easy-going way was de rigueur in the RFC. Nothing much seemed to have been thought out and troubles were not generally anticipated.' Such was certainly the case with battle flying in the last period of the war.

12
GLAMOUR – THE ACES

Scale was perhaps the greatest problem in the Great War. In one week during third Ypres, for example, the British army dispatched two million shells and had 3,000 dead and 14,000 wounded in the Ypres Salient alone. For the combatants, war on such a scale meant loss of meaning. As one subaltern put it: 'The barrages became so enormous and mechanical, the succession of persons and places so rapid and their characteristics so obliterated that I doubt if anything was ever so clear as it had been when we began.'

This scale produced in addition the feeling that all a man could do was just hang on. Another infantry subaltern wrote: 'Few of us knew the importance of the events in which we took part and we cared as little. I asked one of our men what his thoughts were. He answered: "I wonder if we're going to be relieved."'

Propoganda was never adequate counter. At best, the huge anonymous desolation of the battlefield might yield the name of a particular division or regiment, but for the most part the individual was without significance. 'Everything appeared to be moving along with me,' wrote infantryman Manning of an attack on the Somme. 'Figures were popping up and down on every side and I felt the rush of others coming on behind. The waves in front were merged in smoke, moving like animated figures projected on a glaring screen. I felt stunned and hardly conscious of anything. The noise was deafening.' From such anonymity even the selection of particular men to receive a decoration in the hollow square of the recipient's battalion came to mean the chance recognition of a deed seen by higher authority as against hundreds unseen, the ribbon diminished by the distance from high explosive of those who awarded them.

The air was different. There, a handful of men fought in a virgin medium, seeming to personify skill in arms, individual judgement and sustained ferocity in single combat leading to a calculated

GLAMOUR – THE ACES · 133

killing. The power of such an image was first realized by the French, whose press created in Pegoud the first 'ace' in the summer of 1915. The Germans followed quickly. By the end of 1915 Max Immelmann had been officially filmed and his aeroplane put on display in Berlin. His postbag was made up of forty letters daily from civilian admirers. Such propaganda was equally effective among fighting soldiers – Ludendorff rated the name of Richthofen the equivalent of three infantry divisions.

The British never used the activities of the RFC to such advantage. What corps commander Ivor Maxse termed 'the extreme reticence and horror of all forms of publicity evinced by the professional soldier' prevented it. Thus Sir Douglas Haig in September 1917 said: 'I feel sure that officers of the RFC are proud of being anonymous like their comrades in other branches of the British army.' The result was that, even when the war ended, the name of leading marksman Edward Mannock was known to very few, while even air chief Salmond thought Beauchamp-Proctor (fifth highest-scoring ace) unremarkable for his final tally.

In the freemasonry of trenches and aeroplanes it was different. When the call for pilots came to the St Omer pool, one of the first checks was always on squadron number: 1 meant the spirit of Bell-Irving and Fullard; 24 spelt Hawker and Hazell; 46 Maclaren and so on. Even Trenchard, who privately thought aces a waste of time and effort, since a single night bomber could destroy in one night more enemy machines than all aces in a week, had in public to declare that 'Albert Ball was the most audacious, the most skilful and most marvellous pilot in the RFC. Every pilot in the corps considered him a perfect model and strove to imitate him.'

If fighting men gave such prestige to successful fighter pilots it must often have been for what they represented rather than what they were, for most aces seem to have been physically unimpressive. Pilots after all had no need to march long distances with heavy packs, then hurl grenades or fight with bayonets at close quarters. Like ground snipers, pilots killed sitting and so bantams could compete with giants. Indeed, small men always seemed better fitted to the medium. Beauchamp-Proctor and Rochford stood around five feet; on the German side Udet and Wolff were five foot three inches. In the second war, historian Sims found the same strong tendency towards the small and whiplash among high-scoring fighter pilots.

In temperament there was often similar lack of charisma. There were certainly cheerful extrovert killers like William Barker, who would smack his thigh and shout 'Well, that's that, boys' at the end of each patrol. But most seem to have been neurotic, distant men. Fry described Albert Ball as an unfriendly, uncommunicative man without friends. He slept alone in his own hut, cultivated his vegetable garden alone off duty or played a violin. Grinnell-Milne noted squadron opinion of McCudden as ruthless, ambitious, unwilling to share. Of Bishop, Douglas wrote: 'There was something about him that left one feeling that he preferred to live as he fought, in a rather hard brittle world of his own.' Mannock certainly began his fighting life as a moody, aggressive, unpopular outsider. Mellowness came only with the recognition of skill.

What qualities, then, made these small, moody men into successful killers? Even fighter pilot Sholto Douglas, with experience of aces in both wars, thought their composition a mystery. Flying skill in the conventional sense had little to do with it. Balfour noted just how many brilliant pilots failed in war flying. In his own squadron, William Barker was outflown by Linke-Crawford, while in crack 65 Squadron, Caldwell was acknowledged a finer pilot than Albert Ball and participated in more combats, yet he finished well down the scoring list. Duke, a colleague of Beauchamp-Proctor, described the fifth-highest scorer as 'not a good pilot'.

Shooting rather than flying seems to have been the essential skill. As McCudden put it in a lecture to cadets early in 1918: 'Good flying has never killed a Hun yet. You just get on with sighting your guns.' What counted above all was not flying the aeroplane but converting it into a flying rifle, held steady to the pilot's shoulder. Such skill might find flamboyant expression. McCudden enjoyed demonstrating his ability with the impossible deflection shot from 400 yards and at right angles, saying that hitting at such a distance was just as easy as from 40 yards. On the German side, Dossenbach likewise enjoyed the prestige which went with kills at 500 metres. But the surest measure of shooting capacity was economy. Immelmann reckoned on a killing with every twelve to twenty-five bullets fired. Fonck got the figure down to between twelve and fifteen. On one occasion – 9 May 1918 – he even scored six Germans with fifty-two bullets. Such shooting was the ace trademark in both wars.

As a component of such shooting ability, flying skill cannot be omitted. It often went unrecognized, since it was so different from any conventional type. In the schools it meant slow, smooth curves combined in a fluid geometry, like a self-absorbed ballet dancer practising in front of a mirror. The requirements of war flying were very different, as novice Cecil Lewis discovered from that great French flier Guynemer:

> I was considered one of the best pilots in 56 Squadron, so when Guynemer challenged me to mock combat over the airfield, I accepted with alacrity. I knew our machines were fairly evenly matched and judged that my own flying skill would give me the edge over the Frenchman. But soon I found it otherwise. Guynemer's little Spad was smaller and more manœuvrable than an Se5a. He had the better climb and could turn in a smaller circle. The result was that as I sat in a vertical turn with the stick right back, circling as tightly as an SE5a could go, Guynemer just sat right on my tail in a slightly smaller circle so that he always kept his sights on me. Had I been an enemy I should have been dead five times in the first minute. Do what I would – spin, half roll, dive, climb – there he sat just as if I had been towing him behind me.

In this vignette, the essence of war's flying skill had been displayed, for all that counted was the rough, brutal handling linked with the telepathy of experience which told what an enemy was about to do and allowed one machine to be held tight in relation to its prey. Manœuvres executed in isolation were nothing. War flying meant a capacity to cling. The art was that of the bare-knuckle street-fighter compared to the Queensberry of the schools.

Boelke brought out the significance of such skill when Richthofen asked him the secret of high scoring. 'I fly close to my man, aim well and then of course he falls down,' was the reply. The whole point was that, whatever a pilot's shooting skill, flying ability, which allowed shooting at close quarters, made success very much more certain. René Fonck liked to open fire between 40 and 60 yards from his target, Ira Jones from 75 yards. Collishaw always thought that hitting anything beyond 200 yards required a miracle, given slow-firing guns delivering bullets of tiny calibre from a violently vibrating machine. Even with the superior equipment of the second war, ace of aces Hartmann liked to open fire at just 50 yards before breaking off in a split S.

High scoring therefore involved getting close, ideally directly behind, so as to cut out deflection adjustments, and then holding this relative position however the target tried to escape. It meant too the skills of hiding, seeing, evaluating and diving so as to be able to get into such a position.

In his memoirs, Bishop suggested a balance between these skills: 'By this time I had learnt nearly all the fundamental principles of fighting in the air and had decided upon exactly what tactics were best for me to use. I had learnt that the most important thing in fighting was shooting. Next, the various tactics in coming into the fight. Last of all, flying ability itself.'

Lethal shooting. Flying skill of a particular sort. There was still one vital physical capacity remaining without which no man survived long enough to use his potential – the negative skill of not being hit. It was recorded that Fonck knocked out thirty-two enemy aeroplanes before he received the first bullet hole in his own fabric, while Dorme on the Somme fought a hundred combats for just three bullet holes. Late in 1916 McCudden and Jennings were chased down from 10,000 to 800 feet by an enemy circus. McCudden was not hit; Jennings riddled. On the German side, Udet wrote of Gontermann:

> His very presence was re-assuring and seldom did his coarse peasant features show the slightest excitement. He had unlimited faith in himself. But there was one thing about him which caused me to wonder. If when he landed bullet holes were found on his machine, he was intensely annoyed. He regarded them as proof that there had been something wrong with his flying.

The final result of such skill in evasion was that of the top fifty-two pilots in the RAF scoring list, thirty-eight survived the war.

The root of this spatial instinct may have been akin to the *coup d'œil* of the chess grandmaster, a single glance round the sky sufficing to sense the position of all machines and calculate instantly the likely trajectories of future bullet streams. Perhaps more than others it was a skill practically acquired. Douglas once gave an opinion that 'a pilot's worth doubles for every week he survives in battle conditions'. It may thus have been an apprenticeship in the rear seat of a reconnaissance machine which allowed the accumulation of experience by means of long periods surveying a wide arc of sky in combat, protected by the flying skill of the more experienced pilot - or just good luck. McCudden was in the rear seat for a year. Barker likewise. Bishop served four months and Fonck two months, with twenty artillery spotting flights and twenty-nine photographic missions during which he was involved in eleven combats. But the value of such experience was never discussed in print by a successful pilot.

The finest illustration of the aces' three physical qualities – marksmanship, positional flying and awareness of the enemy – comes from one of the classic combat reports of the war:

On 27.10.18 William Barker observed an enemy two-seater at 21,000 feet N.E. of the Foret du Normal. E.A. climbed east and Major Barker followed, firing a short burst from underneath at point blank range. E.A. broke up in the air and one of the occupants went out with a parachute. He then observed a Fokker biplane 1,000 feet below stalling and shooting up at him, one of the bullets wounding him in the right thigh. He fell into a spin from which he pulled out in the middle of a formation of about fifteen Fokkers two of which he attacked indecisively, both E.A. spinning down. He turned and getting on the tail of a third which was attacking him, shot it down in flames from within ten yards range. At the moment he was again wounded in the left thigh by others of the formation who were diving at him. He fainted and fell out of control again. On recovering, he pulled his machine out and was immediately attacked by another large formation of between twelve and fifteen E.A. He at this moment received a third wound from the remainder of the formation who were attacking him. The bullet shattered his left elbow. He again fainted and fell out of control to 12,000 feet and, recovering, was at once attacked by another large formation of E.A. He then noticed heavy smoke coming from his machine and under the impression he was on fire, tried to ram a Fokker just ahead of him. He opened fire on it from two to three yards range and the E.A. fell in flames. He then dived to within a few thousand feet of the ground and began to fly towards our lines but found his retreat cut off by another formation of eight E.A. who attacked him. He fired a few bursts at some of them and shaking them off, dived down and returned to our lines a few feet above the ground, finally crashing close to one of our balloons.

On a single flight therefore Barker had taken on about sixty enemy machines and shot down four. Barker's own comment later to Ira Jones was: 'Taffy, it was damned funny. I thought that morning I was meeting the whole of the German air force. They were everywhere. My wounds? Well, they hurt me a bit but it was damned funny.'

Combined physical skills gave ace potential, but it was only the addition of certain mental attitudes which gave consummation.

A compulsion which drove skilled pilots frequently into the air came first of these attitudes. 'Two jobs a day are no good to me,' Albert Ball once said. 'I want to be up all the time.' He therefore had a telephone fixed in his hut and took off whenever it rang, pyjamas under his flying coat if need be. Mannock likewise was seldom seen in the mess once his run of successes started. He seemed to live in his flying boots, colleagues remarked. Guynemer was often in the sky eight to ten hours daily. His mechanics noted the look of ecstasy on his face when he landed or of depression if the clouds were too low for the enemy to take off in worthwhile numbers. His opponent and contemporary, Oswald Boelke, at that time was taking off about seven times daily. Fischer, his servant, wrote that Boelke was cheerful only after scoring. His successor as squadron commander, Richthofen, would bring the squadron aerodrome to within enemy artillery range and take off five times daily if the game warranted it.

In part the motive for such frenzied flying may have been pleasure in the sudden fruition of difficult skills. More important with most was ambition. When Fonck equalled Nungesser's score, the latter, who was in hospital with one foot in plaster, immediately discharged himself and returned to his aerodrome. In the same spirit Bishop once wrote:

> I began to feel that my list of victims was not climbing as steadily as I would have liked. Captain Ball was back from his winter rest in England and was adding constantly to his already big score. I felt I had to keep going to be second to him so I was over the enemy line from six to seven hours daily, praying for some easy victims to appear. I had had some pretty hard fighting. Now I wanted to shoot a rabbit or two.

Ira Jones, an ace himself, said that he could never understand why flying men were so jealous of one another's achievements, but the facts were plainly seen on the ground as well as in the air.

Guynemer would personally sew newly awarded stripes on to his own uniform, while Immelmann signed every letter with a full list of his own decorations - as did Albert Ball DSO, MC, in his combat reports. Nungesser, it was rumoured, even flew wearing a full chest of medals.

The second crucial mental quality was the aggression which finished the job towards which ambition had driven the pilot. When Nivelle asked Nungesser the secret of his high scoring, Nungesser replied: 'I go for the enemy when and where I find him.' 'Attack everything' had been squadron policy laid down by the first British ace of the first fighter squadron, Lannoe Hawker. In this spirit the shy, stuttering Geoffrey Cock, monocle in his eye and flying the lumbering Sopwith Strutter, bagged nineteen Germans in ninety-seven sorties. On one occasion he accepted odds of four to one, his CO on that occasion adding to his combat report the comment 'Gallant, but against all common sense'. Of the Americans, Rickenbacker described Douglas Campbell as 'quiet and thoughtful in manner and gentle of speech on the ground. In the air he was a quite different character. He went after every enemy pilot like a tornado, often exposing himself to deadly openings.' Perhaps like the French pilot Navarre - 'the sentinel of Verdun' - Campbell found relaxation only after killing a German. 'Only then is the wild beast in me sated,' explained Navarre. Recalling such hyper-aggression later, Cecil Lewis wrote: 'The fighting aces of world war one as I remember them were young men of high fettle and great energy. They seemed to burn. Perhaps their metabolic rate was greater.'

Such flying and shooting skills, combined with driving ambition and aggression, can be expressed statistically. Fullard scored four on one day and three the next, while Campbell, in the same squadron, got three in forty minutes. Claxton, Trollope and Fonck all scored six in a day, while Bishop got seventy-six in six months - the last twenty-five in twelve days, including five in one afternoon. Scoring about the same rate, Raymond Collishaw registered twenty-nine killings in the months of June and July in 1917.

The last mental quality of the ace was an unexpected one and - for the sake of co-existing with desk soldiers who gave advancement - seldom spoken of: caution. Wrote Bishop: 'I have come to the conclusion that to be successful in fighting in the air, two things were required above all. One was accuracy in shooting and the second was to use one's head and take no unnecessary risks. Constantly my plans from this time were to take the minimum of risks.' In the same spirit McCudden wrote 'caution was ever the watchword in fighting the wily Hun'. Rhys Davids, who had successfully made the transition from head boy at Eton to high-scoring fighter pilot, was a byword for recklessness, but in conversation with Trenchard's adjutant Maurice Baring, Davids remarked that the Buddhist maxim 'Don't be stupid' was his touchstone. Always in Rhys David's pocket was a miniature edition of Blake's poetry, lest he should be shot down and taken prisoner. The same spirit might be put in reverse form. Captain H. Lewis noted of the leading Irish ace McElroy 'his reckless bravery used to make me dubious of his having a long fighting career'. Aces, reckless in every combat, burnt briefly like meteors, but survival long enough to build a big score required more penny-pinching qualities.

Caution began with the pilot's own body. Abstinence, fitness and confidence were rated by Fonck as the three greatest virtues in a fighter pilot. Mannock, too, set much store by long periods of sleep.

Aeroplane health was important as well. McCudden was always tinkering with his engine, machining cylinder heads till his SE5a was able to reach 3,000 feet over its official ceiling. On the German side, Werner Voss invariably wore mechanic's overalls on the ground, adjusting the engine of his triplane as lovingly as that of his own motor bike. Only in the air did this son of a poor Jewish tailor wear silk shirt and best uniform. Baron Richthofen, in contrast, was shot down wearing mechanic's overalls. Fonck and Guynemer, the two leading French marksmen, were both often photographed arm in arm with their mechanics. Such social priority was unusual on either side of the line – and adversely commented upon.

Twin Vickers guns needed even greater care. Firing at twice the speed of ground machine guns, the aerial Vickers accepted only the most perfect ammunition. High or deep-set caps, thick rims or bulging cases would all jam a gun. Buffer, pawl and fusee springs were constantly losing critical tension and threatening to produce a double feed capable of defeating any amount of crank-handle wrenching or hammer beating, and such things could kill. Fullard was once shot down clearing a jam, his vision of the sky temporarily obscured by the needs of his guns. All experienced pilots knew this. The memoirs of Mannock, McCudden and Guynemer therefore specifically mention the minute care they took with the tools of their trade. The American Lufberry checked each single bullet for calibre three times before testing diameter in the barrel and rim by passing the bullet through extractor grooves. Some went further and weighed each propellant charge in each cartridge. Fed individually into belts, the full belts would then be slid into containers whose rollers had been checked for ease of rotation and whose ammunition blocks had been tested for alignment with the feeder blocks. Killing in the air was always a matter of millimetres and milligrams.

Sighting and testing were as elaborate. 'I am a stickler for detail in every respect,' wrote McCudden. 'A lot of my time during the first few days with the squadron was taken up with gun testing and aligning my sights.' On one occasion he tested his guns continuously for two days and even then 'could not get them to my liking. All my comrades and grandpa, our dear old recording officer, simply chaffed me to death and suggested when my guns did not go when I got into the air it was because I first wore them out on the ground. By jove, how those fellows chaffed me. But for a gun to fire forty rounds and then stop was not good enough for me.' Likewise Fry wrote that Albert Ball was very particular about his favourite Lewis gun, spending hours on the ground shooting range, testing the gun and aligning the sights. 'I practised shooting constantly,' said Bishop. 'I became more and more expert at it with the result that I finally had great confidence in myself and knew for certain that if I could get a shot in from one or two of my favourite positions, I would be successful in downing an opponent.' With this object, Bishop had his own personal ground target for practice - his Petit Boche.

Guns loaded and sighted, experienced men planned their flights with care. By early 1915 Guynemer had already worked out his own method, flying deep into enemy territory at the then remarkable height of 13,000 feet so as to be able to make a diving attack from an unexpected quarter. On leave early in 1917, Mannock had told his friend Jim Eyles that, though age was against him, he had decided that there was room for brains which would allow him to counter his one blind eye by careful formulation of tactics. He spent hours with pencil, paper and protractor before saying to Eyles: 'Watch me bowl them over when I get back' - which he did. Even Albert Ball with his berserker reputation thought long over his trade. When he plunged into the middle of an enemy flight, like Fonck he relied on enemy reluctance to fire because of the high risk of hitting their own aeroplanes. There was similar calculation behind Ball's favourite mode of attack on two-seaters which broke all established rules by coming from underneath an opponent. Zooming under his prey with his Lewis gun mounted at 80 degrees on a Godfrey mount, he would with slight oscillations of his control column rake the enemy from ten yards range – just as German night fighters in the second war intercepted Lancaster bombers. With such attacks in view Ball's own machine was rigged so tail-heavy that it almost looped off the ground and needed hard forward pressure on the stick to fly level at most altitudes. At the chosen combat height of 10,000 feet, however, it flew hands-off and allowed Ball to hold his Lewis in both hands. Of Ball's skill in holding the base position, squadron leader Hill was once unnerved to find that Ball had flown a long distance beneath him without Hill once suspecting his presence.

With so many swarms of aeroplanes stacked up in the battle zone between 6,000 and 20,000 feet, few men could survive flying alone after the middle of 1917. On one occasion, just to prove to himself that he could still 'see' the enemy and hit him, McLanachan went up by himself in 1917 and fell for the bait of a lone canary-coloured two-seater. The penalty was to be jumped on by six Albatrosses. He escaped by a whisker with a zero-altitude bout of crazy flying. The necessary conclusion was drawn and McLanachan survived to complete his memoirs. Fonck also ruled out solitary flight when the circuses appeared. Protection then came from formation flying, many cautious aces adding a personal bodyguard in the form of a wingman. Boelke always had a man covering his tail, while aeroplane-maker Fokker thought a wingman in attendance the chief reason that Richthofen survived so long.

In the same way Mannock never flew without Larry Callahan or Clements in attendance. Even as early as May 1917 an official publication pronounced that 'single-handed attacks by single-seaters require a gift of observation, a familiarity with the gun and a skill in manœuvring which are possessed only by a first class pilot'. Killing was teamwork.

The choice of victim was a matter for some deliberation. Two-seaters made up 60 per cent of Richthofen's bag, so that during Bloody April, 1917, for example, he claimed eight BEs and five

FEs as against a single Spad and two Sopwith Strutters. McElroy specialized in low-flying artillery observation machines which assumed immunity by reason of top cover. Others rationed themselves to an upper limit of combats or victims, so that euphoria might not disturb their concentration. And even the method of killing was a matter of pre-planning. To cut down the risk of jamming and to have a bullet surplus for future dangers, like all seasoned fliers, aces used their guns as little as possible. Bishop reckoned to fire in bursts of three bullets and bring down a target with about four bursts.

If in combat the enemy seemed in danger of gaining the upper hand, aces had no compunction about breaking for it. 'He who fights and runs away lives to fight another day,' said McCudden to his pupils. Bishop would have agreed with him. 'Whenever things looked doubtful or bad, I made my escape immediately and waited patiently for another opportunity. The patience part in carrying out this campaign was hard but I managed to control myself and found it more effective than constantly blundering into danger like a bull in a china shop.' Mannock too: 'My system was always to attack the Hun at disadvantage if possible and if I were attacked at disadvantage, I usually broke off the engagement for in my opinion the Hun in the air must be beaten at his own game which is cunning. I think the correct way to wage war is to down as many as possible of the enemy at the least risk, expense and casualties to one's own side.' A comparison of this philosophy with the policy statement of Haig or Trenchard suggests just how much the experience of being shot at daily over long periods concentrated the mind.

Aces were therefore men with much in common in physique and temperament, in ways of flying and shooting, in their combination of aggressive and cautious qualities. Perhaps it was typical of the British part in the Great War that no attempt was ever made to isolate these qualities with a view to recruiting particular types of men or to adjust training schedules.

13
THE DARK SIDE – PHYSICAL STRAIN

Most soldiers thought that the RFC fought a cushy war, and even today surviving veterans smile at the memory of a corps so small, so seldom seen. At the time, some pilots half agreed with them. Wrote Cecil Lewis: 'Under the most arduous conditions we were never under fire for more than six hours a day. When we returned to our aerodromes the war was over. We had a bed, a bath and a mess with good food and peace until the next patrol. Though we always lived in the stretch or sag of nerves, we were never under bodily fatigue, never filthy, never verminous or exposed to the long, disgusting drudgery of trench warfare.'

A visitor to a fighter squadron might easily have got the same impression. The pilots he saw would be swimming, playing tennis or slumped in armchairs. But for those who looked rather than listened the signs were always there of a range of emotions unknown in civilian life, carefully hidden beneath the façade of civilian leisure activities. First in faces. Like Richard Hillary in the second war, Sholto Douglas in the first remarked on how old the faces of young pilots suddenly became after a short experience of active service work. Springs thought too that the faces of twenty-four-year-olds on a fighter aerodrome were like those of men of forty. Already on his first leave in April 1915, friends were surprised by the new seriousness of Lannoe Hawker's expression, the loss of his former carefree boyishness with a single tour. At the bottom of such changes were facial muscles which maintained a posture during each patrol suited to depth of anxiety, uncertainty and fear unknown to most men since infancy. Not death but the waiting for death and the undignified, self-destructive thoughts which went with the waiting carved on the skin those sustained tensions which a later wartime generation were to see in the urgent press photos of first-wave combat troops or perhaps of liberated concentration camp inmates.

Closer examination of pilots off duty in the mess would reinforce this suggestion. Shaking hands unable to pick up cups of tea. Twitching eyelids. Men constantly glancing at the clock or unable to keep still. A double Dubonnet before a patrol. Lapses of memory and blurred vision. Meals returned untouched. Perhaps there might be these sudden flare-ups, showing the hint of hysteria beneath the calm. When McLanachan told Mannock that it was the duty of escort men to stay with reconnaissance machines until they were safely back over the line, the two friends almost came to blows. On another occasion a pilot in Hawker's 24 Squadron put a spoof notice on the board calling for volunteers for a Spad squadron. At this time 24 Squadron was flying DH2s, the 'spinning incinerator'. When the practical joker was identified and severely beaten up, Hawker passed no comment. Men knew the odds well but seldom mentioned them, since talk would only bring to the conscious mind uncomfortable facts which could not be changed.

Sleep above all showed the price. Almost every memoir mentions it. Ira Jones once wrote in his diary:

Had a terrible nightmare last night. Jumped out of my bed eleven times even though I tried to stop myself by tying my pyjama strings to the bed. Each time I jumped up, there was a devil of a row. Poor old Giles got fed up to the teeth as I kept waking him up. It was the usual old business of being shot down in flames and jumping out of my aeroplane. One of the nightmares took a new line though. I was forced down and crashed on top of a wood. As I wasn't hurt, I slid down a tree and tried to hide in a bush but the Hun kept chasing me and shooting me up, wounding me every time. At last he landed in a clearing and chased me with a revolver until he caught me and killed me. Feel very weary today. Did two shows. The clouds have been low and some rain. No luck.

In his diary for June 1917 Mannock wrote of how much he was looking forward to leave, since he couldn't sleep. Unable to eat a meal or sleep, Balfour's diary noted 'old troubles coming back'. During August 1918 Springs found himself fighting Germans all night, as did Lee. 'Trench strafing was beginning to get on my nerves. Apparently I was yelling in a dream and Thompson had to come into my cubicle and waken me. I was shaking and sweating with it. In the nightmare I was diving, diving into a black and bottomless pit with hundreds of machine guns blasting endlessly up at me.' In his autobiographical novel Yeates wrote of men waking up at night covered in sweat, men jerking up in bed with twitching faces, men walking about their huts at night smoking. So it was in both wars, for the night gave time for reflection denied by the fighter pilots' crammed day. Then thoughts and face, kept severely apart during the day by conscious effort, came together. Just occasionally too, at night and in the privacy of a small hut, such things might be discussed. Finding himself during the battle of the Somme unable to sleep for thoughts of next morning's early patrol, Balfour and his wingman lit candles 'to hide the dark'. Then 'we admitted mutual feelings of terror and foreboding. In those days such thoughts were too sacred, too intimate to bring up. Each one of us had such thoughts and secrets closely guarded and treasured.'

The effects of those thoughts and of the strains which generated them could be expressed statistically. Lannoe Hawker thought nine months the longest a fighter pilot could endure. McLanachan reckoned several weeks necessary to gear a man up and then a few months to wear him out. 'Even at the end of two months,' wrote Oliver, 'I am sick to death of France and machines and above all the lines and the look of the area we work over. This flying job is rotten for one's nerves and although one is supposed to last six months with a fortnight's leave half way, quite a lot of peoples' nerves conk out after four and a half.' More precisely, the air service medical laboratory reckoned that 80 per cent of groundings were nervous and that 50 per cent of pilots developed serious neurosis during their tour of duty.

The most immediate of these accumulating strains was the physical. In 1912 an RFC booklet remarked that all pilots on the ground over-estimated their capacity for work in the air and that aviation, like arsenic, had to be taken in small doses, 'for the strain reduces all men by stages until it becomes as dangerous for the best pilots to fly a machine as for a beginner'. These words were written before pilots in open cockpits flew regularly above 10,000 feet or had become the target of machine-gun bullets and anti-aircraft shells. They related simply to the sequence of physical forces progressively operating on a pilot as he gained altitude.

These began even before he took off – an engine warming up at full revs generated about 120 decibels and propeller tips revolving at about 30,000 feet a second added a second sound source at 125 decibels. These figures compare with an unsilenced pneumatic drill at 110 and meant that about a quarter of all war pilots suffered marked permanent hearing loss.

In addition to rotating a prop shaft, the engine also vibrated in its wooden mounting. Bearing in mind that vibrations of one tenth of a Hertz are detectable by the human body, a fighter aeroplane at full throttle vibrated between 100 and 200 Hertz, which was sufficient to arouse sensations of fear and make the pilot physically unable to relax.

On take-off, the increased force of the wind blast was perhaps the first change to become noticeable. Expressed statistically, a 40 mph wind represents about 1 per cent of total wind at ground level. At the relatively low fighting altitude of 10,000 feet such winds become 25 per cent of the total, cutting the lips, chapping the skin, altering breathing rhythms and increasing general body metabolism by about 30 per cent.

The cold of high-altitude work was another big enemy because a comfortable ground temperature of 60 degrees Fahrenheit would have dropped progressively to 45 degrees below freezing at the top cover altitude of 20,000 feet. The sort of temperatures a fighter pilot faced in his open cockpit during winter flying can be imagined. Again, the effect upon the working of the body can be precisely stated. At 50 degrees Fahrenheit, the body is reckoned to work efficiently. By 30 degrees below freezing, a common temperature at fighting altitudes even in mid-summer, 75 per cent of efficiency would be lost, with circulation slowed, breathing diminished and body temperature falling. The combined effect was almost to turn the pilot into a sleep walker.

But fighter pilots never bothered much about percentages. Theirs was a knowledge made up of sensation. Hands and feet were lost first, then back and chest, finally abdomen and legs. Parsons described one occasion when he felt the bitter cold through five pairs of gloves, with shooting pains throughout his body and the sensation of a contracting scalp, while during December 1916 McCudden felt so cold on one occasion that he didn't bother to look round and didn't care if he was surprised and shot down. Flying at 17,000 feet Crundall described a similar experience, writing of a feeling of breathing ice and of crouching down in his cockpit and steering blind, just relying on his compass. The only actual physical danger of this acute cold came from frostbite, the aerial version of trench feet. Collishaw experienced the condition once when his goggle elastic broke and his whole face swelled up like a balloon. Feeling no pain, he would have shrugged it off but for the insistence of his medical officer, who knew the dangers from gangrene and insisted on rest, warmth and the drinking of hot fluids.

Lack of oxygen at high altitude was altogether less uncomfortable than the cold yet much more dangerous in its effects. In the autumn of 1914, when machines were flying only at about 2,500 feet, there were no problems, but when anti-aircraft shells and diving fighter attacks began to develop, so aeroplanes were forced higher and higher. At the start of 1916 they were at 8,000 feet; by the end of 1916 the Sopwith Pup was operating at 18,000 feet. By the summer of 1918 the Sopwith Dolphin had become the first fighter specifically designed to perform efficiently above 20,000 feet and reach as high as 24,000, at which heights lack of oxygen was more critical than cold, though it was well into 1917 before the fact was realized. An American mission was the first to remark on how many pilots otherwise A1 fit became unfit for flying after prolonged work at altitude. RFC doctors Birley, Corbett and Flack then got to work and demonstrated that units with bottled oxygen showed less 'staleness' and could fly double the hours of pilots not so equipped. They discovered too the critical height to be 10,000 feet, at which level oxygen pressure in the lungs became insufficient to saturate the haemoglobin of the blood. The conclusion was that oxygen was necessary at 10,000 feet and essential around 16,000. Indeed, in the second war pilots went on to oxygen at 9,000 feet and later tests found that 14 per cent of pilots needed oxygen even at 8,000 feet.

The immediate danger of oxygen starvation was difficulty in recognizing its dulling effect and taking corrective action. 'During July 1917 I took my Camel up to 22,000 feet,' wrote RNAS ace Rochford.

This was the greatest height I had ever reached. I was testing a new oxygen supply apparatus. A cylinder containing the oxygen and a tube leading from it and attached to a mask could be clamped over the mouth and nose when desired. A valve controlled the supply of oxygen and this was operated by hand. I did not experience any discomfort at this height of 22,000 feet but when I turned on the oxygen and breathed it into my lungs through the face mask, the effect was amazing. It was comparable to an overcast sky changing to brilliant sunshine and I felt very much more alert.

Similar experiments done after the war using a pressure chamber to simulate altitude showed that the practical effects of oxygen starvation were even more diverse than pilots had imagined during the war. Around 10,000 feet some chambered men became over-confident, some silly, some irritable, some just apathetic. As height increased so some developed an irrational fixed idea, others talked like drunkards, some even fell asleep and, most dangerously of all from the point of view of a man on active service, such sleepers were completely unaware of having been asleep when they were taken from the chamber.

Most pilots who wrote memoirs after their war mentioned the effects of oxygen deficiency. During his period of acclimatization in 1915 McCudden described crippling headaches at about 11,000 feet. Even when he had achieved greater tolerance, he was several times forced down abruptly by severe headache in his attempts to reach German two-seaters at 22,000 feet. Indeed, Wortley thought that all pilots at around 19,000 feet experienced persistent pain at the back of the eyes and drastic reduction of powers of concentration which made it difficult to spot enemy aeroplanes. Without any oxygen, all that pilots could do to counter these effects was to take longer periods of sleep and abstain from cigarette smoking, which was later shown to have the effect of generating the symptoms of 14,000 feet at 10,000.

Intense cold. Oxygen deprivation. There remained one final major problem to be faced at high altitude – increased blood pressure. On the ground, a healthy pilot would probably have a blood pressure round about 120. By 6,000 feet this would have become 200, causing all dental fillings to throb and congesting the surface blood vessels of the brain, so that by 10,000 feet the gap between brain and skull would have disappeared, to give pilots the sensation of the flying helmet holding the skull in a vice-like grip. Fullard, though, was probably just unlucky when, flying without goggles at 12,000 feet, he burst a blood vessel in an eye and was temporarily blinded. For most, work at height brought much physical discomfort but seldom direct physical hurt at the time. The real cost would come only later in life.

Combat generated a set of abrasive physical forces which, like those of oxygen deficiency, were unsuspected when the war began and not fully understood even by the end. These were the gravity or G forces which were measured in multiples of the earth's attraction and were dangerous in proportion to the speed and suddenness of violent manœuvre. They were of two types. Turns and inside loops, forcing blood away from the brain and pinning the pilot with increasing force to his seat, imposed positive G force. Inverted flying and outside loops, on the other hand, spun blood towards the brain and induced negative G force.

Expressed in terms of physical strain, a left-handed spin with full engine power imposed about 2Gs, at which force the skin would be reddened from subcutaneous haemorrhage, the eyes would show symptoms of mild concussion and the pilot would be unable to move off his seat. Zoom up from a power dive of 175 mph, common enough in combat or even in fooling about over the aerodrome, would register at least 5Gs and possibly up to 9. Positive G force would then be at its maximum, the pilot physically helpless and unable to move, his face elongated with his mouth forced open and his cheeks pulled in on to his tongue. Characteristically he would be fully conscious at the terminal point of the dive, grey out as soon as he pulled the stick back, then completely black out after three seconds of the zoom as blood was drawn from his brain. For all the severity of these symptoms, the pilot would nevertheless regain full clarity of vision and complete muscular control within thirty seconds. All post-war experiments found no lasting harmful effects from such positive G stress, which was perhaps just as well in a fighter war, with so many fast turns and dives.

Negative G was altogether more dangerous because the body seems to be designed only for direction change in an upright direction. Symptoms at −1G were thus rated equal to those at +2G in virulence. −2G forces made the head throb and between −3 and −4G the eyes bulged from their sockets and the head felt as if it was bursting. At −4G the pilot would suffer red-out and feel confused for several hours afterwards. Indeed, just a few seconds at −3G in an inverted roll or inverted turn would leave him dazed for fifteen minutes, the tangible physical effect of such a force being to bloat his face and raise the lower eyelid to cover the eyeball.

As the pilot completed his patrol and lost altitude for his return to the aerodrome, so the temperature increased, the oxygen became richer and he would be relieved of the necessity to make sharp turns. Physical strain had nevertheless not finished with him. Increased oxygenation and brisker circulation were both intensely painful initially, so that Fry wrote of often climbing for short periods several times during his descents to slow down the agonizing process of thawing out. Vincent reckoned that the high point of pain came around 3,000 feet, at which height it would become impossible to clutch the control column. Ears would be playing up as well, for though in ascent regularizing pressure movements maintained equilibrium in the ears' eustachian tubes, there was no such natural counter in descent. Though pilots would be chewing and blowing their noses continually, 15 per cent of them were nevertheless in hospital with ear trouble of some sort during the war. Udet wrote of such a grounding during the great battle of March 1918, his medical officer working daily to extract masses of pus from his ears with a spatula. Rickenbacker described the same copious and painful discharge in his memoirs. If a man had a cold, the sinus could become as painful as the ears, and a haemorrhage might strip the whole sinus membrane. The sensation would resemble that of a hammer blow inside the head. Reascent would then be imperative, with immediate heat treatment and vigorous use of vasoconstrictors during the mandatory rest period of three months. Even if a pilot did recover from this sinus stripping, all his future work would have to be below 10,000 feet.

The final act of landing served only to confirm the combined effect of the flight's physical pressure. In addition the muscles would be tight from having had to turn constantly during the two hours of flight to check the tail, and the eyes needed to adapt suddenly to a fixed, three-dimensional landscape lit from 180 degrees. Indeed, the whole nervous system would be showing signs of acute fatigue and the accurate manipulation of complex machinery would be impossible. The number of crash landings on fighter aerodromes served as exact measure. Rickenbacker's solution was to circle the aerodrome twice so as to give himself time to calm down and adjust focus. As a veteran, Rickenbacker would well have known the hazards of crash landings, of which 70 per cent wrote off the aeroplane and 50 per cent injured the pilot.

The conclusion was clear. Theoretically every day, in practice every second day, a Great War fighter pilot would have to experience the same physical strains as an Edwardian mountaineer in the Himalayas in terms of height, unsuitable clothing and lack of oxygen, but with the ascent from base camp to summit and the return compressed into two hours and the discomfort exaggerated in proportion. In addition, the lightning dives and zooms of a pilot had no parallel in a mountaineer's ropework, so that even without meeting an enemy aeroplane the apparently simple business of going out on patrol imposed more physical strain on more parts of the body than any fighting man had experienced in any past war. The impact on the pilot's mind of bullets and anti-aircraft shells was quite another matter.

14
THE DARK SIDE – DYING

Dead and missing in the air service on active service fronts during the war totalled about 9,000, according to official figures. When this figure is set against the million or so soldiers dead, such a relatively small number might seem a small matter, and certainly today's traveller among the war cemeteries of the old west front seldom sees airmen's headstones. The 20,000 who died on the first day of the 1916 Somme offensive make the 9,000 deaths in four years seem like a bagatelle. The loss was a severe one nevertheless, because the air force had a structure unlike any other arm of the fighting services, and when the number of deaths is set against the total number of men who formed the fighting end of the air war, the grievous nature of the loss becomes clear, for pilots constituted only 2 per cent of the RFC/RAF, which itself at most formed just 3 per cent of the British Expeditionary Force. Put more simply, on Armistice Day there were only 5,182 pilots on the west front and, set against this tiny strike force, the figure of 9,000 makes better sense.

The scale of loss is suggested by the Americans who served with the British. Of the 210 who flew with the RFC, fifty-one were killed – a one in four ratio directly comparable with the infantry figure in the ground war. One man a week was killed on average throughout the war in 43 and 56 Squadrons – taken at random – which loss must be set against a squadron strength starting at twelve pilots and ending the war at just twenty-four. Expressed in another form, Lee calculated that during 1916 the average pilot had a life expectancy on the west front of three weeks – a figure reduced to two during the early months of 1917. Even among the more cautious and professional French, René Fonck found early in 1918 that at twenty-four he was the oldest pilot in his squadron and suggested that a plucky French pilot tended to last three months and a prudent one perhaps six months.

Greatest time of killing was always during the great set-piece land battles. First came the Somme offensive in the second part of 1916, in which the RFC flew for the first time against the enemy's newly organized fighter squadrons, whose twin-machine-gunned aeroplanes and superior interruptor gear combined more than six times the RFC's punch per machine. The effect overall was suggested when in April 1917 Lloyd George tried to find out what the casualties over the Somme had been. RFC headquarters replied that all communications from London had to be direct with Haig's headquarters, and anyway the RFC did not have the Somme casualty figures, which related to a battle Trenchard always rated 'the greatest success the air had in the first war'. Henderson in London certainly knew the exact figures as soon as the offensive had been called off in November 1916 – 800 RFC machines lost against the German loss of 359 and 252 RFC pilots killed to forty-three dead Germans.

Cecil Lewis described what such figures meant on the aerodromes:

I dumped my kit in the billet and walked to the mess. The gramophone was on wheezing 'I'll see you tonight, dear. Your eyes will be bright, dear.' Two chaps were playing vingty and drinking port. The gramophone stopped. The lamp was smoking. They hardly greeted me. I was eighteen, conceited, unpopular.

'Had a good leave?'

'Fine, thanks.'

I ordered coffee. The place smelt of stale smoke. The chairs wobbled. The tablecloth was stained and dirty. The wire that held the lamp was thick with dead flies.

'Orderly!'

'Sir?'

'Whisky!'

'Sir.'

'Where's Rudd?' I asked. Only four chaps here. Where are the others?

'Killed. Archie. This morning. Orderly!'

'Sir?'

'Cigarettes.'

'Sir.'

'Both of them?' I couldn't believe it somehow.

'Suppose so. Machine took fire. Couldn't recover the bodies.'

The boy who spoke was only eighteen too. A good pilot. Brave. Rudd had been his room-mate. God. How quiet the mess was.

'And Hoppy?'

'Wounded. Gone home.'

'And Pipp and Kidd?' I was almost frightened to ask.

'Done in last night. Direct hit. One of our own shells. Battery rang up to apologize. New pilots coming.'

Kidd with the funny quirky laugh! Pip who had seen the poppies with me! I turned instinctively to the piano. After dinner he was always there. Never again those yellow keys under those gentle hands. It was so still. Surely they were near? The door would open and ...

'By the way, congrats on your Military Cross.'

Echoes. Congrats. Congratulations. Five ghosts in the room. Five friends. Congrats.

'Thanks,' I said.

The Arras offensive in spring 1917 produced similar large-scale killing. The reason was threefold. Withdrawal of the French air service for refitting after the battle at Verdun allowed the Germans to concentrate their aeroplanes against the RFC and, in addition, as Trenchard wrote to the War Office in December 1916, the Germans were producing new types of scout machine of greatly improved type which he had not warned the War Office about early enough. The Germans had also become active more rapidly than he had anticipated, so that orders for improved aeroplanes on our side had gone in too late. The result was that SE5s and Sopwith Triplanes arrived after the main fighting in the spring offensive, leaving the DH2 (86 mph at 6,500 feet and reaching 10,000 feet in twenty-five minutes) to take on the new Albatrosses (124 mph at 6,000 feet and reaching 16,000 feet in twenty minutes). Given the immutability of the Haig–Trenchard constant offensive policy, the result was predictable. 'There is no doubt in my mind,' wrote Trenchard in January 1917, 'we shall have enormous numbers of machines brought down by the enemy.' On 8 April, as the battle developed, Trenchard wrote: 'Hard fighting is inevitable and heavy casualties are bound to occur ... continual pauses allow the enemy to recover.'

Expressed in statistical terms such 'heavy casualties' meant a flying life for RFC fighter pilots in April 1917 officially calculated at $17\frac{1}{2}$ flying hours. It meant too the RFC losing 20 per cent of its flying personnel in the six weeks of the battle, including the loss of twenty-eight machines on Easter Sunday alone, the Richthofen circus claiming thirteen aeroplanes for themselves the following Saturday.

In the remainder of 1917 there was little improvement, for no sooner did the SE5a, the Camel and the Bristol Fighter appear than the enemy in June 1917 initiated the 'America programme' as counter to the US entry into the war. Given priority second only to U-boats, the German air force grew so fast that by the end of 1917 the number of fighter squadrons had been doubled within a year and monthly production of equipment was running at 1,500 machine guns, 2,000 airframes and 2,500 engines. The result of such development was noted by corps commander the Earl of Cavan writing to the king during the battle of Third Ypres: 'The enemy is stronger in the air than I have ever seen him, having concentrated the bulk of his fighters opposite this (the 5th) army.' At aerodrome level such a concentration meant that 9 Squadron, fighting for two months over the Passchendaele position, had its fighting strength wiped out twice over. Indeed, looking back over the whole of 1917, Trenchard spoke of 'an unhappy year' with regard to events in the air.

Sustained by their America programme and equipped with perhaps the best fighter of the war – the Fokker D7 – the Germans proved hard opponents through 1918 as well, though strangulated increasingly by shortage of petrol. In his memoirs Sholto Douglas indicated such continuing strength by comparing 15 September 1940, climax of the Battle of Britain, with 30 October 1918, just one day in that sustained pursuit of the retreating Germans in the war's last hundred days. On that day in the second war, the RAF lost twenty-six aeroplanes and thirteen pilots to the Germans sixty aircraft; in the first war, the single day meant losses to the RAF of forty-one aircraft and twenty-nine pilots to the Germans sixty-seven aircraft.

These were the battles. Between them, death ran like the scarlet thread of a rosary:

Lt Glyn left the aerodrome at 6.40 pm and got into a spinning nose dive on a turn and crashed into Marcelcave cemetery 200 yards east of the aerodrome, bursting into flames. Lt Glyn was killed.

On 11th June 1917 a machine left the aerodrome at 3.5 pm and east of Ypres was run into in the air by a French Spad, Captain Mackay being killed.

On 28th May 1917 while Lt Johnson's machine was taxying, a sudden burst of wind turned it over. The aeroplane caught fire and before Lt Johnson could be released, he was badly burnt. Just before his death he said the accident was due to a gust of wind.

20.12.16. Immediately before his fall Lt Simpson had looped a dozen times and then flew upside down for some distance before turning somersaults. Afterwards he drove along the ground at an enormous pace and rose again suddenly as if to loop again when the right wing gave way as the machine was perpendicular. He righted himself and started to volplane down, at first successfully, but suddenly the machine dropped like a stone from a height of 500 feet and Lt Simpson was killed.

Quite apart from death from enemy action during routine patrol in the quiet periods, such accidents were constant in the spasms between battles. During their war service in France 24 Squadron lost sixteen men from accidents as against twenty-seven in aerial fighting.

The relation of survivors to squadron dead was not immediately apparent because dead men were seldom mentioned in the mess. 'I steeled my heart against the intimate kind of friendship with my comrades,' wrote Rickenbacker. 'When Jim Miller went down, I learnt the necessary stoicism. Later Jimmy Hall went and Lufberry. Many others were to follow and well I knew it. Close as our friendships were, living side by side with a common purpose and mutual interdependence, all pilots of 94 Squadron I believe came eventually to look with callous indifference upon the sudden death of their dearest friends.'

An outside observer might therefore see little emotion anywhere. 'I was mighty sorry to see old Rhys Davids go.' 'Afraid he bought it. Have a drink.' 'Hell of a war isn't it!' Perhaps not even so much. When a flight commander of 43 Squadron crashed, Balfour noted the reaction of a hut-mate who was shaving: – 'Dear, dear. That must be G. He's made me cut myself.'

After news of a death, the dead man's effects would be methodically cleared:

The next morning Tom and Williamson cleared up Seddon's effects. When they opened his kitbag, they found on top of everything an envelope addressed to C or W. It contained a letter and a sealed envelope marked 'For my wife if I am killed'. The letter was dated 22 March 1918. 'Dear Tom and Bill, if you read this it will be when I am wounded, missing or dead. If you know for certain that I am dead, please send the enclosed letter to my wife and I should like you to let her know any particulars you can of my death. If I am a flamer, don't say that. Just say shot down and killed. If there is any doubt about my death, please burn the letters to my wife. Burn all the correspondence, especially a bundle of letters and papers tied up in a bootlace. Please be certain of this. Put it if you can on a hot fire. If I am wounded, please keep the bundle, if you can, until I write to you. If you can't, then burn it. I would like you to have something in memory of me. There is nothing very valuable among my stuff. Have my silver cigarette case and my fountain pen or anything else you like. If I am alive when you read this, au revoir. If I am dead, goodbye and may you both be more fortunate. If there has been any bright spot for me in this war, it has been living with you two blokes. (signed) P. B. Seddon.

'You have the cigarette case. He was more your friend than mine. Razor? Unorthodox memorial but it'll keep him in daily memory.'

They close the kitbag. Tom went and sat with his head between his hands. Williamson went and rolled up and strapped the valise.

'Well, that's done. I've had the job often enough. Thought I was quite hardened but I must say I haven't liked it this time.'

Tom did not reply for a minute. Then he burst out: 'It isn't only losing Seddon as a friend. It's such a bloody waste. He was a man in a million. He'd had little enough chance caged in a bank. The war brought him out, gave him courage to think and now ... and look at the way Smith's life was thrown away.'

'Yes, I know. Authority always lets you down in the end

sooner or later. But the personal grief of losing a friend is bad enough. Don't mix up other things with it. You'll only make yourself mad and do no good.'

Perhaps death in the air needed nothing beyond such cursory ceremony, because the actual process of dying may have been equally matter of fact. In his classic war autobiography, Richard Hillary wrote at length of his feelings when death in his Spitfire seemed certain. He thought first of his fellow squadron pilots returning home, next of his mother and finally of whether or not people would miss him. 'So this is it,' he said to himself, then fainted. In the first war, too, some men survived to talk of certain death. Noble, like Cecil Lewis, wrote that an out-of-control dive was not terrible and that he had talked with many survivors who said that they too had felt very calm and been reconciled to dying. Richey when hit and spinning felt isolated and detached from his body. He remembered thinking: 'God, if I'm to be killed, I won't feel it.'

The initial appearance of cursory ceremony was nevertheless incorrect. Death did always go to the root of a squadron. At the least it gave survivors experience of their own death, because the man who had died had worn the same uniform, flown the same type of aeroplane and had done the same sort of work as the survivors. '*Hodie mihi, cras tibi*,' wrote Guynemer in his diary. On the German side Dossenbach told Schroder: 'Everyone of us has to die sooner or later. We scout pilots are all doomed to death. I'd only like to know who will be the next of us.'

In a tight-knit mess, survivors would grieve for the dead as well as fear for themselves. The Stork Squadron wept and told stories about Dorme for a fortnight after his death, as did 40 Squadron when McElroy went down. In the privacy of their huts men grieved more candidly, so that we hear of Mannock weeping like a child for Dolan and Kennedy, or Hawker writing six months after the killing of Gordon Bayley that 'He was still very much in my thoughts.' With his squadron wiped out three times over during 1917, Arch Whitehouse felt desolate and alone. He wrote of going for long, solitary walks and of becoming so thin that his clothes hung on him like a scarecrow's.

Udet described such emotions on the other side of the line:

The others had already landed and I found them standing in a group on the flying ground, dejected and talking in low voices.

Glinkermann stood a little apart from the rest, immersed in thought and scribbling designs in the sand with the point of his walking stick. His dog was beside him, rubbing his nose against his master's knee. But Glinkermann was beyond taking notice of the animal. His thoughts were elsewhere. As I approached him, he lifted his head and looked at me. 'You mustn't blame me, Knagges,' he said. 'I really couldn't prevent it. He came down at us straight out of the sun and by the time I had realized what was happening, it was all over.' Pain had distorted his features. I knew him and realized that he would torture himself with reproaches and doubts for weeks to come. Having flown in line with Puz he would keep telling himself that he ought to have prevented his death. But I knew too well that it was no fault of Glinkermann's. When I flew in his company I felt absolutely secure, knowing full well that he would let himself be shot to pieces rather than allow me to be vulnerable from the rear. 'Don't take it too badly, Glinkermann,' I said, placing my hand on his shoulder. 'No one can do anything about it and if anyone is to blame, all of us are equally responsible.' I then went to my room to write my first official report and then a letter to Hanisch's parents. But death had not finished with us yet. An orderly woke me up from my midday nap. There had been a phone call from Mortiers to say that one of our machines had come down. The pilot, acting sergeant major Muller, was dead. I went to Mortiers. Two old campaigners, grey and weathered like the Champagne mud, received me. They had placed Muller in a barn to which I was taken. His features were calm and peaceful. His must have been an easy end. I asked for an account of what had happened and then returned to Boncourt. It was very quiet at the aero-drome. In the afternoon all the machines had gone up and towards evening they returned in two's and three's. Glinkermann had not come back. The two men who had been flying with him had lost sight of him. He had disappeared into the clouds and was last seen flying towards the west. The old story. The old, bitter story. On the flying field, plunged into the soft turf, stood a walking stick. A military peaked cap hung from the handle. Glinkermann's talisman. When he started out on a flight, he left them there and on his return he took them away with him. A big wolf-like Alsatian wandered restlessly up and down near the stick. As I walked over the field, he trotted to meet me. He never

8. British 13-pounder anti-aircraft guns in operation during March 1916 in the town square of Armentières. Cobbled streets and bleak brick architecture capture the feeling of most towns on the British front. More interesting is the gunner's lack of range-finding equipment. In the anti-aircraft field the Germans always led. Already in 1909 they could fix height and angle within three seconds and from a battery of four 77s fire fifteen shells per minute accurately to 13,000 feet at a velocity of 2,000 feet per second.

9. A German rear gunner. His swivel mounting was altogether more effective than the British Scarff mounting, which looked like a present-day geriatric's walking frame and was as cumbersome. Calibre and rate of fire of the German weapon were about equal to our Lewis equivalent, but the rotating drum of the enemy carried altogether more ammunition. Throughout the war, speed, height and rear fire power of German two-seater reconnaissance machines combined to produce a formidable antagonist.

30. Each pilot flew with a POW kit of shaving outfit, spare underwear and pyjamas in case he should survive being forced down. Pilots were often roughly treated by the infantry of their opposing armies and hoped for early 'capture' by enemy aviators. The custom of offering prisoners the hospitality of the Mess continued into the second war.

31. Since a pilot sat on his petrol tank and all pilots loaded their guns with a high proportion of tracer and incendiary ammunition, fire in the air was frequent and dreaded, the more so by the RAF since our machines carried no parachutes. Many pilots like Mannock carried a revolver for shooting themselves in this contingency; most dreamt often of becoming 'flamers'.

2. A successful crash landing was the mark of a seasoned pilot, but the irregularities of old battle areas would cause a machine to nose tip or even flip on to its back. If the pilot were still strapped in with his Sutton harness, the prognosis would be good, though the pressure on the body in such a landing would be somewhere around 9Gs. Enemy machines in such condition would be cannibalized by infantry before RAF men could claim their scalps - numbers and Maltese cross cut out of the fabric; British machines would be taken apart and re-assembled for further flying.

3. A wrecked British FE2b, the inevitable swarm of spectators, and a collection of Crossley lorries, ammunition limbers and GS waggons on a typical French road. The FE was a pusher aeroplane, its propeller and engine mounted behind the pilot. This allowed the gunner at the front in the nacelle a free shot in the days before interruptor gear allowed a machine gun to fire through the propeller.

34. Fourth-ranking British fighter pilot McCudden, who started the war as a professional soldier and NCO. A distant, formal man, colleagues respected his shooting skill and fanatical devotion to detail without getting close to him. Ironically he was killed during the war in attempting a beginner's manœuvre – trying to turn back shortly after take-off with a suspect engine.

did that at other times. He was essentially a one-man dog and growled fiercely at anyone who came near Glinkermann. Now he buried his cold, damp nose affectionately in my hand. I had the greatest difficulty in concealing the despair which I felt. But Gontermann had handed over his Staffel to me and I was determined that no one should see me displaying signs of weakness. Night came slowly. I sat by the open window and stared into the gathering darkness. A new moon rose from behind the big trees in the park. The noise of the crickets was unusually loud and unbearably irritating. The atmosphere was sultry; there would be rain before morning. I had Glinkermann's dog in my room. The wretched animal could not settle down but walked continually backwards and forwards to the door. Occasionally he howled dismally. Glinkermann! Glinkermann! A week before he had brought down a Spad that was about to dive on the tail of my machine and on the next day I drove off an enemy plane which was making things rather uncomfortable for him. He had to come back! I could not be left alone! At 10 o'clock an orderly rushed into my room. 'Herr leutnant, you are wanted at once on the phone by an infantry unit near Orguevalles.' I heard a deep gloomy voice. Yes, a German machine had come down near them. The pilot had black hair parted in the centre. That was the only description he would give me – the rest was burnt beyond recognition. As I replaced the receiver without a word, the dog howled so appallingly that I had to put him out of the room. I lit the lamp on my writing table and told an orderly to bring me Glinkermann's possessions. I found a tattered wallet containing a little money and the photograph of a girl. There was also a love letter which had just been started. At noon on the following day an army lorry drove into the camp. Inside it there was a wooden box. It was unloaded and taken into Glinkermann's tent. We placed his cap and his walking stick on the top and then we covered the bare wood with flowers and green foliage. Two days later, Glinkermann was buried and on the morning of that very day came the news of his promotion to lieutenant. Had he lived, it would have been the greatest day of his life. I got a man who was going on leave to Mulhausen to take the commission to his parents together with the dog. The poor brute had to be dragged from Glinkermann's tent and as it was driven away in the car, its howls were heart-rending.

A disturbing degree of visibility often accompanied aerial death. Shot infantrymen would fall unnoticed in a vortex of artillery noise among thousands of other men. Shelled artillerymen would disappear into a few lumps of red meat. But the dying airman, encased in wood and canvas and so far up, would seem to amplify his death by a fall in slow motion which watching pilots never forgot.

One instance can be taken as typical of death in the air:

The Hun put a bullet through Roberts' rudder controls. The machine immediately went into a spin. Roberts was a crack pilot and if human skill could have got that machine out, he would have done it. His elevator and ailerons were still intact and by shutting off the engine he almost managed to avert disaster – but not quite. He could not stop the machine spinning but he could stop it going into a vertical spinning dive. He tried every combination of elevator and bank. No good. The machine went on spinning slowly, round and round, all the way from 8,000 feet to the ground. It took five minutes. He and his observer were sitting there waiting for death all that time. The machine fell just this side of the lines and they say that a man in the trenches heard shouts, as it might have been for help, coming from the machine just before it struck the ground and smashed into a pile of wreckage.

Fire, almost as slow and more visible, was always the greatest fear among pilots and orchestrator of the most sickening deaths. A machine like the SE5a after all carried twenty-six gallons of petrol in its main tank behind the pilot's seat with a further three gallons in the gravity feed tank in the upper wing, which was sufficient both for a two-hour flight and for a fierce blaze. Armouring the tank would have made it too heavy for the slight engines of those days, when relative speeds were so close and 1 mph might mean the difference between life and death. The sheathing of petrol tanks in uncured rubber which would swell when wet and thus fill any bullet hole was, on the other hand, a technique acquired only at the very end of the war. Tanks were thus throughout the war the most profitable target for discriminating machine guns. A bullet through the gravity tank would cause a leak on to the hot engine or exhaust pipes, while penetration of the main tank would generate a cloud of white vapour which was always likely to ignite given the high proportion of tracers or incendiary bullets which most pilots fitted into their ammunition belts.

The appearance of these fires was described in Mannock's last diary entry before his own death: 'To watch a machine burst into flames is a ghastly sight. At first a tiny flame peeps out of the tank as if almost ashamed at what it is about to do. Then it gets bigger as it licks its way along the length and breadth of the machine. Finally, all that can be seen is a large ball of fire enveloping in a terrifying embrace.'

The only way to survive a petrol fire in an aeroplane doped with highly inflammable material was to first shut off the petrol supply, then sideslip vertically, tail first to keep flames from the wings. Few succeeded and all who saw it happen never forgot. Mannock frequently told stories of flamers in great detail in the mess, assuring young pilots: 'It will happen to you next, laddie.' His particular butt was Caldwell, who would retaliate with the sounds Mannock's burning machine would make in the air. Cairns once asked Mannock what his first thought would be if he found his own machine on fire. Mannock quietly replied that he would reach for his cockpit pistol and blow his brains out.

Rickenbacker, the cold and restrained American ace, wrote about the end of one of his friends.

I rushed the enemy from the rear when suddenly old Luff's machine was seen to burst into flames. He passed the Albatross two-seater and proceeded for three or four seconds on a straight course. Then to the horrified watchers below, there appeared a figure in a headlong leap from the cockpit of the burning aircraft. Lufberry had preferred a leap to death rather than endure the slow torture of burning to a crisp. His body fell into the garden of a peasant woman's house in a little town just north of Nancy. A small stream ran nearby and it was thought later that poor Lufberry, seeing this small chance of life, had jumped with the intention of striking the water. He had leapt from a height of 200 feet and his machine was carrying him at a speed of 120 mph. Jumping into a car, we sped across the intervening miles and arrived at the scene of the tragedy less than thirty minutes after Luff had fallen. But already loving hands had removed his body. The townsfolk had carried all that remained of poor Raoul to their little townhall and there we found him, his charred body covered with flowers from nearby gardens.

And so on the other side of the line. 'We climbed to a height of 6,000 feet,' wrote Udet:

> The sky was clear and one or two small clouds, very high up, were all that was to be seen. Far and wide there was no sign of an enemy machine. Periodically I turned round and waved to the others. They were still in formation behind me – the brothers Wenzel, Puz and Glinkermann – all was in order. I am not prepared to swear that there is such a thing as a sixth sense but certainly on that flight I had a sudden feeling that all was not well, that some hidden danger threatened us. I made a half turn and a moment later I saw Puz's machine enveloped in smoke and flames. Puz was sitting perfectly still, his body stiffly erect in the cockpit, his face turned towards me. He slowly raised an arm to his helmet. It might have been a last struggle but it looked exactly as though he was saluting me for the last time. 'Puz,' I shouted. 'Puz.' But in that instant his machine broke up, the engine dropping like a flaming meteor and the broken wings fluttering down after it. For several moments I was incapable of thought. I simple stared overboard at the falling wreckage.

However caused, the death of a British pilot was always made worse in the mind of pilots who saw it by knowing that the enemy had always a good chance of surviving a jump. German ace Jacobs jumped successfully twice and Udet once, using parachutes of British design, changed only by a cord attachment to the fuselage which ripped open the chute when needed. Such a parachute had been demonstrated in a jump from an airship in 1913, while by November 1917 Major Orde-Lees showed when he jumped from the parapet of Tower Bridge that parachutes could open successfully within the 153 feet available to him. Nevertheless, parachutes were never issued to the RFC or RAF. Perhaps the fact that they weighed as much as a machine gun had something to do with it, but not until 1935 did serious testing take place under Air Ministry supervision.

Death therefore became a close acquaintance of the fighter squadron. Even if a pilot were registered as 'Missing', such an unseen killing would be represented by proxy in an empty chair, a catch in the breath, an absent voice, a sense of waiting and desolation. In the end the line between the living and the dead became so blurred that survivors would hear the things dead men used to say, feel their vitality, expect them suddenly to appear or sense their presence in a patrol, and all the more strongly since death was already in a way throwing its shadow forward on the squadron.

Trenchard's assistant Maurice Baring noted Rhys Davids' certainty that he would soon die. Mannock's last letter to his sister remarked: 'Occasionally I feel that life is not worth hanging on to. I had hopes of getting married but ...' Udet described a similar feeling.

We walked along the loose gravel path leading through the park to the castle. A small, white garden table stood close by us. Gontermann halted and picked up a leaf, a handful of pebbles. Placing the leaf on the table, he opened the palm of his hand and slowly released the stones. As each fell, there was a sharp metallic sound as the pebbles hit the tabletop. 'It's like this, Udet,' he said. 'The bullets fall all round us' – he pointed to the leaf – 'and gradually they get nearer and nearer. Eventually they hit us. We're bound to get hit in time.' With an impatient movement of the hand he swept his playthings from the table. I was watching him from the side. Obviously he was in a highly emotional state and my desire to get away from the place increased a hundredfold ... Gontermann died three months later.

For some, the exact time of death was revealed. McLanachan described two such cases on a single aerodrome. The first involved twenty-year-old Canadian Binnie,

a quiet type of Scottish descent with fairish hair and less than medium height. I asked him if he would care to join us but he looked up with a quiet smile and answered simply, 'No thanks, Mac. I've got some letters I want to write.' I left him sitting placidly on the edge of his camp bed. When we returned about 10 o'clock he had just finished writing and stood up, stretching as I entered the tent. Very, very quietly he spoke. 'I've written a couple of letters and gone all over my kit. If anything happens to me tomorrow, Mac, will you post the letters for me and see that my kit is sent off to the two addresses where I've labelled it to go?' I said I would. But what words can one utter at such times? Soon after, we all turned in. Beyond the narrowing V of the tent opening, trees shut out all but a tiny strip of sky. Cool, sweet air came in under the turned-up flap at the bottom of the bell tent. On his camp bed opposite me, my comrade of the past three weeks slept peacefully. In the distance a cock crowed throatily. Binnie died next day.

Another time Kennedy and McLanachan missed dinner and so mixed eggs and whisky with condensed milk as a meal filler. Unable to sleep before the imminent patrol, Kennedy played over and over again on the gramophone:

> I shall see you tonight love
> in our beautiful dreamland
> and your eyes will be bright dear
> with the lovelight that gleams for me.
> To my heart I will press you
> I will kiss and caress you
> So goodnight and God bless you
> I shall see you tonight.

Kennedy told McLanachan that he had a hunch he would not last another day. Next day, he too died.

Death was thus bewilderment, anxiety, despair and as much part of the war as the chilling mists and rancid sweetness of aerodrome grass at dawn; or that great wedge of darkness which from the air seemed to force patrols back to earth while squadron commanders fired Vereys like the bonfires of All Souls night to guide their men home. Yet in one sense death was unlike any other part of a pilot's war. The essence of war to a fighting man is a powerful concentration on the present, whether in the overwhelming sense of joy in being alive or in the introverting sense of gathering self together to face up to the worst possibilities. Death formed no conscious part of such an orientation. Dying perhaps, but never death, for death had happened and would happen, but to men so fixated upon the present, death meant always a violation, a surprise, a finality which never really fitted into the many practicalities in a fighter pilot's agenda. Willy Coppens expressed perfectly such a position: 'One day Olieslagers chanced to go into the squadron workshop and saw one of those crosses of propeller walnut standing in the corner, beautifully polished. We had not lost a pilot for some time and he was not a little surprised. "Who is this cross for?" he asked. And the carpenter replied simply, "The next." '

15
THE DARK SIDE – KILLING

With much experience of aerial fighting in both world wars, Canadian ace Raymond Collishaw judged that the spirit of the Great War, with its dropped messages and wreaths, had been very different from the second, all hatred and impersonality. Such a view, with its undertones of 'chivalry' and of 'knights of the air', has always been behind most writing on first war pilots and draws attention away from the central point of combat ethics throughout that war – never to give the slightest chance to any enemy in the sky at any time. The simple reason was expressed by Mannock: taking the number plate from the engine of a burnt-out aeroplane, his thirty-third victim, Mannock spoke for all fighter pilots when he remarked: 'It was he or I and I would prefer it to be him.'

Displays of charity were indeed so rare that, if suspected, the recipient would be as shaken as if one of his spars had been shot through. Fighting the French ace Guynemer on one occasion, the German pilot Udet's guns jammed. Against such a master of manœuvre and marksmanship as the Frenchman, Udet became the coldest of cold meat. Guynemer nevertheless disengaged and flew off. On landing, Udet had to be grounded for seven days, so certain had he been of death, so disturbed by an unprecedented let-off. Ira Jones noted his bewilderment on being allowed to fly away when his single Lewis gun had been ripped from his machine by slipstream. He could only imagine that his opponent had been one of the rare enemy sportsmen.

Another element giving benediction to a killing without guilt was duty. As fighter pilot Balfour put it, though pilots might admire the technical skill of their opponents, the job was to kill and eliminate the enemy's air force. No published memoirs of the first war express doubts at the rightness of this task, and many took pleasure in it. 'To see an enemy going down in flames is a source of great satisfaction,' wrote Bishop. 'You know his destruction is absolutely certain.' Leading Irish marksman McElroy watched his own flamers with the pleasant sensation of a job well done, a job essentially right. This spirit of destruction could be taken further. Springs described his friend Hilary Rex being machine-gunned on the ground long after he had crashed. Buckley, too, wrote of the same experience with some feeling when he himself was the target. Fokkers dived at him for ten minutes while he lay pinned under his crashed machine. Our men could do the same as easily. Mannock's diary for April 1918 records chasing an enemy two-seater down to the ground, then taking half a dozen strafing dives at the marooned crew. Questioned afterwards, his comment was: 'The swine are better dead. No prisoners for me.'

Two forces of a more personal nature than the imperatives of survival or national duty reinforced the business of killing with a quiet conscience. The first and most direct was that of revenge. McLanachan remarked that for some time his only purpose in flying had been to avenge his friends Bond, Rooke and Jones. Before each fight he would pray: 'Please let me kill one at least before I die.' It is curious to note though that such personal feelings had to be kept within limits, for when McLanachan ordered his ammunition drums to be filled just with armour-piercing and Buckingham incendiary bullets both Davidge, his air mechanic, and Mannock protested.

The other personal factor was sporting instinct. 'When I left for my leave to England,' wrote Bishop,

> I was not keen on going. The excitement of the chase had a tight hold on my heart strings and I felt that the only thing I wanted was to stay right at it and fight in the air. It seemed that I had found the one thing I loved above all others. To me it was not a business or profession but just a wonderful game. To bring down a machine did not seem to me like killing a man but more as if I was just destroying a mechanical target with no human being in it at all. One had the great feeling that one had hit the target and brought it down – that one was victorious again.

In other words Bishop, like many others, found in killing in the air a piquant mixture of stalking and chasing, clay-pigeon shooting and fox hunting. Or, as Mannock put it to Caldwell, 'I think an airfight quite the most thrilling sport there is apart from doing one's duty. In beating the Hun one realizes the same satisfaction as in winning a keenly contested game of golf or tennis.'

Likeness to hunting came out in many ways. First there were the trophies. As Mannock said in a letter to his friend Jim Eyles in August 1917:

> I sent the parcel off to you yesterday. Pilot boots which belonged to a dead pilot. Goggles also belonging to him. The cigarette case and holder were given me by the captain observer. The piece of fabric with the number on it is from the Hun two-seater. The bayonet is the one I pulled out of the body of a dead Hun who was lying near the crashed bus. It is one of our own bayonets and I had to crawl out on my stomach to get it and there was not much cover. I have several other things which I cannot send home. They will do later.

After such trophies came the counting of the game bag's contents. When McCudden's squadron shot down their 200th victim in five and a half months, forty Verey flares were sent up in celebration. In the same spirit 74 Squadron raced 65 Squadron for the record of the quickest century, individual pilots blob-painting the fabric of their machines or notching walking sticks or control columns to keep record of their individual contributions.

So killing wore many glamorous disguises, yet the disguise could never be complete. In contrast with the second war, the first produced no systematic propaganda effort to dehumanize the opponent or turn the enemy into a sinister threat with whom there could be no commerce. Individual pilots might feel modern hatred and refuse to stand when Richthofen's health was drunk or agree with McLanachan that 'We were ever conscious of being opposed by an inhuman weapon and by the system and logic of an almost invincible foe.' But for the majority, killing was confined to the sky. German pilot Stark seems to have reflected majority opinion on both sides after he had shot down a two-seater Bristol Fighter:

> His machine sits there like a big butterfly with its cockades shining peacefully. It is a strange spectacle – a thing that I have been fighting, a thing that was turning its guns on me, a thing I could hardly see at all in the hustle of our turning and now it stands quietly before me. We greet one another almost like old acquaintances. We bear no malice against one another. In a kind

of way we are one big family. We meet at the front, we get to know the respective badges of Staffel and squadron and are pleased to meet these old acquaintances in the flesh. The fight is over and we are good friends.

In the same way, when 'the Black Knight' Von Schleich had shot down Lieutenant Reece and found his prisoner in plimsolls and flannels, Schleich took him to the Staffel tennis court to play out the deciding set in Reece's outstanding match, which had stood at 3-2 just before Reece's last take-off. The distinction between fighting and not fighting seems thus to have been as distinct in the air as on the ground, with its lengthy unofficial truces and scaled-down aggressiveness on non-essential fronts, so hated by the desk soldiers.

Reinforcing such lack of virulence outside the specific context of combat was another peculiarity of the Great War – a front static for a long period, with the two sides in close contact. In the air as on the ground this produced constant communication between the antagonists.

First was the communication requesting information. 'No information has been received about Captain Von Osterroht, missing near Arras since April 23rd. Information is requested.' Or again '23rd August 1917. German flying corps. We would be very pleased to have news about our famous pilot first lieutenant Dostler who came down on the 21st about 12 o'clock in our time between Frenzeberg and St Julien just in your first lines. He was distinguished by the Pour la Mérit.' Another typical dropped message read: 'To the British Flying Corps. The 4th September I lost my friend Fritz Frech. He fell between Vimy and Lievin. His respectable and unlucky parents beg you to give any news of his fate. Is he dead? At what place found he his last rest? Please to throw several letters that we may found one. Thanking you before, his friend K.L. (Postscript. If it is possible send a letter to his parents, Mr Frech, Koenigsberg i.Pr., Vord Vorstadt 48/52.)'

Then there came information on our own losses. In the Public Record Office is an original German list dropped during the war giving a full tally of RFC machines shot down between 1 April 1917 and 29 July 1917. Individual deaths were notified more frequently. 'Biplane 133 was shot down yesterday in an air battle by Lt Likinarge (pilot) and Lt Trilsche (observer). The two officers were dead. One wing broke off already in the air. We regret the dead of your fellows. The had bravely defended till the pilot received a shut in the head. (signed) Felmy.' Cr a note informing his home aerodrome that a pilot had been buried with full military honours like the note for Lieutenant Maurice Basden in May 1916, signed 'Bavarian aviators' and enclosing four photos of the burial ceremony.

In the same way, prisoners were notified: '13.7.17. I permit me to send the parents of Mr Vantin my respects. He tolled me he is your only son. I know and I hope that he is well treated also in the next time. I think it is a consolation for you because you see him positive after the war. He fought with me very bravely on 8.7.17 and I am proud to have combatted with such a sport and a gentleman. His genteel behaviour at us was the reason that we have treated him as a guest. With respectful regards, Gerhard Folmy, Obert. (address after the war Germany, Wierck a/Darss in Pommern).' The message might even be written by the prisoner: 'Monday 4th June. The RFC, BEF. I have been wounded in both legs and am being well looked after. T. Malcom Dickinson. 16th cavalry. 1a and RFC.'

Such combination of personal contact with lack of ideological commitment often seems to have given to aerial killing a dangerously personal quality, itself reinforced by the slow speeds and closenesses of the fight, and the possibility of finding a victim's remains in the compact war flying zone. Fighting a black and purple machine in August 1917, McCudden found himself very close each time his opponent produced quick negative G manœuvres to get beneath him. McCudden's response was bewildered. 'By jove, there is a man in it, I said to myself. At times I have fought a Hun and on passing at close range have seen a pilot and been quite surprised.' Sholto Douglas likewise recorded his sense of shock when seeing an opponent clearly visible: 'Queer feeling. Fellow like myself. Damned silly and senseless. Bloody futile all this.'

The appearance of an opponent in person seems always to have disrupted the simplified emotions of the chase. Coppens once saw a German machine disintegrate in the air, the fuselage falling fast and the rest of the machine descending in a slow mist with the observer spinning endlessly down. 'Poor man, poor man,' Coppens found himself saying as his own machine flew through the debris and one of the observer's maps brushed his wing-tip. Vincent also wrote of being sickened at the sight of an aeroplane losing its tailplane and the observer jumping out. Of his first flamer McLanachan wrote that he was 'horrified and sickened' and Ira Jones wrote of 'a horrible sight. It made me feel quite sick.' He at once flew home without daring to look back.

German pilots seem to have felt the same. Udet once fought a single combat with a British machine. They had made four head-on passes at each other.

It looked as though at any moment we would ram each other. A quick movement and he passed just over my head. I could feel the draught of his propeller and smell his engine fumes. I saw in black letters painted on the fuselage the number 8224. For the fourth time we faced each other. I felt my hands grow damp. It was he or I. There was no alternative. A memory flashed through my mind of something I had witnessed above Lens. An air battle was in progress in which two machines crashed head on. The fuselages plunged to earth while the wings flew on a bit ... I flew back to my aerodrome, my skin soaked in sweat and my nerves in a desperate state of excitement. At the same time I felt a dull, persistent pain in my ears. He who fights should not look at the wounds he inflicts, but on this particular occasion I felt an insatiable desire to know who my opponent had been. A field dressing station stood quite close to the spot where he had fallen. I asked to see the medical officer and when he came, his white coat had an uncanny appearance in the hard light of the carbide lamp. My opponent, he said, had been shot through the head. His death had been instantaneous. The doctor handed me his wallet. On a visiting card I read 'Lt C. Massdorp, Ontario. RFC 47.' So he had been a member of the RFC! Also in the wallet were a picture of an elderly woman and a letter. It said: 'Don't be reckless. Think of father and me.' A hospital orderly brought me the number of his aeroplane which he had cut out of the wreckage. It was covered with little spots of blood. I drove back to my unit. Somehow one had to try and get rid of the thought that a mother wept for every man shot down.

Even so cool a customer as McCudden was disturbed by such sighting of a victim at close quarters. 'I felt sorry, for shooting a man down in your own lines is very different from doing it in Hunland. You can see the results of your work. Shooting Huns is very good fun while we have to do it but at the same time it makes one think, as I say, when one views such an object as I was doing then' (a dying pilot on a stretcher from the two-seater McCudden had just brought down).

In the end there was no way the contrary emotions of aerial combat could be reconciled. On the one hand was the joy of impersonally downing an aerial target and the satisfaction of doing a national duty. On the other hand there was revulsion at killing the pilot's own analogue and awareness of the dead man as both German and human being. 'I hate this game,' wrote Albert Ball in one of his last letters. 'I do get tired of always living to kill and am really beginning to feel like a murderer.' Or, as Mannock put it in a letter, 'I sometimes wonder if my whole nature has not been altered under the stress of this business.' Aerial killing thus became for many pilots a thing of mixed emotion. Less tangible than the physical stresses of flight or of being a permanent target for German guns, killing was nevertheless an occupation which conflicted with a basic taboo of civilian life, and was a disturbing exploration of a dark area in the mind of which none had previous experience. Ball and Mannock, after all, were two aces noted for their hatred of the enemy and for relish in service flying.

16
ENDURING

Fighter pilots were among the most isolated of fighting men, and necessarily so. Bound to a round-the-clock routine of patrol work, they could very seldom enjoy those longer periods of 'rest' between periods of front-line service which were part of the infantryman's war.

The result was a high degree of introversion which Lee describes:

> Isolated from the rest of the world we really didn't care for it and we were not interested in it. Certainly we would read newspapers a day or two late and with eagerness. Otherwise we would not have known how our war was progressing. But we soon forgot even the boldest headlines and took such events as the Russian revolution or the death of Kitchener in our stride as being of lesser consequence than reports that Baron Richthofen was shooting down too many of our airmen. Our strongest links with the outside world were letters to and from home but those we wrote were usually brief and perfunctory. We had little contact even with other RFC squadrons though some were within easy flying distance. With Other Ranks we had little to do except with particular NCOs and mechanics who serviced our aeroplanes and guns.

Such isolation within the squadron meant that few knew whether Trenchard or Henderson was in charge of the RFC or even what date it was. One writer described a fierce debate on the date, ending with a decision that the calendar be put to the vote.

If stress was an important factor in the fighter pilot's war, relief had therefore to be found within the framework of the squadron. And so it was, much assisted by the freedom given to a new service, just two years old when the war began. Much new machinery, such as machine guns or tanks, could be castrated at birth by a graft into the Royal Engineers – as indeed the aeroplane had been before the war. But in war, fighting in a new medium and linked only tenuously with ground activity, looking like no other fighting unit with its subdivision into tiny fighting units in which officers did all the fighting while Other Ranks lived in gentlemanly safety, the RFC was left alone by the army and allowed to build for itself a ground structure best suited to sustain its pilots.

The first supportive institution was a rigid insistence on obedience to flying orders. Pilots might continue to loathe their patrol routine deeply but, by removing it from the level of personal decision, it was as if an omnipotent outside force had decreed what must be done with a weight and authority which demanded acquiescence. The result was an almost oriental passivity among pilots with regard to the major things in service life which contrasted strongly with the squadron's anarchic ebullience with regard to all things minor, as Lee records:

> We lived to a rhythmic pattern, mounting into the air perhaps two or three times a day to do battle, then returning to our pleasant Mess to enjoy an exclusive, comfortable existence like cattle being fattened for the slaughter house. But we didn't see it that way. We had our daily job to do and it was strange how overnight we became accustomed to our routine of having a good breakfast after a good night's sleep, then going up on a mid-morning patrol, taking part in a frantic dogfight three miles up, killing a young German, then probably narrowly escaping death oneself before coming down, having a swim, a drink and a good lunch. All quite normal. One hardly commented on it after a while. Like going to the office.

The strength of the imperative was described graphically by Balfour:

> Even after a lapse of fifteen years I feel that the names of units or of any of those concerned should be left out. Sufficient to relate that there was a squadron which had for one of its flight commanders an individual who though in himself an above average pilot, possessed neither in the air nor on the ground a good influence. In the air his patrols were not led with any keenness or desire to cross the lines if it could possibly be avoided. On the ground his conversation was defeatist and not

likely to induce any esprit de corps among young pilots. Captain A then went to a new unit where the CO was an active member of patrols and where A's previous disinclination to cross the lines could not be continued without being noticed by all concerned. There arrived at the squadron shortly after his posting, orders for a low bomb raid on an enemy aerodrome to take place the following morning. This was a fairly hazardous task for all concerned but Captain A was detailed to lead the raid and the CO announced his intention of following as one of the patrol. Soon after he had given his orders, Captain A came to him in the office and said he did not feel he could take part in the next day's operations. He was asked if he definitely declined to go. He replied in the affirmative. The CO told him to return to the office in one hour's time and meanwhile communicated the refusal to HQ. At the end of an hour Captain A reported and was informed he was to proceed to Base the following morning. He asked if this meant he would be court martialled and was informed this was likely to occur. He left the office and within an hour had gone into the officers' lavatory and shot himself dead.

In the same way, when Mannock was CO of 74 Squadron, he would rip the tunic wings off any pilot requesting a desk job and order their replacement by a strip of yellow cloth. As Roberts remarked, the CO was basically a little god.

Strict obedience to orders was not the result only of the CO's overriding authority. Hesitation in any member of a flight endangered the whole unit, whose safety depended chiefly on tight formation work, so men who returned prematurely from any patrol reporting boiling radiator, oil pressure trouble or the like came under suspicion from everyone else. In his early days with 40 Squadron, Mannock himself had deserted his colleague Keen when both were jumped on by three of the enemy. The incident resulted in his being sacked from 40 Squadron and being transferred to 74, where his reputation followed. McLanachan recalled a warning against drinking with newcomer Mannock, who was not allowed to take part in discussions of aerial work since his condition might prove infectious. Even McLanachan ran into trouble when he quit a dogfight with Lewis gun trouble:

> I showed them the broken pieces of bolt but even then they did not acquit me. There was the bald fact. I had left in the

middle of a dogfight and when Captain Bath and the remainder returned, it appeared that I was going to have a rough time. Mannock dismantled my Lewis and came back with the broken bolt in his pocket. Steve Godfrey expressed interest in how I had managed to dismantle a gun whilst spinning. I was still a stout fellow.

The pressure which maintained the flying timetable of active service was thus a combination of the squadron commander's formal demand with an equally strong informal pressure in the same direction from the pilots collectively, and was the expression of a fundamental dichotomy at the foundation of the squadron. On the one hand was Roberts' 'little god' who, as 60 Squadron's commander Smith-Barry had shown on the Somme, had power to refuse to send inexperienced men over the line, ignore Trenchard's orders to the contrary, then publicly call them 'bloody murder'. Such formal authority came from a Standing Order in 1915.

The guiding principle is that so long as the work of the squadron is done satisfactorily and in accordance with the system laid down by RFC headquarters and so long as the squadron is kept at a high level of efficiency, there is seldom any call for the intervention of the wing commander. If initiative is to be encouraged, allowance must be made for individual characteristics and the wing commander must often be content to see his subordinates deal with matters in a somewhat different manner from that which he himself would adopt if he were a squadron commander.

Yet on the other hand were the squadron pilots, close in rank to the CO and manipulating complex machinery in a war which often called for tactical decisions by the individual. Authority over such men could never be satisfactorily imposed in an arbitrary way whatever the latitude indicated in the 1915 Standing Order. Indeed, the authority itself had always to be justified. Thus in 1916 Bishop wrote with approval of a CO who flew alone over enemy trenches stunting so as to attract anti-aircraft shells and enemy headhunters, making a point without putting anyone else in the squadron at risk. Then, when COs were forbidden to fly over the line early in 1917, Yeates wrote of a newly appointed squadron commander making the same point by stunting smoothly at 1,000 feet over the aerodrome, passing his wing tips to within a few feet of the ground before sideslipping into his hangar – just as newcomer Bader felt he had to at Tangemere a war later but for the same reason. Even then, a squadron major's was no easy command. A man of such proven bravery and flying ability as Sholto Douglas wrote of his charge during 1917. 'There were lots of arguments as to how we should operate. Were we to fight in flights or as a squadron? There was bound to be some opposition from some individualists in the squadron since the flying corps was so largely made up of individualists. I found that they did not hesitate to argue and press their views.'

In practice, therefore, the major's style had to be a form of democratic dictatorship, a formulation of majority opinion, a leadership of equals. Orders had always to be clear and decisive, but at the same time many areas had to be left free from imperatives, and even in areas where orders gave necessary structure they had to accord with perceived good sense and be presented in such a way as to preserve self-respect.

Fry wrote of his squadron commander: 'Charles Bryant was the perfect gentle knight, sans peur et sans reproche. His orders, usually given in the form of suggestions, were invariably obeyed.' Balfour's Robert Lorraine had a more oblique approach.

The officers' mess was filled with patent bells and alarm gongs which might go off at any moment, each one indicating some different event such as the start of a patrol or the sighting of an enemy aeroplane. Always when one of these went off it was the custom that not an eyelid should quiver. Scarcely altering the tone of conversation Lorraine would turn to whoever was concerned. 'Gregory, I think there is an enemy around. I think you had better go.' And then on with the game of bridge. On the other hand, I have seen him on the floor allowing himself to be rolled about by his junior officers, for always a commanding officer must be able to be a boy amongst boys if he is to play his part to the uttermost.

Spit-and-polish majors, or majors unable to argue and convince or unbend and play, were quickly sent home to training squadrons, where such rigidity did less immediate damage. Even Brocard, of the crack French Stork Squadron, was relieved of his command early in 1917 because 'il refusait s'évoluer'. D'Harcourt, who replaced him, was a man who it was said presented orders to his pilots with such courtesy that they seemed almost like prayers. The RFC acted likewise, but sacked with less publicity, recognizing the importance of the CO as organizer of those attitudes which maintained morale.

The second sustaining institution in the squadron was total relaxation on the ground, a counterpoint to the strain of the air. Again it was the squadron commander who led. 'If we have to fight,' said Major Foster, 'let us fight in comfort, for we can fight better when we are comfortable.' He then acquired Marjorie, a milch cow, and the cock Robert with fifty-four attendant hens to serve the mess table, a jazz band to serenade it and four horses for recreation, borrowed from the adjacent 16th Lancers in return for the lancers' use of the squadron tender to visit Amiens weekly. More often though the CO's benediction would be by carefully limiting his area of decision. Thus Fry wrote of Bryant: 'He rarely interfered with the pilots in any way but he was sometimes moved to protest mildly when we sat in front of the fire wearing hip-length flying boots which were of untanned sheepskin with wool inside. It was certainly rather over-powering.' Fry did not think it necessary to remark on the fact that the major sat with his pilots in the officers' mess, for such proximities were commonplace on a fighter aerodrome.

Mess and anteroom were the focal point of off-duty relaxation, the embodiment of the style of a London gentleman's club, due allowance made for the austerity of west front furnishings. At the centre was a cast-iron stove surrounded by assorted settees and easy chairs covered in balloon fabric; around the perimeter would be an upright piano, a half-sized billiard table, papers and magazines on a table, an improvised bookstand with its collection of battered popular novels. Place of honour was invariably occupied by the single most important item of furniture, the wind-up gramophone with its horn like a giant ear trumpet, battle-scarred from past rough-houses in the mess. The only indication that this hut was the home of a fighting squadron might be the names of leading scorers pencilled on the wall. Perhaps a propeller or cut-out enemy aeroplane number with cross might be set over the anteroom door to make a triumphal arch for entry into the mess proper. More often there would be nothing of this. Just walls roughly pasted with cretonne wallpaper and brightened by Kirchner's pin-ups. In the mess, men wanted chiefly to forget. Mess kit underlined the fact – slacks without puttees, town walking-out shoes, tunics with castor-oil flecks and accumulated leather reinforcement, with pyjamas correct dress for summer meals.

In this setting, the only briskly mobile figures were likely to be the mess waiters, moving between pilots slumped in assorted chairs. McLanachan remembered the odd heated discussion on Spinoza or Rochefoucauld, but quietness was the rule, for, as Collishaw observed, flying every day and with just half a day off weekly, men were simply too tired for the least exertion of energy. So it was on the other side of the line among fighter pilots. Wrote Stark: 'We lounge about the aerodrome or go to sleep under the shade of a tree. Sleep is a great necessity for the airman. Sleep is the food of the nerves. How much time we have often frittered away uselessly with cards, talking and the like.' There would, too, be encouragement of somnolence by the airlessness of the mess. Men who flew daily into bitter cold valued warmth too highly ever to open windows. For much of the year, therefore, the mess atmosphere would be one of hot flying kit, hot pets and what an official RFC pamphlet termed 'those unpleasant odours which any group of persons in a closed space of relatively small volume will soon generate. These arise principally from smoking, foul breath, sweat and sebaceous excretions, expelled intestinal gases, decomposing organic matter on clothing or skin.'

Those few not dozing could be reading. Whitehouse might get through the novels of H. G. Wells but, for most, light novels or newspapers represented the heaviest reading strained men could handle. Indeed, Balfour wrote specifically that the pilots he knew never read. Non-readers might keep their minds away from flying by making sleeveless jerkins or slippers from old flying boots ('lost owing to the exigencies of the service'). Perhaps they might write letters home requesting extra thick vests, balaclavas or supplementary cardigans.

The only sounds would be the flop and shuffle of flying boots on the roughly tacked linoleum and the wheeze of the gramophone. But always the gramophone in the background, for flying men were afraid of silence. Each man on each leave had an iron obligation to bring back one record, and though Yeates thought that few consciously listened to the music, it was always there, quietly reassuring and stopping minds wandering back to the sky. Hawker thought the gramophone the single most essential piece of squadron equipment, and the record of 'Mum's Darling' always reminded him of his father returning tired after a day's shooting on his home estate. With Mannock it was the 'Londonderry Air'. Each man had such a personal link with his civilian memories – perhaps Violet Lorraine and George Robey singing 'If you were the only girl in the world' or Jose Collins with 'Love will find a way'. Later the records would have the reverse effect. After the war Yeates could never hear 'Any time is kissing time' or 'The bells are ringing' without being transported back in memory to particular little villages in France amongst the ghosts of dead men. Beethoven's Seventh to McLanachan meant the air still and warm with the distant rumble of Ypres gunfire. Wrote Norman Macmillan:

I should like to have all those records now that were made before the days of electric recordings of singers whose method of voice production was so different from those of today and more natural. I can still picture a meadow, a clear sky on a summer's day, a full moon tracing long shadows on bordering poplars across grass half ringed by bell tents – and this music changing the harsh reality of guns and aeroplanes into a sound of beauty.

Pets played the same role as music in reminding a fighting man of the gentler side of his nature. Dogs were the great favourite, and they were easily acquired in a war zone in which strays always regarded uniformed men as their particular friends. Bishop kept three chows, McCudden his bulldog 'Bruiser'. In the evening, such dogs ringed the mess stove; by day they waited on the field like squires for the return of their masters:

Stood on the tarmac today watching my flight take off. Chilly's little fox terrier was there with me. That little beggar has more sense than the average human being. Sat on his haunches and wouldn't be coaxed away until the flight came back. Didn't even cock his ears when B flight came in a little while after ours had taken off. But when A flight returned, watched each machine as it landed and when Chilly climbed out of his bus, he jumped all over him. Some bishop, asked if dogs had souls, said he couldn't imagine a heaven without dogs. Damned right. Best little friends in the world.

Animals other than dogs served also to take thought away from the air, perhaps more strongly for not being associated with particular masters. Bishop's memoirs are pleasantly filled with such animals.

We tried hard to train our farmyard ducks to walk on the ground in formation in the same way as we flew in the air. One afternoon we got sixteen ducks and after giving them a good luncheon, by way of celebration of their outing we put them on the roof of the mess where they all sat in a stately row quacking in spasms. The French people who owned them did not seem to mind. We then secured a large sow and painted a black cross on her nose, a little one on her ears and a large one on each side. On her back we painted the words 'Baron von Richthofen'. So that the other pigs would recognize her, we tied a squadron leader's streamers to her tail. This trailed for some three feet behind her as she walked. When the 'Baron' returned to her farmyard, chickens and ducks and pigs and geese all followed the big sow round as she walked. Upon the express condition that we must not paint them, the farmer let us have his rabbits in the afternoon. He must have had over 200. We would sit under the trees and play with them or watch them eat. They were very amusing little things and passed away many hours for us.

The third supportive mechanism of the squadron was the reverse side of that quietness and withdrawal into the private self symbolized by the mess. This was creation of a corporate unity, a team feeling, a bonding of the eighteen or twenty-four men of the fighter squadron's strike force.

Much work was needed here, since so many factors operated to split the squadron apart. The incidence of death in a small group was constantly bringing the loss of the known and replacement by the unknown. Veterans anyway tended to split into smaller groupings – leader and wingman, dominion pilots, men from particular public schools or training squadrons. At any time, questions of rank might cut across such sub-divisions and brutally demonstrate the shallowness of war's unity. When Zulu Lloyd became a flight commander in 74 Squadron and boasted his experience with 60 Squadron, the seasoned men like Hall, Bond, Godfrey and Mannock sat quietly by. Similarly, the promotion of Mannock over Bond was resented because the taint of cowardice in Mannock's early career had never been forgotten. Even McLanachan left

Mannock's next patrol early in protest. So excellent a war flier as Rhodesian Arthur Harris, a flight commander with five killings to his name, protested at having to serve under a newly appointed commanding officer, his junior in the service.

Perhaps even more important than these easily grasped, always changing groupings in distancing the men from each other was a force which operated evenly and at all times upon them. This was the random way a small group of total strangers had been put together in an isolated place to face an unbroken sequence of intensely dangerous war missions. Those who served for a time in the easy atmosphere of home service squadrons giving air cover to London were always surprised how much more quickly than on the front they got to know colleagues' first names and how much more relaxed such relationships were. The greater pressures and darker fears of the service squadron always made for distance and gave to acquaintance a sharp edge suggested by Yeates:

> They arrived at the squadron mess and Williamson joined in a game of Slippery Sam. Allen went to the hut to write letters as usual so Cundall joined the group sitting round the fire. Desultory talk about the war was going on. Thompson was there (A flight commander) and Bulmer (commander of B flight) and Robinson who called everyone 'Old Bean' or 'old tin of fruit'. And Franklin, vast and sleepy, who was utterly unaffected by the chances of war. He got into frightful scrapes and would come home with his machine full of bullet holes and tears. Not content with the usual two shows a day, he often went up alone to look for something to shoot at. But unlike most sportsmen, he appeared to enjoy being shot at as well. To Tom Cundall he was a mystery. Did he think? Had life any value or meaning to him? He was completely good natured and good tempered and did not appear to dislike anyone or anything, certainly not the Germans. To him war seemed a not too exciting big game hunt, Tom imagined. The efficiency of McAndrew, C flight commander with a bag of twenty-six, was tremendous and he was a first-rate leader. He was now playing poker with some of the Canadians. At about ten he strolled over to the fire.
>
> 'I guess I'll turn in now. Don't forget we've got the dawn show, Cundall. Bombs.'
>
> 'Right you are, Mac. Are you taking Allen?'

'Aye, he's going to be a good lad. He's keen.'

Tom wondered how to take the last sentence. Was it a hit at him? He was never quite sure how to take Mac.

The first and easiest way of preserving harmony was for the squadron commander to use his powers in the selection of men. This could be done officially. 'Lt Algernon Anthony. A1. Aged 19. 87 hours solo. Indifferent pilot. Disinclination to cross the lines. I do not consider his services to be of any value as a pilot. Not suitable officer. Jockey, so to cavalry?' Such confidential reports could be sent at any time to wing HQ, which in its turn might at any time reply in irritation: 'It has been brought to my notice that officers the subject of adverse reports or of COs not wanting them, being given letters to staff officers at the War Office to the effect that they are not wanted in France and that there was no objection to their retention in England' or that 'There was a case of flight commanders not being recommended till there was a vacancy in their own squadron. This procedure is quite out of order.'

Once he had chosen his own team, the squadron leader often seems to have cultivated an eccentric flamboyance which made him a common point of reference in the squadron, the acceptable embodiment of an authority which made such great demands of fighting men; a man whose vividness made him a slightly frightening figure like a dangerously volatile headmaster.

Such an extrovert was the legendary Jack Scott. Wounded in 1915, he had always to walk with the help of two walking sticks yet invariably flew his Nieuport before breakfast in pyjamas and dressing gown. In combat, Douglas thought him even braver than Beauchamp-Proctor. By personal example Jack Scott turned 43 Squadron in training and 60 Squadron in the field into great fighting squadrons.

Macmillan's Nethersole seems to have been another of similar type.

He was a great believer in encouraging the offensive spirit among his pilots and he adopted two methods. Not far from the airfield was a steep hill. Near the bottom of the hill he had a trench dug. On the higher side of the trench, he had a sloping ramp constructed. His idea was to dash down the hill on a pedal cycle, rise up the ramp and take off. The trench was filled with water to make a soft landing. At his own third attempt, he succeeded. Thereafter he expected all pilots to make the run. He considered it a splendid test of nerve and guts for new arrivals to his squadron and it was not until a broken leg resulted from one run that the cycle jumping test of the offensive spirit was ended. At other times, he lined his pilots up to face each other at about forty yards range and armed them with tent mallets which they had to hurl at each other as hard as they could.

The fact that Macmillan and his men did these absurdities without question is alone measure of the commander's success in image building.

There were other, more institutionalized ways in which the squadron commander could take the lead in bonding the process. The most common of these were squadron rituals involving communal absorption of alcohol and past history, the CO presiding.

> After dinner we played rugby for a while with a rolled-up Sidcot flying suit as a football. The game was rapidly becoming too expensive so those of us who were sober enough stopped it. Then Simkins began thumping the piano and we gathered round and sang squadron songs. Most of them were local productions sung to well-known airs:
>> 'Twelve young pilots from squadron ...
>> took the air one morn at eight.
>> They met fifty Huns, they say
>> over the middle of Tournai.
>> chorus: so early in the morning,
>> so early in the morning,
>> so early in the mor-r-r-rning,
>> before the break of day.
>> Hep was leading A flight then.
>> Murray followed with the B flight men.
>> There were eight old Fokkers in the sun,
>> that is the way of the wily old Hun.
>> (chorus) So early in the morning etc.
>> Hep got a Hun right on his tail.
>> He did a half roll without fail.
>> Then his gun went dud they say
>> So he came home and left the fray.
>> (chorus) So early in the morning, etc.'
> Practically everyone who had taken part in the scrap had

contributed some verses to this epic. A number of verses were omitted altogether in deference to the jovial visiting padre. No one knew all the verses but each man knew some of them and the solo was carried on by different members as the song progressed. But at the end of each verse we all roared out the chorus with vast enjoyment. The singing was thirsty work and before long there was a yell of 'Drinks all round on the CO!' Our good-natured squadron commander promptly gave his consent and Bobby Westcott climbed on to a table with his glass in his hand to make the CO a speech of thanks.

In all these matters, the pattern of the squadron commander sanctioning spontaneous behaviour from his own men was maintained as it had been in the insistence on the disciplines of patrol flying or in the establishment of a perfect go-as-you-please framework outside the constraints of war flying. The spontaneous behaviour in this case was that horseplay which was constantly breaking through the somnolent and casual attitude customary in the mess. Its purpose would seem to have been twofold. On the one hand it relieved combat tension; on the other it joined the squadron together.

One type of saturnalia involved the whole squadron against the world. The quiz section of 24 Squadron's history after the war indicated its form. What was the squadron that was jealous of our settees but failed to smash them with their combined weight? Did our neighbours object to our nocturnal band parade and was that why they kicked out the side of our anteroom? In such rituals Mannock wrote of collecting a sore shin and black eye in a massed fight with 10 Squadron, while Ira Jones recorded a bombing raid on 1 Squadron, using 200 oranges as the ammunition. Counter-retaliation came in banana form, and both squadrons celebrated a reunion at the George Robey café in St Omer.

Then there were the games which brought together separate groups within the squadron. Macmillan wrote of a squadron dinner at which a dominion flier was hit over the head with a plate. A general rain of crockery then fell, to the vast amusement of the CO and the horror of the visiting padre. In the same squadron, Mannock always relished the organization of anteroom fights between 'colonials' and the rest, or 'shooting up the boche' (colonials), using gas (flit sprays), flamethrowers (siphons), bombs (tennis balls) and armoured cars (cane chairs). In any squadron, spasms of gardening invariably ended with the gardeners throwing each other into the ornamental pond, a signal for the rest of the mess to come rushing out to join in a massed water fight in which watering cans supplemented chamber pots.

Animals took a prominent part in this boisterousness. Lee wrote of cows being driven into tents at night and chickens being used as retaliation. Bishop wrote of pigs appearing in bedrooms after much pushing from behind.

> When we begin to feel a little bored we can always have a good hearty quarrel with the lady of our farm billet. She is really a very kind hearted old dame but she has peculiar ideas about the noise we make in her loft at night. She seems to object to any stampeding or water throwing or about any of those amusements which make life worth living. A few days ago we had a row which went on for a complete day resulting in half the interpreters (interruptors) in France being present. But she is such a good hearty talker that there was little to do but listen. She started off early in the morning and one of the fellows, half awake, asked what the new gramophone record was! However, on the whole things go very well and we try to do good. The other day, though, there was a bit of a fuss. We had nothing much to do so we captured one of her cocks and after a good chase got another from a neighbouring farmyard. Things were becoming interesting when the good lady came in so we had to scatter the cocks in a hurry. The major who had wandered up and was enjoying the show had to scurry round one side of the building while she came round the other side and cut for it. You see, it is most improper for COs to attend cockfights.

The outside observer might often have taken such behaviour as simply the expression of high spirits in young men, more particularly young men with a public school upbringing involving many japes and practical jokes. Often they may have been. When Kay put up a punchbag in his hut for exercise, he soon had to take it down when the whole squadron insisted on punching it at all hours or swinging on the shock absorbers. Best to send to London for babies' rattles, Kay wrote in disgust. In the same frivolous manner six men dived on a one pound tin of chocolates which Thieta got in a parcel from home and 'fought a tremendous scrap before the chocolates were handed round in the usual civilized manner'.

The degree of violence used, nevertheless, seems to imply that more was involved than just high spirits on many occasions. Black eyes and sore elbows were only at the start of things. Even games quickly got beyond Queensberry, so that Fullard once reckoned himself saved from a breakdown by breaking a leg in a football game and gaining leave. Two examples from many may serve for example, the one of a typical squadron rag, the other equally typical of horseplay between men in the squadron.

One of the squadrons at Izel le Hameau were having a party when some of its members decided to raid the mess of another squadron. Armed with Verey light pistols, one or two climbed on to the roof and fired them down the chimney. This started off a 'battle' between the two squadrons and very soon Verey lights were being fired off into the air in all directions. Some of the more sober fellows on the aerodrome climbed up and kicked these off before they could start a fire. It was like a gigantic Guy Fawkes' night celebration and those concerned seemed to be enjoying it a lot until someone firing a Verey pistol at random hit the CO of another squadron behind the ear, severely injuring him. He was taken to hospital where he died during the night. It was a tragic end to a very wild evening.

It was no good going to bed if you did not feel like any more of the hilarity. During the pause someone would ask 'Where is so and so? Let's get him out'. The whole flight would then crowd into his small room and throw themselves on to his bed. It was a frightening experience in the dark. One night, they were all on top of me and making a frightful racket and refusing to go away. I got rather desperate and picked up my oil lamp which had the usual glass funnel and hit Eustace Grenfell over the head, shattering the glass. He hardly noticed the blow. The paraffin flowed over the bed. I felt something warm dripping over my hand and shouted all the more since I realized it was blood. I shouted that someone was bleeding badly. They only laughed and shouted all the more. It took several minutes to make them understand that something was really wrong. Someone fetched a torch and we discovered that Grenfell was bleeding from a deep cut in the head. He appeared next day with his head wrapped in bandages.

I had visions of trouble for striking my senior officer but all was smiles right up to the CO. I think I had established myself by standing up for myself in that rowdy C flight.

This was the same flight which used to throw cigarette tins filled with petrol down anteroom chimneys!

Such incidents suggest strongly that there was a deeper root to horseplay than just youthful exuberance. In this horseplay those tensions usually hidden were by common consent allowed to have expression, and through this shared display of deepest feelings men could come together and assert their unity in seeing the job through.

Yet however sustaining all these institutional devices might be in drawing out a man's endurance, in the end the pressures of flight broke every pilot and always it was the CO's task to measure the process of wear. He would stand by the runway as each flight took off and receive each flight back to base, notebook in hand. In this flying book, each sortie would be noted in ink against the name of each pilot, with hourages or notes on morale added in pencil. Army book No. 129 with its A4 pages was ideal for the purpose, neatly fitting the CO's commodious patch pockets.

The CO had the power to break routine if he noted signs of wear. When Balfour crash landed his DH2 and then almost immediately crushed his fingers in a deck chair, CO Smith-Barry sent him for a spell of leave without question. Dispatch to base or to Paris to pick up a new machine was a favourite pretext for such periods of recovery, since it was tacitly accepted that the ferryman might wait for the skies to clear for up to a fortnight before returning. Style of behaviour was tacitly accepted too. In a letter to the War Office in September 1916 embassy man Leroy Lewis wrote that 'Navarre [the French ace] is a respectable mechanic and certainly not the leader of a gang of apaches [name for Parisian hoodlums at the time]. He is rather mad and on one occasion took all his clothes off in a restaurant here. He behaves quite as well as our aviators whose conduct the assistant provost marshal informs me leaves on occasions much to be desired.'

But in the end there was no substitute for home leave as a stabilizer. Bishop once wrote: 'When I reached England, I found I was in a very nervous condition. I could not keep still. After a week I found I was getting quieter and realized that my leave was doing me the world of good.' Such leave, introduced in November 1914 and originally for seven days, had by late 1917 grown to fourteen days, which came after about two or three months' active service or so Ira Jones thought. Six months' fighting and three resting had become a common pattern in the last two years, when fighter activity became intensive. The essence nevertheless was flexibility, the CO's judgement. Balfour thought himself twice saved from total collapse by being suddenly granted leave. In the early days of the war and after fifteen engagements with five killings, Lannoe Hawker likewise thought himself saved by such a leave – during which a lady in Exeter presented him with a white feather.

Memoirs all seem to recall leave with photographic clarity contrasting with the blurred memories of combat and aerodrome life. The crowded leave train departing with the excitement of a Derby day crowd in London. Clean sheets and pillows at Boulogne with clean clothes and a bath. The difficulty on board the Channel steamer of distinguishing between ASC clerk and front-line sniper. Then the homecoming, the startling sense of unreality and the awareness of just how much a civilian turned airman had come to accept tension as a normal state.

Perhaps pilots even more than soldiers sought solitude and silence and avoided civilians, because few in the England of 1917 seemed to grasp the size of the European war, let alone the experience of those fighting by proxy for the community. In 1917, 20 shilling Rolls-Royce shares stood at 64 shillings and the promising young composer Eric Coates was offering for sale 'four songs of the air services'. Customers were assured that 'they will enjoy singing these invigorating songs written in the vernacular of the service' whose titles were 'Ordered Overseas', 'Five and Twenty Bombers', 'Billy', 'The Finest Job of All'. Lee always thought the smell of France cleaner, and Whitehouse, like many, felt that he was shirking his responsibilities while on leave. Some, like Sholto Douglas, however, reacted to the remission from sentence of death by wilder behaviour. 'I must confess we often took the bit between our teeth.' Such men would link with old friends, drink the free champagne offered by Mrs Rosa Lewis at the Cavendish Hotel in Jermyn Street and then enjoy the open house and dry-fly fishing of rich society women like Mrs Dawney at Hillingdon Hall in Norfolk. Finally perhaps an extra day squeezed out of leave by volunteering to pilot a new machine back to France, using the day in London to buy oddments like a pipe, a propelling pencil, or a waterproof watch, and have flying kit dry-cleaned (cap 6d., tunic 2s., warm 3s. and gloves 6d.).

Shrewd use of such leaves by the CO could keep a man fighting right through, but if men cracked suddenly the CO would have to bring in the wing's medical officer. Diagnosis was the important thing. Men with over a hundred hours of flying were always likely to make a recovery, bachelors doing better than married men. In the short term, the prognosis for psychopaths was surprisingly found to be excellent and of anxiety-state men even better. Depressives and hysterics on the other hand were poor risks – like poorly educated men, men who in peacetime were in clerical work, pilots who had been involved in aerial fires or in direct hits from anti-aircraft shells. Such men would be sent quietly to the lines of communication. The rest would be given eight hours of sleep in a warm room followed by periodic doses of barbiturates to give periods of forty-eight hours' sleep with 5-gram caffeine tablets every ten hours between sleep. Just as with shell-shocked infantry, the speed of diagnosis and the selection of treatment were the crucial factors. War's mental casualties had to be prevented from becoming fixated upon their own symptoms. In the end, 48 per cent of those treated for what at the time was called either Flying Sickness D or Aviators' Neurasthenia were returned to full flying duty, 60 per cent to partial duty.

War was after all the game of young men and the resilience of young men was the capital freely given which squadron commanders invested. There had always been, in addition, an original decision in becoming a fighter pilot which, together with the supportive mechanisms evolved within fighting squadrons and personified by that subtle blend of leading and following implicit in a good squadron commander's exercise of authority, meant that the great majority of fighter pilots saw the business through. In addition, every pilot knew that as a last resort he could declare himself a coward without risking the firing squad which faced an infantryman making such a decision. Perhaps this safety net was the necessary supportive mechanism which underpinned all the others.

17
AFTER THE WAR

The end of the war was greeted on the fighter aerodromes in the same unexpected way as in the infantry regiments. Wrote one pilot: 'On news of the armistice, the thin spread of enthusiasm which bound the fighting services together seemed to snap. I remember the next three months with greater horror than all the rest of my experience – the depression, the demoralization.' RAF Christmas cards for that first Christmas of peace certainly support the subjective impression of Lieutenant Baker. Typical was the card of 82 Wing, which showed an aeroplane dropping bombs labelled back pay, pensions, civilian suits and blood money. The mood on aerodromes was thus one of resentment at the loss of four years, resentment at the uneven way in which burdens had been shared.

Air minister Sir William Weir was well aware of this mood. 'The situation regarding demobilization in France has ugly possibilities,' he wrote. 'We would appear to be on the edge of a volcano due to the amount of unrest among the men. It would be an excellent thing if we could induce Trenchard to go round all units in France explaining to the men the position and the steps being taken. His influence with the force is so great I feel sure he could prevent any trouble.'

In the end the job was successfully done with a judicious combination of discretion and veiled coercion. Regarding the first, crucial men like Sergeant-major McQueen of 3 Squadron would be startled to receive Rumanian medals 'for continuous devotion to duty and setting a splendid example'. Aerodrome NCOs in turn would find an extension of off-duty ease and lessons arranged for civilian rehabilitation. Such military duties as remained would be most carefully cushioned. 'Send twelve lorries of men. On no account are the lorries to be overcrowded. The comfort of the men is the first consideration. Do the journey in easy turns.'

The veiled coercion came in the actual demobilization process.

35. The pilot's nightmare – an enemy on the tail. Distance about 100 yards, the ace's favourite. The victim's plan would be to delay until the last moment, then turn hard into the opponent's firing pass. If the opponent was diving or climbing on to the tail, a climbing turn was standard evasion. But at the distance in the photo, if the machine behind was guided by an ace, prognosis was poor.

36. The Canadian William Bishop (middle) was second in the British scoring list. Seventy-six enemy were claimed for him in a flying career of six months, twenty-five of them in the last twelve days. Bishop's trademark was that he was one of the few who could survive and score in the crowded skies of 1918. He represented too the spearhead of the Canadian fighter pilots who made up about one third of the RAF by the end of the war and supplied a disproportionate number of our high-scoring pilots.

37. The professionalism of the German back-up service is suggested by the policy of moving aeroplanes by train or road so as to cut down loss of life away from the battle zone. The village here is typically northern French. Attitudes in the photo are identical to those of our own RFC mechanics and ASC labourers.

38. Werner Voss, highest-scoring Jewish ace of the war, was the son of a Frankfurt tailor. He looked after his own machine and invariably flew in full dress uniform with a silk shirt. McCudden, one of the team who shot him down, wrote after a classic duel: 'As long as I live I shall never forget my admiration for that German pilot who, single-handed, fought seven of us for ten minutes and put some bullets through all our machines. His flying was wonderful, his courage magnificent.' The possession of a highly tuned motor bike he shared with many fliers; the Blue Max which hangs at his throat in the photo he shared with few.

39. During 1917 and 1918, the years of hardest fighting, German aeroplanes were at least our equals.
Prince of them was the Fokker D7, with its welded-steel fuselage and thick-section cantilever wings.
The specially developed BMW engine was a model of reliability and particularly good at high altitude,
where it was more agile than any of our machines. It was therefore the only aeroplane mentioned
by name in the Treaty of Versailles. Here in the photo is Ernst Udet, with sixty-two victories
the highest-scoring ace to survive the war for Germany.

40. Oswald Boelke was probably the greatest
German fighter pilot. A pupil of Immelmann,
he was the pioneer of team fighting and set an
aggressive example. When he was killed in an
accident, Richthofen, who took over Boelke's
squadron, maintained its customs. They would
live under canvas just fifteen miles from the
front, sitting in deck chairs and waiting for the
allies to appear. If necessary, the squadron
would go up five times daily. Even Richthofen
was puzzled by Boelke's ability to score a
victory on almost every flight. Boelke's
explanation was that, since he flew so close, his
opponents were bound to fall down. The strain
of fighter fighting is seen vividly in Boelke's
taut face and claw-like hands. The decoration
round his throat is Germany's highest — the
Pour la Mérite, or Blue Max.

41. Preparing for a flight. A quarter of all wind over 10,000 feet blows at 40 mph or more, while a ground temperature of 60 degrees Fahrenheit would become minus 13 at 20,000 feet. To counter this, the pilot would have underwear of cellular cotton and silk, with several thicknesses of pullovers over it. Fur boots and muskrat-lined gauntlets over silk inners protect the hands and feet, while a Nuchwang dogskin-lined leather flying helmet would be fitted later over the balaclava. Fur-lined triplex goggles would be surrounded by whale oil smeared over the face, then covered with a leather face mask. Even so, bitter cold was an enduring experience for the fliers, since by 1918 much fighting was taking place around 20,000 feet, at which height breath iced goggles and the propeller barely gripped the rarefied air. Although the two rankers in the photo look like RFC men, they are in fact German. The pilot is Baron Richthofen.

All drafts would be made up of one officer, five NCOs and 250 men, and travel was arranged in such a way that these units were kept apart: 5, 7, 25 Squadrons were separated by two-day intervals at the staging points of Argus and Dunkirk before dispersal in England at widely separated points – Lincoln, Bicester and Salisbury. There the men would first be given form P4A C10913, which placed them formally on the unemployed list and gave a date on which last pay would be drawn. In the form, a pilot would find that though he retained the rank of lieutenant or captain, 'this does not confer the right to wear uniform except on state or ceremonial occasions. If uniform is worn, dress must be that which is appropriate to the occasion.' In addition came the *Service & Release Book* which gave re-mobilization instructions and warned that the Official Secrets Acts of 1911 and 1920 made it an offence to divulge information acquired in service overseas. The all-important Clearance Certificate would be handed over only after the pilot had digested the cheerless information which served for the thanks of the service. It might seem that higher authority regarded its own men with greater suspicion than the enemy they had been shooting down. Certainly the men seemed undisturbed by it all. They wanted only to forget, so that though several squadrons advertised re-union dinners in 1919 there were few follow-ups in 1920. More common were advertisements like Lieutenant Wright's in the *Aeroplane* – 'RAF blue suit. Breeches. Overcoat with khaki tunic, cap and badges. Nearly new. £18.'

Aeroplanes were dispersed with equal briskness. Reduced from 188 to fifty-one squadrons within twelve months, the RAF sent its surplus machinery to its salvage store at Waddon, near Croydon, as if the peace of the world were assured. Disabled service men at Waddon – with much trade-union protest – sorted surplus ranging from 10,000 airframes and 30,000 engines to 667 yards of white shock absorber cord, a third of a million sparking plugs, 1,000 tons of ball bearings and 85 hundredweight of aircraft glue. There was little interest. By 1920 anyone could buy a complete Bristol two-seater fighter with a 300 hp Hispano Suiza engine for £800 or a Sopwith Snipe with a 200 hp Bentley rotary engine for £700. A reader of the *Aeroplane* might find even better bargains: 'Avro 504K in perfect order. £40 or would take motor cycle in exchange.'

This spirit of the bargain basement seemed to apply to the whole air service after the war, as if it were an unwanted, illegitimate child. 'Make up your mind whether you would like to go to the War Office or to the Admiralty and let me know by tomorrow,' wrote Lloyd George to Winston Churchill in December 1918. 'You can take the air with you in either case. I am not going to keep it a separate department.' Such indifference was not peculiar to the prime minister. When during August 1918 the Air Council had circulated both army and navy with a memorandum calling for ideas on the post-war function of the air service, neither bothered to reply.

In an immediate sense, authority was quite right. A strong case might be made that the way in which an expensive air service had been used for over three years bore no relation to the way in which the land war had developed after the initial period of single trench line and simple frontal attack by both sides. In this earlier phase the problem had been straight-forward. Eye and camera, by pre-empting surprise and directing counter-offensive artillery, made war as staff college men knew it impossible. The role of the RFC was thus to prevent enemy reconnaissance machines from operating while getting their own information at the same time.

The Trenchard–Haig policy statements of RFC, GHQ expressed the British solution in formal language. Ira Jones put it more expressively with the authority of intelligent man and ace fighter pilot.

What was the function of the airman during the war? It was to obtain information quickly and with as much accuracy as the conditions allowed. This job was almost confined to the slow, cumbersome two-seater. What was then the fighter's duty? His duty was to shoot down the enemy's two-seaters with high-speed scouts. What then was the most important task in the air as the war developed? To shoot down the enemy's fighting scouts so that our two-seaters could carry out their vital duties of reconnaissance and cooperate with the infantry and artillery. A contest between a high-speed scout and a slow, cumbersome two-seater was an unequal contest and however valiant the occupants would invariably end in the downfall of the two-seater. It was therefore the gladiatorial affrays between the high-speed fighters which became the acknowledged combat. Shooting down a two-seater was regarded as good and essential work but nothing to boast about for the fighter pilot. By carrying the fight deep into enemy territory, the British established the ascendancy of a superior attacker and thus won renown for offensiveness which puzzled and irritated the enemy to the point of despair. Boelke at first called it stupid and impudent. Richthofen called it foolhardiness and recklessness. This constant cracking of the whip of the offensive, this unending defiance of the grim Prussian-disciplined Moloch produced an inferiority complex which finally hampered the offensive spirit of the enemy airmen and pinned them over their own lines.

The fact that Jones was incorrect on the effectiveness of the German two-seater or of the tactics of German single-seaters is less important than his endorsement of the Haig-Trenchard policy line and indeed at the time, there were few doubts among fighting men. Samson's Standing Orders for the Royal Naval Air Service spoke of the need to attack the enemy whenever he was sighted. Evasive manœuvres were never to be used in the RNAS, for they were 'not the conduct required of a naval officer'. Samson need not have worried. As Richthofen wrote, 'I hardly ever encountered an Englishman who refused battle.' The typical flight lieutenant (and future air marshal) John Slessor thought that the offensive spirit alone pulled the RFC through Bloody April 1917.

The great question, unasked until well into 1917, is just what was being achieved by this offensive policy or, put another way, whether it mattered at all if German two-seaters flew over the British army and reported on its intentions. During 1915 the enemy certainly had to be checked, for British attacks aimed at surprise in the spirit of Henderson, who had been the chief teaching influence at Camberley Staff College on the Great War generation of generals. Haig for example was intensely proud of the ruses he used at Neuve Chapelle in the early summer of 1915 was not to try again until the Cambrai raid late in 1917. In the years between, the British army fell under the influence of Pétain's papers analysing the great French offensives in the Champagne during 1915. According to Pétain, surprise had been made ineffective by the construction of trench lines in depth, on reverse slopes and protected by wire and machine guns. Against such positions, weight of artillery was the only possible means of breach. Each battle therefore saw new permutations in weight, duration and type of barrage, width of front attacked and numbers of infantry involved in order to hold the ground captured by artillery, but since there was no way in which the amount of artillery pieces involved could be concealed, little attempt was ever made to hide it and add the element of surprise. Instead, the new aim was to wear the enemy down with artillery attacks at a number of places and then break through in a breach made by artillery on a wide front where the enemy could not afford to give ground.

Haig put these guiding views succinctly on many occasions. In May 1917 he wrote, 'The guiding principles on which my general scheme of action is based are those which have proved successful in war from time immemorial viz. that the first step must always be to wear down the enemy's power of resistance until he is so weakened that he will be unable to withstand the decisive blow.' Of battles involved in the wearing and breaking, Haig wrote in February 1917, 'As a result of past experience it may definitely be said that in view of the great and prolonged preparation required, the enemy cannot be suprised as to the general front of an attack on a large scale but only to some extent as to the exact limits and the moment of assault.' In this way, it only made sense to launch a massive air attack barring the skies to enemy two-seaters at most just on the eve of a land assault.

From First Ypres onwards on the other hand, German offensive strategy was of an altogether different type. In his *Notes on Offensive Battles* published during February 1918, Ludendorff remarked on the contrast with British strategy. Their attacks, he observed, were based invariably on artillery schedules, skilfully worked out but rigid, whose aim was to carry forward the infantry who supplied no impetus of their own. Despite very considerable initial tactical success, he wrote, the fact that commanders ceased to have influence on their own men after zero condemned such artillery-based attacks to failure. Describing his own attacks, he required that artillery activity should be dependent on infantry advance with infantry commanders at every level having full discretion right up to the high command, whose place was on the battlefield and whose function was to direct reserves so as to get behind the rear of units on the flank of the breach and so roll up and widen the gap. With papers of his own on Verdun and the Russian front, Haig well knew the German pattern, which didn't change throughout the war. As he wrote in March 1917, 'The Germans are wholehearted believers in the principle that offensive on the greatest scale driven home with the utmost rapidity, violence and determination is the only method of forcing a quick decision.'

If the German break was to be achieved with minimum of artillery, the secret massing of infantry was crucial. The enemy therefore devised ways of defeating aerial reconnaissance as it was then practised. In their only major west front offensive before 1918, the Germans at Verdun made use of broken, forested ground to conceal their concentrations. A year later on the east front at Riga in 1917 the Germans hit on yet more efficient methods of obtaining surprise. Artillery was put in position by night just five days before the attack, and heavy mortars just two days before. Assault infantry had meanwhile been gathered 120 km back for final training, then moved up by stages at night to arrive in the jump-off trenches the night before.

The success of such methods was such that Haig's intelligence summary five days before the great German attack in March 1918, which all but drove the British army out of France, read as follows: 'No serious attack is to be expected south of the Bapaume road', where the critical attack was in fact delivered. The British were not alone in their blindness. In a paper analysing the German attack of 27 May 1918, the French Second Bureau noted that their aerial photographic work had detected no abnormal movement and that in five days the Germans had moved twenty-three divisions by road undetected at night. The paper's conclusion was that a major German attack gave few preliminary signs. Whether that should have been the case is another matter. Dining with British ministers during July 1918, King Albert of Belgium expressed incredulity that the enemy should have been able to move up such large bodies of men undetected, to achieve an overwhelming surprise. Where had the night fliers using searchlights been, he asked. Then he went on embarrassingly to note the fixation of the RAF upon fighting and bombing rather than on reconnaissance work. Though superior in numbers and bravery, Albert concluded, the Germans made better use of their smaller forces and were superior in the strategy of the air. The documents fail to record any British answer.

Whatever the justice of Albert's strictures, it seems clear that both sides invested disproportionately in fighter aeroplanes, imagining that the blinding of the aerial eye was important and could only be done through single-seater work. Yet whatever the divergence in battle strategy, reconnaissance by either side after the early days seems to have become almost irrelevant. Haig made no attempt to conceal his intentions; Ludendorff's could not be divined from the air.

The surface appearance of quick rejection of a fighting service with little practical value and of dispersal of personnel without trace or effect is nevertheless incorrect. The impact of the Great War in the air proved as disproportionately large as the resources invested for the duration in such a numerically insignificant arm.

But the most immediate impact was on the pilots involved. Trenchard had shrewdly remarked that the man who had gone straight from school to a short-term commission was unlikely to make a satisfactory civilian, for some years at any rate. War had meant living in the short term, and ingrained habits and rhythms of living unrelated to anything outside the war zone. It had left memories too. As Sholto Douglas wrote: 'The years of the first war provided us with an experience that was so extraordinary that it was impossible to understand immediately what it all meant, so profound that it was to alter the whole course of our lives. We had scarcely more than begun to know what living meant but we all knew about dying and for many, the experience was to leave upon some minds the deepest scars.'

Writing much later, Cecil Lewis identified the most enduring of such scars:

How different a battlefield looked from the ground. It was a desolation unimaginable from the air. The earth no longer had its smooth, familiar face. It was a diseased, rancid thing stinking of death. Yet (oh the catch at the heart!) among the devastated cottages, the tumbling twisted trees, the desecrated cemeteries the poppies were growing. Clumps of crimson poppies. As we stood gazing, a lark rose from amongst them and mounted over the diapason of the guns. We listened, watched and then I remember trudged slowly on down the road without a word. That morning seems stranger than most to me now for Pip is dead, twenty years dead, and I can still see the lark over the guns, hear the flop and shuffle of our rubber-soled flying boots on the dusty road.

Combined with such deep memories were habits which made re-integration into civilian life the more difficult. Early in 1919 the *Aeroplane* was already warning against the continued use of such wartime specifics as morphine, heroin and opium and remarking too upon the notoriety of RAF Clubmen for the speed and recklessness of their driving and their habit of leaving cars parked in the road outside the club – a thing unusual at the time. Similar erratic patterns showed in the sky. Hartney noted how few pilots adapted to civilian flying after the war. Barker and Beauchamp-Proctor both died in post-war flying accidents. So did Carter (thirty-one killings), when the Fokker D7 he was stunting collapsed in the air. Meanwhile Coli, Navarre (flying under the Arc de Triomphe) and Nungesser (crossing the Atlantic solo) were killing themselves flying abroad. Perhaps more typical than such spectacular indiscretions was the issuing of a summons to Captain Jones in November 1920 for dropping a wreath from an aeroplane on the Henley Cenotaph on Armistice Day. The issuing agent was police inspector Adlem, himself a former war pilot, who dropped the summons from an aeroplane before looping over Jones's house. Such wild men were not easily digested. The following was typical of many. 'Over 2,000 flying hours. Requires post as pilot. RAF Captain. Practical engineer and understanding of rigging and erecting of machines. Prewar pilot. Any type of machine. Go anywhere. Box 4587. The *Aeroplane*.'

The parents of those reported 'Missing' during the war formed a larger group of scarred people than the former fighter pilots. Death in the sky miles above the ground made certainty even rarer than in the ground war, with its high-explosive blast.

To get immediately in touch with the Red Cross in Geneva, which handled all such correspondence from both sides, was the first task of a missing man's parents. Geneva's request was just for name, regiment, rank and date of disappearance. No photos were wanted, money would gain no advantage, handwriting had to be as legible as possible. Then there was nothing to do but wait.

After the war, the grave hunt began. For the purpose, twenty officers had been chosen by the War Graves Commission, paid 15 francs daily and issued with motor cycle and sidecar. They worked from lists supplied by the German Graves Commission and from the April 1918 issue of the newspaper *Die Welt*, which put all machines shot down in place on a handsome wall map. Typical of the thoroughness of the Commission's work was a report on a body which was unrecognizable but had a DFC ribbon on rotting uniform and the tailor's name of Lewis Moses of New Oxford Street still decipherable.

Certainty was nevertheless established only after a protracted searching. John Caldwell was an example. Reported missing on 29 August 1918, the telegram reached his parents on 1 September, though classification as 'Dead' rather than 'Missing' occurred only on 4 April 1921, when the Berlin Red Cross discovered that Caldwell had fallen victim to Jasta 5. Shot down in flames, artillery action had prevented his burial. Parents wrote back whether the body survived. They gave a description – fine teeth, height of five feet ten inches, always a green handkerchief in the top pocket. Then three weeks later they wrote asking if he might not still be a prisoner of war. Only in August 1922 was the correspondence concluded with the War Office payment of £94 18s. 4d. in back pay, after £1 16s. 8d. had been deducted for over-issue of mess allowance and flying pay covering the last three days of the week in which he had been killed.

For a bereaved family all that remained of their son was the contents of a little parcel sent home from the squadron. A. J. Fisher is an example. He had been a member of 21 Squadron, with sixteen and a half hours' dual and seventeen and a half hours' solo flying experience before being ordered to France on 13 September 1916. Two days later he was killed in combat by Richthofen with just four hours and twenty-five minutes of war experience. When his flight got back to aerodrome, they opened the envelope on his bedside table and found a cheque to pay for champagne all round. Razor, cigarette case and propelling pencil went to Fisher's pilot friends. What remained was sent home: four shirts, six collars, nine pairs of socks; two uniforms and flying kit; brushes and combs; dirty washing; a squash racket. Finally a letter from West End tailors Welton and Head. This letter stated that the firm was sending two pairs of puttees for Fisher's choice. There was a cloth pair at 12s. 6d. and a silk pair at the same price – 'the last word in swank'. This letter then referred to a previous purchase by Fisher. 'We have done our best to give you a topping pair of swanky bags that will make your brother officers blue with envy.' The body from which this letter had been taken had been so badly broken that the squadron had difficulty fitting it into its coffin. On receiving

the news, Fisher's parents requested that his age (twenty-one) be
specially engraved on the headstone with the inscription 'He lies
with England's heroes in the watchful eye of God'.

Another memorial document which survives in the RAF
museum is the last letter home of the Irish ace McElroy. It is dated
29 July 1918, just two days before his death, and has deep fold
lines and torn edges.

> Dear Mother. This morning I received your letter and also
> one from Eileen. I am glad you are having a good holiday. I am
> sure little Jack is very happy. Quite at home and very happy.
> The weather here continues to be rainy and hazy so we are doing
> little flying and I have seen no Huns for a week. I am anxious
> to get started as I am now third on the list of leading airmen. I
> expect my DSO to get through in a few days. I still expect my
> leave towards the end of September. I shall probably spend four
> or five days in England. Of course I shall have to give Drogheda
> a day. High flying seems to take a lot out of me but I am getting
> an oxygen set. Otherwise I am feeing very fit. Love to all at
> Killycreighton. Your loving son, George.

To families bereaved, the cost of such things was beyond calculation. Long after the reparations of war had been declared void
and handsome annuities paid to commanders, the overwhelming
burden remained. Albert Ball's father bought the field in which his
son had come down and laid a concrete path along the route taken
by his body to the nearby field hospital. The circumstances of
Ball's death could never be mentioned in front of his mother right
up to her death in 1931.

In another critical area the air fighter war left an impression
whose depth could not possibly be gauged in the immediate post-
war period: its effect on the second war.

The first impact was in the area of aircraft production, the defence
of London and the involvement of Britain's ablest scientists in all
aspects of technological developments in the air.

In June 1919 Grey, editor of the *Aeroplane*, described that war
as having been short and fairly virulent, leaving less damage than
the Thirty Years War. Later, he predicted, the Great War would
come to be seen as having performed a valuable function as a short,
sharp scrap giving a useful lesson in organization for the real race

war which would be coming in ten years or so. Grey, after all, was well connected. The *procès-verbal* of the war cabinets of 1918 show that such practical views were frequently discussed by the well-informed.

So far as bulk production of a complex engineering proposition like the fighting aeroplane went, Grey was correct, the first three years of the Great War demonstrating at what cost the idea of two basic fighter types and the techniques of rapid production had been developed. On the eve of war, the British aeroplane industry was producing about a hundred aeroplanes annually, with a firm like Sopwith's needing to turn their factory into a skating rink each weekend to remain solvent. The problems associated with developing from such a slender base were inevitably numerous – shortage of skilled men, absence of electrical components, lack of experience with the internal combustion engine and so on. Practical examples best show the scale of the problem. As late as spring 1917, when 1,500 separate firms were involved in aeroplane manufacture and forty separate engines were being used, it was reckoned to take thirty-four weeks from approval of an airframe to bulk production, or sixty-four weeks for the same process with a new engine.

The peak of crisis was in fact touched early in 1917. British factories were then managing to produce only thirty magnetos weekly and half the number of ball-races required. Needing 2,000 engines monthly, the RFC were getting 600. Even the supply of silver spruce was critical. Only the piracy of 1,122 tons of West Virginian spruce en route to Russia saved the situation. Rolls-Royce, meanwhile, makers of the only fully satisfactory aero engine, were called before the Air Board and threatened with direct take-over by the Ministry of Munitions for obstructionist methods. Rolls-Royce merely replied by restating their view that dominion of the air in the long term was a higher task than fighting the war and made no effort to increase production beyond a couple of dozen engines weekly, or even to release design details to Pearce Arrow, their American contractors.

This crisis was settled with remarkable rapidity. Between October 1917 and August 1918 the air force required 22,000 engines and got 31,240. Then, during the great German offensive of March 1918, the RFC requested 1,993 machines to replace those lost and got 2,259. These improvements were reflected even more strongly in components. When the war began, annual production was of

1,140 magnetoes and 5,000 sparking plugs; when the war ended the figures were 128,637 and 2,148,726 respectively. Even Rolls-Royce had turned out 6,554 engines by the time of the armistice – more than any other single manufacturer.

Crucial catalyst in this transformation was Lloyd George, who, in the words of his parliamentary private secretary, 'gathered round himself in the early days a general staff of British industry'. At the top he harmonized private enterprise by separating design and supply and then put the Ministry of Munitions and Air Board into a single building – the Hotel Cecil – so that all operations were under a single roof. For designers and producers in the scattered units of manufacture the Ministry produced 'Instructions to builders'. 'Nothing is to be left to the experience or judgement of manu-facturers' this pamphlet announced – and then went on with a numbered list of instructions, phrased with beautiful clarity and accompanied by illustrations at every step 'that may be readily understood by any sub-contractor'. Then in the wake of such booklets, which gathered the best practices of the time, came a host of inspectors, so that every single part of a military aeroplane required the official stamp before it was accepted. Nor was the Welsh Carnot without that shrewd touch which was necessary to lubricate such radical changes in technique. Profit margins he increased from 6 to 20 per cent. It was LG who thus showed how the skills and cupidities of private industry could be reconciled with the national interest, thereby placing the roots of the great Battle of Britain fighters firmly in the later stages of the Great War.

The fighter aerodromes of the Battle of Britain likewise repre-sented just re-birth, for in June 1918 there had been a workforce of 65,000 building such aerodromes as Biggin Hill, Rochford, Hainault, Suttons Farm, North Weald and Woodham Mortimer for the defence of London and to a standard 100 acre pattern. The very system of London's defence overall was simply based on Percy Scott's original formulation to beat the Gothas and Giants of the Great War. Scott's system laid down a ring of 475 AA guns, 500 searchlights, thirty-three airfields equipped with flares for night landings and early warning stations on the coast or on ships moored in the Thames estuary which phoned warnings straight through to the Horse Guards, which in turn phoned them through to the aerodromes. Even the radar, which played such a crucial role, had begun its life in the earlier war when young Watson-Watt was

using cathode ray tubes to track thunderstorms on behalf of the
Meteor weather reporting service which gave information in advance to GHQ in France.

Indeed, the intimate link between university scientists and engineers on the one hand and the war effort on the other symbolized
by radar had been created during the first war and largely for the
air service. It went back to Thomas Hopkinson, professor of applied
mechanics at Cambridge University, who had joined the sappers
at the start of the war. Realization of the technical complexities of
the new war led to his being brought home to head Lord Fisher's
Board of Inventions and Research and empowered to select his
own men. This he did largely from among promising young dons
at Oxford and Cambridge like Lindemann and Tizzard. Though
Hopkinson relied chiefly on twenty or thirty pilots at a time on
leave from France to man his Experimental Flight, the scientists
themselves realized the need for direct experience in the new field.
Their most famous flight was probably Lindemann's in bowler and
winged collar, notebook and pencil on knee to record instrument
readings in a downward spin and thus finally cauterize the fears
which attached to the spin with a closely argued paper. Tizzard,
too, went solo after only three hours of dual flying and filled his
diary with notes on propellers dropping off, cylinders shed at
altitudes around fifty feet and flights into thunderstorms to see if
the wires would glow. He even came under artillery fire in the
course of his duties – from his own side – when delivering an early
model of the Sopwith Dolphin to France. Unknown in shape to
our gunners, it must have seemed distinctly Hunnish in wing
configuration.

The advanced state of experimental work in 1918 seemed
generally to be pointed ahead to a new type of war. The Farnborough wind tunnel in that year was analysing the wind flow of
prototypes, variable-pitch propellers were being built and a blind
flying device featuring radio beams of dots and dashes were indicating correct flight path. Camel fighters based on Biggin Hill were
also talking to each other in the air with two-way radio systems,
while their pilots sat on Wynn self-sealing rubberized petrol tanks
and parachutes weighing 30 pounds were squeezed into lockers
just fifteen inches square. Such developments were clearly the
result of this new marriage of science and war, with the patenting
of a gas turbine engine in 1920 followed by a jet engine patent in

1924 and indication of what might be achieved if the union were sustained.

The second aspect of the Great War's legacy to the second war was in the continuity of pilot tradition, passed from mouth to mouth, lying in files of letters, read in books, running underground like some medieval heresy. In this way Battle of Britian pilot Hall wrote of Immelmann, Voss and Boelke as having been the heroes of his boyhood; of his own anxiety too on joining up lest the same spirit did not still permeate the RAF. Later, flying over the wide plains of the Pas de Calais and Flanders, climbing the same spiral staircases as the Great War aces, he felt himself deeply moved, remembering how the burnt out machines of an earlier war had gathered like stubs in an ash tray. In the same spirit Hurricane pilot Paul Richey wrote of a posting to Berry au Bac, close to the Chemin des Dames:

> Poking about in the wood by the airfield we came across plenty of evidence of the Great War - old shell holes and trench systems, shrapnel scraps and even a sniper's tree post with neat steps cut up the trunk ... a memorial stood at the crossroads on the Laon-Rheims road with a plain granite crucifix, completely simple but bearing an inscription so beautiful and so striking that I have never forgotten it:
>> Ossements qu'animait un fier souffle naguère,
>> Membres épars, débris sans nom, humain chaos,
>> Pêle-mêle sacré d'un vaste reliquaire,
>> Dieu vous reconnaîtra, poussière de héros!

I thought of my father who had spent four long years in the trenches in the first world war and of the courage of millions of fighting men who had given their lives between 1914 and 1918. In peacetime, their sacrifice had been taken for granted and forgotten. But now that we stood on the ground on which they had fought and died, we shared a common bond. We caught something of the atmosphere of the old British Expeditionary Force and the RFC. And we all felt, I think, that we had a fine tradition of bravery and endurance to live up to. For myself, throughout the French campaign, I was strongly conscious of the example, the presence beside me almost, of my father.

LIST OF NAMES

(IWM: Imperial War Museum archive; RAF: RAF museum archive at Hendon; PRO: Public Record Office papers in Air 1)

Armstrong, W. — Fighter pilot and author of *Pioneer Pilot* (Blandford, 1952).

Bader, D. — Second war fighter pilot whose life is in P. Brickhill's *Reach for the Sky* (Collins, 1980).

Baker, J. — Fighter pilot with a brief memoir in PRO 2389.

Balfour, H. — Fighter pilot and author of *An Airman Marches* (Hutchinson, 1933).

Ball, Albert — Fighter pilot described by contemporaries Maund and Hill in PRO 2387 and in Chaz Bowyer's *Albert Ball* (Kimber, 1977).

Baring, Maurice — Trenchard's personal aide whose account is in *Flying Corps Headquarters* (Blackwood, 1968).

Barker, William — Fighter pilot ranking seventh in the British list. Short biography in W. Musciano's *William Barker* (Hobby Helpers, 1964).

Bartlett, C. — Two-seater pilot and author of *Bomber Pilot* (Allen, 1974).

Beauchamp-Proctor, A. — Fighter pilot ranking fifth in the British list. Personal material in RAF 77.38.2 and 73.35.

Bewsher, P. — Fighter pilot and author of *Green Balls* (Blackwood, 1919).

Biard, H. — Fighter pilot and author of *Wings* (Hurst and Blackett).

Bishop, William — Fighter pilot ranking second in the British list. Author of *Winged Warfare* (Bailey, 1975).

Boelke, Oswald — Fighter pilot ranking tenth in the German list and described in J. Werner's *Knight of Germany* (Arno, 1972).

Brancker, Sefton — Director General of Military Aeronautics 1914-15, then Director of Air Organization 1916-17 before going to the Air Council in 1918. Described by N. Macmillan in *Sefton Brancker* (Heinemann, 1935).

Bridgman, L. — Author of *The Clouds Remember* (Gale and Polden).

Buckley, H.	Author of *Squadron 95* (Arno, 1972).
Burge, T.	Fighter pilot with a brief memoir in PRO 2389.
Burn, D.	Fighter pilot with a brief memoir in IWM pp/mcr/193.
Butcher, P.	Fighter pilot and author of *Skill and Devotion* (Radio Modeller, 1971).
Caldwell, John	Fighter pilot with material in RAF 72.2.1-2.
Campbell, Douglas	Fighter pilot ranking fourth in the American list.
Capper, J.	In charge of the school of military engineering 1911-17.
Cavan, 10th Earl of	Commander of 14th Corps and 10th Italian Army 1918.
Cheesman, J.	Fighter pilot with material in RAF 74.68.1.
Churchill, W. S. C.	Minister of Munitions with a seminal paper on the role of air in war, 21 October 1917.
Cloete, S.	Infantry subaltern. Author of *Victorian Son* (Collins, 1972).
Cock, Geoffrey	Fighter pilot, 'King of the Sopwith Strutters'.
Collishaw, Raymond	Fighter pilot and author of *Air Command* (Kimber, 1973). A brief memoir in PRO 2387. Ranked third in the British list.
Coppens, Willy	Fighter pilot ranking first in the Belgian list. Author of *Days on the Wing* (Hamilton).
Courtney, F.	Fighter pilot and author of *Flight Path* (Kimber, 1972).
Crundall, E.	Fighter pilot and author of *Fighter Pilot on the West Front* (Kimber, 1975).
Dorme, R.	Fighter pilot ranking ninth in the French list.
Douglas, Sholto	Fighter pilot and author of *Years of Combat* (Collins, 1963), with material in PRO 692 and 2386.
Dowding, H.	Fighter pilot described in B. Collier's *Leader of the Few* (Jarrolds, 1957).
Dugdale, G.	Infantryman. Author of *Langemarck to Cambrai* (Wilding, 1932).
Ellwood, A.	Fighter pilot with a brief memoir in PRO 2392.
Fisher, J.	Fighter pilot with material in RAF 76.99.1.
Flack, M.	Adviser on physiological research to the Medical Board, with a paper in the *Aeronautical Journal*, January-March 1919.
Fokker, A.	Leading German aeroplane manufacturer and author of *Flying Dutchman* (Routledge, 1931).
Fonck, René	Fighter pilot ranking first in the French list. Author of *Ace of Aces* (Doubleday, 1967).
Foster, R.	Fighter pilot with a brief memoir in PRO 2398.
Fry, W.	Fighter pilot and author of *Air of Battle* (Kimber, 1974).

Fullard, P.	Fighter pilot ranking ninth in the British list.
Garland, E.	Fighter pilot with material in IWM p359.
Gates, H.	Fighter pilot with material in RAF 76.58.
Gibbs, G.	Fighter pilot with a brief memoir in PRO 2388.
Grey, C.	Editor of the *Aeroplane*, which he founded in 1911.
Grierson, J.	Outstanding general earmarked for high command who died of a heart attack on the way out to the war.
Grinnell-Milne, D.	Fighter pilot and author of *Wind in the Wires* (Jarrolds, 1933).
Guynemer, G.	Fighter pilot ranking second in the French list. Described in *Guynemer* by H. Bordeaux (Chatto and Windus, 1918).
Haig, D.	Appointed Commander in Chief, BEF, in December 1915. The patron of Trenchard.
Hall, Bert	Fighter pilot and author of *One Man's War* (Hamilton).
Hall, R.	Fighter pilot of the second war and author of *Clouds of Fear* (Bailey, 1975).
Harris, Arthur	Fighter pilot and later author of *Bomber Offensive* (Collins, 1947).
Hartmann, A.	Fighter pilot in the second war and ace of aces. Described in R. Toliver's *The Blond Knight of Germany* (Barker, 1970).
Hartney, H.	Fighter pilot and author of *Wings over France* (Bailey, 1974).
Hawker, Lannoe	Fighter pilot, commander of the RFC's first fighter squadron and first fighter VC. Killed by Richthofen.
Henderson, D.	Director General of military aeronautics 1913-18. The hand behind the seminal Smuts Report which pointed to the future importance of bombing. Said Trenchard: 'He had twice the insight and understanding that I had.'
Henderson, G.	Staff College professor 1892-7 and perhaps the single greatest influence on the British High Command, with his emphasis on surprise and constant offensive.
Hill, M.	Fighter pilot with material in PRO 2387 and 2389.
Hillary, Richard	Fighter pilot in the second war and author of *The Last Enemy* (Macmillan, 1968).
Hoeppner, E.	Commander of the newly created German air force on the Somme, with Major Thomsen his Chief of Staff.

Hopkinson, H.   Professor of applied mechanics at Cambridge before the war and orchestrator of aerial research during it.

Howsam, W.   Fighter pilot with a brief memoir in PRO 2391.

Hucks, B.   Test pilot with a paper in the *Aeronautical Journal*, October–December 1917.

Immelmann, Max   Fighter pilot and author of *The Eagle of Lille* (Hamilton). First German ace.

Jacob, C.   Commander of the 2nd Corps from 1916 onwards and chosen to succeed Haig by the Smuts-Hankey mission in January 1918. Lloyd George did not act on the recommendation.

Johns, W.   Fighter pilot and author of *Fighting Planes and Aces* (Hamilton) and *The Air VCs* (Hamilton). Creator of Biggles.

Jones, H.   Author of the final five volumes of the official history of the air war.

Jones, Ira   Fighter pilot and author of *An Airfighter's Scrapbook* (Nicholson and Watson, 1938) and *Tiger Squadron* (Allen, 1954), books about his own war and that of his squadron. Biographer of Mannock in *King of the Air Fighters* (Nicholson and Watson, 1934). Material in RAF 76.43.467.

Kay, G.   Fighter pilot and author of *Letters from Bob* (Melville and Mullen).

Kingston-McCloughry, E.   Fighter pilot and author of *War in Three Dimensions* (Cape, 1949). A brief memoir in PRO 2389.

Knocker, A.   Fighter pilot with a brief memoir in PRO 2391.

Lanchester, F.   Aircraft manufacturer and author of *Aircraft in Warfare* (Constable, 1916).

Lee, A.   Fighter pilot and author of *No Parachute* (Kimber, 1968) and *Open Cockpit* (Jarrold, 1969). A memoir in PRO 2389.

Leigh-Mallory, T.   Fighter pilot with a brief memoir in PRO 2388.

Lewis, Cecil   Fighter pilot and author of *Sagittarius Rising* (Davies, 1936, and Penguin, 1979) and *Farewell to Wings* (Temple, 1964).

Lewis, D.   Fighter pilot and author of *Wings over the Somme* (Kimber, 1976).

Liddell Hart, B.   Seminal inter-war military writer while military correspondent of the *Daily Telegraph* 1925-35 and *The Times* 1935-9.

Lindemann, F.   Director of the Physical Laboratory, RAF Farnborough, and experimental pilot.

Long, S.   Fighter pilot and author of *Into the Blue* (Bodley Head, 1920).

Lucas, K.	Inventor of the RAF Mark 2 compass and turn indicator at Farnborough.
Lufberry, R.	Fighter pilot ranking third in the American list.
McConnell, J.	Fighter pilot and author of *Flying for France* (Doubleday, 1917). An American.
McCudden, J.	Fighter pilot ranking fourth in the British list. Author of *Five Years in the R FC* (The Aeroplane, 1919).
McElroy, E.	Fighter pilot ranking tenth in the British list and described in F. Gilbert's *McElroy of 40* (RAF museum).
McLanachan, W.	Fighter pilot and author of *Fighter Pilot* (Newnes). Known in his squadron as 'McScotch' to McElroy's 'McIrish'.
Maclaren, D	Fighter pilot ranking fifth in the British list. Canadian.
Macmillan, Norman	Fighter pilot and author of *Into the Blue* (Jarrolds, 1929).
Mannock, Edward	Fighter pilot ranking first in the British list. Described by Ira Jones in *King of the Air Fighters* (Nicholson and Watson, 1934). Valuable material in RAF 76.43.583 and DC71.51. Given a posthumous VC largely through the efforts of Winston Churchill.
Martin, R.	Fighter pilot with brief memoir in PRO 2391.
Maxse, Ivor	Commander of the 18th Division then 18th Corps before becoming Inspector General of Training in June 1918.
Milner, A.	*Éminence grise* behind Lloyd George, becoming Secretary of State for War in 1918.
Navarre, J.	French ace noted as much for his wild behaviour on leave as for his war exploits. Killed later trying to fly under the Arc de Triomphe.
Nivelle, R.	Replaced Joffre as army commander in December 1916 and architect of the ill-fated allied offensive of spring 1917.
Noble, W.	Fighter pilot and author of *With a Bristol Fighter Squadron* (Melrose, 1920).
Nungesser, C.	Fighter pilot ranking third in the French list.
Oliver, O.	Fighter pilot with papers in the Imperial War Museum.
Oughton, F.	Editor of *The Personal Diary of Mick Mannock* (Spearman, 1966).
Parker, Sidney	Fighter pilot and chief instructor of the Smith-Barry school at Gosport. Papers in RAF 74.181.9.
Parsons, E.	Fighter pilot and author of *Flight into Hell* (Long, 1938).

Pemberton-Billing, N.	RNAS pilot who planned the first long-distance bombing raid on the Zeppelin plant on Lake Constance. Then became an MP, bitterly criticizing Trenchard's conduct of operations. Involved in founding Supermarines.
Pétain, H.	Corps commander during the 1915 Artois offensive. The defender of Verdun, then successor to Nivelle after the latter's failure in spring 1917. Continued as army commander when Foch was made supreme commander in 1918.
Porter, H.	Fighter pilot and author of *Aerial Observation* (Harper, 1921).
Raleigh, W.	The first official historian of the air, appointed while a professor of English literature, never having flown in an aeroplane. Died soon after his appointment.
Reid, G.	Fighter pilot with material in RAF 76.254.10.
Rhys Davids, A.	Fighter pilot with material in PRO 822.
Richey, Paul	Fighter pilot in the second war and author of *Fighter Pilot* (Janes, 1981).
Richthofen, M.	Fighter pilot ranking first in the German list. Described in Gibbons' *The Red Knight of Germany* (Cassell, 1930).
Rickenbacker, Edward	Fighter pilot ranking first in the American list. Author of *Fighting the Flying Circus* (Bailey, 1973).
Roberts, E.	Fighter pilot and author of *Flying Fighter* (Harper, 1918).
Rochford, L.	Fighter pilot and author of *I Chose the Sky* (Kimber, 1977).
Salmond, J.	Director general of military aeronautics 1917 and commander in the field in succession to Trenchard in summer 1918.
Samson, C.	RNAS fighter pilot, first man to ascend from the flight deck of a moving ship in 1912 and author of *Fights and Flights* (Benn, 1930).
Saundby, Robert	Fighter pilot who shot down a Zeppelin in 1917.
Schleich, E. von	The German 'Black Knight' who shot down Dorme.
Schroder, H.	German fighter pilot and author of *An Airman Remembers* (Hamilton).
Scott, Percy	Gunnery specialist in the navy who was put in command of London's anti-Zeppelin defences in September 1915.
Smith-Barry, R.	Fighter pilot who organized the British training system during 1917. His career is described in F. Tredrey's *Pioneer Pilot* (Davies, 1976).

Sopwith, T.	Leading British manufacturer of war aeroplanes described in B. Robertson's *Sopwith - the Man and his Aircraft* (Air Review Ltd, 1970).
Springs, E.	Fighter pilot and author of *War Birds* (Hamilton, 1927). Ranked fifth in the American list.
Stark, R.	German fighter pilot and author of *Wings of War* (Hamilton, 1933).
Strange, L.	Fighter pilot and author of *Recollections of an Airman* (Hamilton, 1933).
Sykes, F.	AAG at the War Office in 1916 and bitter opponent of Trenchard. Replaced Trenchard as Chief of Air Staff in March 1918. Inventor of the RAF motto and author of *From Many Angles* (Harrap, 1942).
Tizzard, H.	Assistant controller of experiments and research, described in R. Clark's *Tizzard* (Methuen, 1965).
Trenchard, Hugh	Commander in the field of the RFC in 1915 with a period as Chief of Air Staff in 1918 before taking command of the Independent (bombing) Force. The biography by A. Boyle (Collins, 1962) must be regarded with extreme suspicion in its coverage of the Great War years.
Turner, C.	Author of *The Old Flying Days* (Sampson, Low) during the war.
Udet, E.	Fighter pilot ranking second in the German list. Author of *Ace of the Black Cross* (Newnes).
Vaughan, Gerald	American fighter pilot ranking fourth in their list.
Vincent, S.	Fighter pilot and author of *Flying Fever* (Jarrolds, 1972).
Voss, V.	Fighter pilot and author of *Flying Minnows* (Allen, 1977).
Voss, Werner	Fighter pilot ranking fourth in the German list.
Ward, H.	Fighter pilot with papers in IWM p356.
Weir, William	On the Air Board 1917-18. Director General of air production in the Ministry of Munitions before becoming Secretary of State for Air in April 1918.
Whitehouse, Arch	Fighter pilot and author of *The Fledgling* (Vane, 1964).
Williams, A.	Fighter pilot with a brief memoir in PRO 2389.
Winslow, C.	Fighter pilot and author of *With the French Flying Corps* (Constable, 1917).
Wortley, R.	Fighter pilot and author of *Letters from a Flying Officer* (Oxford, 1928).
Yeates, V.	Fighter pilot and author of *Winged Victory* (Cape, 1934).

NOTES ON SOURCES

The three chief archives used were the Air 1 collection at the Public Record Office, identified by the letters PRO and the box number of the material cited; the RAF Museum archive at Hendon, identified by the letters RAF and the piece number of the material; and the Imperial War Museum, identified by the letters IWM. Old printed sources I obtained chiefly at the RAF Museum or at the Cambridge University Library. The best easily available source of printed material in London is the West Hill public library in Wandsworth, which specializes in the first war and has nearly everything anybody but the specialist reader could want in its basement collection.

1 : Introduction
Statistics and copies of RFC policy statements are in the official history of W. Raleigh and H. A. Jones in six volumes. The *Digest of War Statistics* published by the Stationery Office in 1922 is also valuable, though one would prefer to see the copies in manuscript which were available to a handful of men at GHQ in the last two years of the war. On the nature of reconnaissance work, H. Porter's *Aerial Observation* (Harper, 1921) is good.

2 : Enlisting pilots
Volume 3 of the official history covers manpower. G. Campbell's *Casualties and Honours* at Hendon gives short biographies of every airman killed up to the autumn of 1917. Colonial statistics are in PRO 2424. G. Drew's *Canada's Fighting Airmen* (Maclean, 1931) gives personal detail. Medical examination is in an Air Council 1919 pamphlet at Hendon: *Examination of Aviation Candidates*.

3 : Learning to fly
Training in 1916 is covered in the official history, volume 3, with the Smith-Barry system in volume 5. Volume 6 covers design defects in aeroplanes. Training manuals at Hendon include the 1914 training manual, the 1915 standing orders in the field, the 1916 hints for young flying instructors and the 1918 official handbook. F. Tredrey, *Pioneer Pilot* (Davies, 1976) is an outstanding biography of Smith-Barry. Material on his method is in PRO 2126, while Hill gives an eye-witness account of Smith-Barry in PRO 2389. Brancker is in the *Aeronautical Journal* of January-March 1917 and Flack in January-March 1919. J. McConnell's *Flying for France* (Doubleday, 1917) covers French training methods. Published books on flying the biplanes of the time include N. Gill's *The Fliers' Guide* (Rees, 1916), C. Barnard's *On Learning to Fly* (Sampson, Low, 1917),

H. Barber's *Aerobatics* (McBride, 1918), and T. Gillmer's *A Simplified Theory of Flight* (Van Nostrand, 1918). A. Rotch's *Charts of the Atmosphere for Aeronauts* (Chapman, Hall, 1911) gives an amusing insight into just how rudimentary knowledge could be.

4: Learning to shoot
Manuals at Hendon include the 1918 instruction notes for Vickers guns, the 1919 handbook on Vickers and Lewis guns and the 1918 General Staff notes on gunnery training for pilots.

5: Finishing school
General Staff notes on air fighting by Captain Strong are in PRO 1625. General Staff notes on aeroplane fighting in single-seaters published November 1916 are at Hendon, as is the Air Ministry pamphlet on aerial fighting of 1918. Best book on aeroplane types is A. Bridgman's *The Clouds Remember* (Gale and Polden, 1924). A. Reid's *Planes and Personalities* (Allen, 1920) is good. Sholto Douglas reported at the time on the SE5a in PRO 2393-24/241. Modern books on the Camel are by J. Pudney (Hamish Hamilton, 1964) and Chaz Bowyer (Hippocrene, 1976).

6: Over to France
24 Squadron seems the best documented, with a readable history by A. Illingworth at Hendon and further material in PRO 627. The analysis of aerodrome personnel is in RAF 72.56.5.

7: Induction
Orders for new pilots are in RAF 74.161. Confidential reports on pilots are in PRO 814. The German air force is very poorly covered. G. Neumann's *The German Air Force in the Great War* (Hodder and Stoughton, 1920) seems to be the only thing about. The *Aeroplane* magazine of 3 December 1919 did an excellent feature on their engines. The Air Board report on German aeroplane construction is in PRO 705. German casualties are in PRO 8.

8: The rhythms of war flying
Assorted squadron histories and personal logbooks are at Hendon. The statistics for infantry service I took from my own book *Death's Men*.

9: Routine work - the pilot's view
Most of the detail here was taken from a mass of memoirs. Those I used most often in practice were by Ira Jones, Yeates and Lee. Ball's combat reports were in RAF 73.82. Details of flying clothing were in RAF 74.22.4.

10: Routine work - the mechanic's view
Air Board notes in 1918, separately for fitters and riggers, were at Hendon. The two best books describing in detail the various stages in making an aeroplane I found to be G. Bailey's *The Complete Airman* (Methuen, 1920) and G. Loening's *Military Aeroplanes* (Best, 1918). The best book on engines was V. Page's *Aviation Engines* (Crosby, Lockwood, 1918). The only attempt to write on air mechanics

is P. Joubert's *The Forgotten Ones* (Hutchinson, 1961), though the Air Council pamphlet in 1918 *A Few Hints for the Flying Officer* gives some unintentionally hilarious advice. Gates's logbook is in RAF 76.58.

11 : Battle work

Most of the material here again came from memoirs. Richthofen's post mortem is in PRO 696. Official historian Jones wrote to the Australian official historian Bean that he had compiled a vast dossier on this controversial shooting down and concluded that the fatal shots came from the air and not from the ground. His dossier is not available for public viewing. G. Hodges's *Memoirs of an Old Balloonatic* (Kimber, 1972) is about the only book to describe the observation balloon by a man who was actually in the basket.

12 : Glamour – the aces

Maund and Hill on Albert Ball are in PRO 2387. Barker's combat report is in PRO 1035. A series of articles in the *Reynolds News* on Mannock is in RAF 76.43.583. E. Sims's *The Fighter Pilots* (Cassell, 1967) takes a number of second war aces on all sides and makes for an excellent comparison with the earlier war.

13 : The dark side – physical strain

H. Anderson's *Medical and Surgical Aspects of Aviation* (OUP, 1919) gives a good view of contemporary knowledge. G. McPherson, in volume 2 of the official history of the medical services (HMSO, 1923), is worth a look. H. Armstrong's *Principles and Practice of Aviation Medicine* (Baillière, Tindall and Cox) was published in both 1939 and 1952 and thus shows the advances made in the second war. K. Read's *Aeromedicine for Aviators* (Pitman, 1971) is good on the present state of play.

14 : The dark side – dying

Casualty figures are taken from the official history, the 1922 digest and the *Aeroplane* magazine of 1919. I found valuable statistical notes and discussion, particularly with reference to the battles, in unpublished material by official historians Jones and Edmonds. Since the majority of archive material is not available to the public today, anything like final adjustment on losses and the policies associated with them is impossible.

15: The dark side – killing; and 16: Enduring

Most material in both chapters was taken from individual memoirs. There is a valuable collection of squadron correspondence between 64 Squadron and 13 Wing in PRO 1867. It also includes a wealth of material on the internal running of a squadron.

17 : After the war

Hendon handbooks include the Ministry of Munitions Instructions for Builders of September 1918; RNAS instructions for the information and guidance of inspecting officers (December 1915) and the procedure book of the Ministry of Munitions (February 1919). Material in the PRO includes items on Sopwiths (PRO 72); on raw materials for aircraft manufacture (PRO 2427); on labour relations (PRO 2427); on the timber crisis (PRO 678); and on experimental work (PRO 6a). Criticism of Rolls-Royce is in the official history, volume 6. The Haig, Ludendorff and Pétain material on the overall air strategy I found in odd unsorted boxes at the War Memorial, Canberra. For the after-the-war material, details on grave searching were in PRO 435; on demobilization in PRO 1132 and on aerodrome sites in the UK, PRO 32.

SUGGESTIONS FOR FURTHER READING

Overall studies of the air war

Peter Simkins' *Air Fighting 1914-18* (Imperial War Museum, 1978) is much the best short study, compressing much information and many photographs into a short space. In a wide field, I thought the best book-length treatment that of A. Norman, *The Great Air War* (Macmillan, 1968). It is not illustrated but has a fine balance between information and anecdote. For the serious reader, there is no substitute for the six-volume official history. The first volume, by Walter Raleigh, is lightweight, but the remaining five, by H. A. Jones, are a wonderful achievement, both readable and informative. Their chief value lies in the fact that well over 90 per cent of the material on which Jones based his work has either been destroyed or is not now available for public inspection. Compared with the west front land war volumes of James Edmonds, which are indigestible in style and disgracefully distorted in the selection and interpretation of facts, Jones retained a high degree of detachment and truthfulness. He looked at problems of supply and higher management as well as fighting, while the appendices contain a wealth of statistical information.

Memoirs of fighter pilots

C. Lewis's *Sagittarius Rising* (Penguin, 1979) is probably both the most elegant and the most easily available. Informative and beautifully written are A. Lee's two books *No Parachute* (Kimber, 1968) and *Open Cockpit* (Jarrold, 1969). Less well written but carrying the weight of the master pilot's own experience are five books written by high-scoring aces: W. Bishop's *Winged Warfare* (Bailey, 1975) probably contains the most practical detail; J. McCudden's *Flying Fury* (Bailey, 1973) and W. McLanachan's *Fighter Pilot* (Newnes, undated) are highly informative as well; E. Udet's *Ace of the Black Cross* (Newnes, 1930) and E. Rickenbacker's *Fighting the Flying Circus* (Bailey, 1973) represent the memoirs respectively of the second highest-scoring German ace and the leading American marksman.

Books about aces

Three books can be highly recommended. T. Hawker's *Major Hawker* (Mitre, 1965) is the beautifully written account of our first fighter VC and ace. Ira Jones's *King of the Air Fighters* (Nicholson and Watson, 1934) not only tells the story of Edward Mannock but weaves in a wealth of background information on the life of fighter pilots. J. Werner's *Knight of Germany* (Arno, 1972) tells the story of Oswald Boelke, usually credited with the invention of the fighter squadron and a pioneer of collective fighting tactics. As the teacher of Richthofen and a man of much personal charm, he is a more interesting and important figure in military aviation than his famous pupil.

Collections of photographs

E. Jablonski's *The Knighted Skies* (Nelson, 1964) has an excellent collection of all leading aces and their aeroplanes. Chaz Bowyer's *Airmen of World War One* (Hippocrene, 1976) is more particularly about the RFC.

Novels

V. Yeates's *Winged Victory* (Cape, 1934) stands by itself. The author was a Camel pilot and the events in his book are mostly autobiographical, hence the vividness. If not quite in the same class as Manning's *Her Privates We* as a study of fighting men in the Great War, Yeates's book is still the finest fictional work of the aerial war. T. E. Lawrence acknowledged its stature when it was first published and Henry Williamson contributed a deeply moving introduction.

The second war

The piston-engined fighters of the second war came only one generation after those of the Great War and so offer many valuable points of comparison. I found four books particularly useful in this way. R. Hillary's *The Last Enemy* (Macmillan, 1968) and R. Hall's *Clouds of Fear* (Bailey, 1970) are two wonderful autobiographical accounts. The first is an acknowledged classic. The second I thought even more powerful. Aero historian E. Sims has written two books whose value is in inverse proportion to their slimness. *Fighter Tactics 1914-70* (Cassell, 1972) and *The Fighter Pilots* (Cassell, 1967) show just how little change there was in tactics between the later stages of the Great War and most of the second, while his volume of monographs on individual second war aces shows the same closeness to the Mannocks, Bishops and Foncks of the earlier war.

INDEX